They Who Give from Evil

They Who Give from Evil

The Response of the Eastern Church to
Moneylending in the Early Christian Era

Brenda Llewellyn Ihssen

☞PICKWICK *Publications* · Eugene, Oregon

THEY WHO GIVE FROM EVIL
The Response of the Eastern Church to Moneylending in the Early Christian Era

Pickwick Publications
An Imprint of Wipf and Stock Publishers
199 W. 8th Ave., Suite 3
Eugene, OR 97401

www.wipfandstock.com

ISBN 13: 978-1-61097-032-7

Cataloguing-in-Publication data:

Ihssen, Brenda Llewellyn.

They who give from evil : the response of the Eastern Church to moneylending in the early Christian era / Brenda Llewellyn Ihssen.

xiv + 208 pp. ; 23 cm. Includes bibliographical references and index.

ISBN 13: 978-1-61097-032-7

1. Basil, Saint, Bishop of Caesarea, ca. 329–379. 2. Gregory, of Nyssa, Saint, ca. 335–ca. 394. 3. Usury—Religious aspects—Christianity. I. Title.

BR60 A65 I35 2012

Manufactured in the U.S.A.

For Tim and Maeve

"If you lend to those from whom you hope to receive,
what credit is that to you?
Even sinners lend to sinners, to receive as much again.
But love your enemies, do good, and lend, expecting nothing in return."

LUKE 6:34–35

Contents

Preface

THIS TEXT EMERGED FROM my doctoral thesis at the University of St. Michael's College. Many—if not most—doctoral projects materialize from a burning desire that a graduate student may have to write on a particular issue or question. This was not my situation. Unlike most graduate students, the only connection I had with usury prior to writing about it was the staggering debt that I accumulated in the course of my life as a student. I still recall, however, precisely when the decision was made to write on usury. My initial thesis proposal had been undercut at the very last minute when a member of the committee—who did not remain on the committee—informed me after all the work had been done that "no one cares about the ramblings of some long dead, long forgotten Byzantine emperor." I sat in the office of my director, T. Allan Smith, and we thought about what to do next. He opened the *Geschichte der byzantinischen Volksliteratur*, by Hans Georg Beck, and read quietly while I sat there in silence. He then looked up at me, shut the book and said "Usury. You can write about usury." I trusted him, and therefore I was going to write about usury. Of course I am glad that I did, because also unlike most graduate students, I was not sick to death of my topic by the time I finished; rather, this project introduced me to the rich social justice theologies of the patristic world, and has thus shaped my scholarly agenda in ways I could not have anticipated at the time. I will, eventually, return to that "long dead, long forgotten" emperor; for now, this is sufficient.

As a thesis, it is expansive in its study of a singular topic, but the rationale and limitations of a thesis are worth noting. The purpose of *They Who Give from Evil: The Response of the Eastern Church to Moneylending in the Early Christian Era* is—after presentation of some of the scholarship done to date on the specific sermons of concern (chapter 1)—to consider the financial and salvific implications of usury on the community and the individual soul as it is addressed within the sermons of a selection of early

Christian Greek authors, in the historical context of the fourth century Roman Empire. The principal limitation of this study is the exclusivity of my primary texts, as they are focused on the Greek East, rather than also including Latin theologians. This is because the two primary texts I work with—St. Basil's *Homily on Psalm Fourteen* and *Against Those Who Practice Usury* by St. Gregory of Nyssa—are Greek texts, and I know that it is not necessary to apologize for a limitation even as it is noted.

Acknowledgments

I WOULD LIKE TO thank the following people for support, guidance and instruction during the life of this project, as it moved from a University of St. Michael's College doctoral thesis to a monograph. I first thank Commodianus, a Christian poet who lived in Africa in the mid-third century, whose poem about the wickedness of lending—*They Who Give from Evil*—provided the title for this text. I would like to thank my dissertation director, Dr. T. Allan Smith, for suggesting a topic that would prove to be both academically and spiritually challenging. I thank also those involved from abstract to defense: Dr. Phyllis Airhart, Dr. Pablo Argárate, Dr. Lee Cormie, Dr. Paul Fedwick, Dr. Alan Hayes. Dr. Robert Sinkewicz, and Dr. James Skedros.

I extend thanks also to family and friends for encouragement and support: to my parents, Paul and Mary Llewellyn, to my sister, Livia Llewellyn, to my aunt, Donna Heath, to my in-laws, Bill and Betterae Ihssen, to my friends Susan Larson Greenleaf, Jill Gardner, Dr. Valerie Hébert, Dr. Sara Humphreys, Dr. Alicia Batten, Annal Frenz, Dr. Brian Matz, Dr. Heracles Panagiotides, Dr. Daniel Peterson, and Dr. Ann Holmes Redding. Thanks also to my friends and colleagues in the Religion Department at Pacific Lutheran University who read an early chapter of this during a fall colloquium in 2005 and offered helpful comments and suggestions. A special thank-you to my very dear friend Abbot Tryphon and the monks at the All Merciful Saviour Russian Orthodox Monastery; I am grateful for your friendship, for good food and drink, for conversation and space for thinking (and space for not thinking). I note especially my gratitude for the encouragement of my friend and colleague, Dr. Michael Zbaraschuk, for the enthusiastic championing of this project in this form. Thanks, Mike, for being a cheerleader.

Most of all, I would like to thank the immediate members of my household; they have had to live with this project for as long as I have, and I am grateful to them for their patience and love. Therefore, a special thanks to my husband, Tim, to our daughter, Maeve, and to every pet in our household who either sat on the manuscript or slept through the process: Maud, Hector, Molly, Gretel, Victor, and little Jimmy Ihssen.

Abbreviations

ACW	*Ancient Christian Writers*
ANF	*Ante-Nicene Fathers*
CPG	Corpus Patrologia Graeca
CSEL	Corpus scriptorum ecclesiasticorum latinorum (Vienna)
FOTC	Fathers of the Church
J	*Gregorii Nysseni Opera Ascetica*. Edited by W. Jaeger
JNSL	*Journal of Northwest Semitic Languages*
LCC	Library of Christian Classics
LCL	Loeb Classical Library
NPNF	*Nicene and Post-Nicene Fathers*
NTS	*New Testament Studies*
NOAB	*New Oxford Annotated Bible*
PG	Patrologia Graeca (Migne)
PL	Patrologia Latina (Migne)

1

Basil and Gregory's Sermons on Usury
A Simple Historiography

USURY IS NOT GENERALLY regarded as a provocative subject. According to authors B. J. Meislin and M. L. Cohen the subject is so low on the stimulation scale that only "the social and religious philosophers, historians and other scholars of the past are still excited by the moral implications of this prohibition."[1] Despite this claim, the amount of texts devoted to the subject of usury—though primarily from an economic rather than a theological or even an historical perspective—suggests that usury is of import to a larger group, and the rising interest in poverty studies and the social justice theologies of early Christian authors suggests that there is clear recognition that the troubling realities of debt remain a concern for early Christians and their bishops as well as modern day citizens of any given location. This first chapter addresses twentieth and twenty-first century historiography of usury scholarship that considers the social justice sermons on usury of Basil the Great and Gregory of Nyssa, and considers to what degree authors subordinate Gregory's work to that of his brother's. This chapter will not include each historian who mentions "usurers" or "money-lenders"[2] within their texts, but seeks to record the more specific projects that deal with the work of the Cappadocian brothers in a significant way.

1. Meislin and Cohen, "Backgrounds of the Biblical Law against Usury," 250.

2. "Money-lenders" is the more popular term used among historians to describe a usurer. For example, A. H. M. Jones makes no mention of usury in his formidable *The Later Roman Empire* 284–602, and only refers to money-lenders rather cursorily; the treatment is similar in his *Roman Economy*.

As a result of Lecky's charges against Christianity and commerce in his *History of the Rise and Influence of the Spirit of Rationalism in Europe*,[3] Patrick Cleary's 1914 *The Church and Usury* demonstrates how Christianity reacted to and changed in the face of developing financial circumstances. Beginning with passages in Acts[4] and I Peter,[5] he devotes a modest section of the text to the "Early Christian Church"[6] in which he discusses early Christian attitudes towards money.[7] Cleary largely confines[8] patristic

3. Lecky wrote that Christianity long desired to fetter commerce, while at the same time opposing it; in Cleary, *The Church and Usury*, v.

4. Cleary notes the works of Tabitha of Joppa, "full of good works and alms-deeds," whose loans were donations. Acts 9:36 (Cleary, *The Church and Usury*, 37).

5. According to Cleary, Peter warns against the greed of ministers: "Tend the flock of God . . . not yet for filthy lucre but willingly" (1 Peter 5:2) (Cleary, *The Church and Usury*, 37). In addition, Paul cites greed as a reason not to elect someone in the ministry for advancement: "Bishops must not be lovers of money, deacons must not be greedy of filthy lucre" (I Timothy 3:3) (Cleary, *The Church and Usury*, 37–38). Cleary includes additional passages in the New Testament that warn against desire for money: Titus 1:7, Titus 1:11, and Acts 15:29; Cleary, *The Church and Usury*, 38.

6. Cleary, *The Church and Usury*, 37–62.

7. He points to the Didache (*Didache*, 1; Cleary, *The Church and Usury*, 39), to demonstrate an early trend towards generosity, Apollonius to proclaim that those who take usury are false prophets (Apollonius, in Eusebius, *Historia ecclesiastica*. 5.18; Cleary, *The Church and Usury*, 40), Clement of Alexandria to demonstrate that usury is against charity (Clement of Alexandria, *Stromata*, 2.18; Cleary, *The Church and Usury*, 40–41), and Tertullian to caution against lending to those who cannot repay (Tertullian, *Adversus Marcion*, 4.17; Cleary, *The Church and Usury*, 41). Cleary quotes Cyprian, who, in his "On the Lapsed," laments the fate of those who put their salvation in jeopardy by increasing "their gains by multiplying usuries" (Cyprian, *De Lapsis*, 5.6; Cleary, *The Church and Usury*, 42). He covers early conciliar statements against usury, beginning with the Council of Elvira and continuing with mention of the Councils of Carthage, Arles, Nice (Nicaea), and concluding with a definition of trading for profit—a form of usury—by Pope Julius (337–52): "It is filthy lucre, when one in the harvest time through avarice not through necessity gets grain at two denarii per peck and keeps it till he gets four or six" (Gratian, *Decretals* 5; Cleary, *The Church and Usury*, 46. This was later adopted by the Council of Tarragona in 526; Cleary, *The Church and Usury*, 44–46). Cleary ends this first section with an interesting discussion on the connection between usury and trade: clergy were discouraged from engaging in trade primarily because the purpose of business transactions is for the two parties to "try to overreach one another," and reaping where one has not sown is highly unsuitable behavior for a minister in any age. These are the words of the second century Pomponius; though Cleary quotes him, he does not provide any citation.

8. Additional authors noted briefly in this portion of the chapter are Sts. Hilary (Hilary, *Tractatus in psalmos* 14, PL 9:307; Cleary, *The Church and Usury*, 53.), Jerome

reaction to usury to Basil the Great's *Homilia in psalmum* 14,[9] Gregory of Nyssa's *Contra usurarios*,[10] and Ambrose's *De Tobia*.[11] He treats all three theologians together, summarizing the contents of their texts, and claiming that it is primarily Basil's text from which the other two have drawn.[12] Cleary notes that all three discuss the fertility of money as well as the revolting conditions in which the debtor must live,[13] to make the point that

---

(Jerome, PL 25:176–77; Cleary, *The Church and Usury*, 54), Augustine (Cleary mentions Augustine's opinion on usury—"St. Augustine would, if he could, impose and obligation of restitution on all usurers for they are murderers of the poor, but, alas, the very laws sanction their practices. He, too, looks at the matter from the point of view of charity, for he would order restitution only to stop oppression."—but, oddly enough, does not provide a citation.) and Chrysostom (Chrysostom, PG 57:61–62; Cleary, *The Church and Usury*, 56).

9. Basil, *Homilia in psalmum* 14; Cleary, *The Church and Usury*, 49–53.

10. Gregory of Nyssa, *Contra usurarios*; Cleary, *The Church and Usury*, 49–53.

11. Ambrose, *De Tobia*; Cleary, *The Church and Usury*, 49–53.

12. "His homily on the fourteenth psalm is professedly used by St. Gregory of Nyssa and by St. Ambrose, and both borrow freely from it" (Cleary, *The Church and Usury*, 49).

13. In fairness, he contrasts their opinions with that of Sidonius Apollinaris, a bishop of the latter half of the fifth century who was more lenient towards usury (Cleary, *The Church and Usury*, 51–52), and Gregory of Tours, who tells of a bishop who borrowed from King Theudericus and promised to pay him back "with usury." As it turns out, the citizens fared so well with the gift that they no longer experienced any financial difficulties. Cleary, *The Church and Usury*, 57. Cleary does not provide details beyond what is stated above, but in the *Historia* it is King Theudebert who makes the loan to the bishop, not Theuderic, as Cleary writes. Although it does not connect necessarily with early Greek Christian authors, and although it is a few hundred years outside of the time period of this project, nevertheless it is such a brilliant example of Jesus's statement to "lend, expecting nothing in return," that it is worth noting the episode: "King Theuderic had done much harm to Desideratus, Bishop of Verdun. After long disgrace, ill-treatment and sorrow, Desideratus regained his liberty with God's help and again took possession of his bishopric, which was in the city of Verdun, as I have said. He found the inhabitants of the city poor and destitute, and he grieved for them. He had been deprived of his own property by Theuderic and had no means of succouring his townsfolk. When he observed the charity of King Theudebert and his generosity towards all men, Desideratus sent messengers to him. 'The fame of your charity has spread throughout the whole world,' he said, 'for your generosity is so great that you even give to people who have asked nothing of you. If in your compassion you have any money to spare, I beg you to lend it to me, so that I may relieve the distress of those in my diocese. As soon as the men who are in charge of the commercial affairs in my city have reorganized their business, as has been done in other cities, I will repay your loan with interest.' Theudebert was moved to compassion and made a loan of seven thousand pieces gold pieces. Desideratus accepted this and shared it out among his townfolk. As a result the business people of Verdun because rich and they

early Christian authors wrote against usury more often because of the difficult situations in which the lenders left the debtors than because usury in itself was unjust.[14] In sum, Cleary's work provides an excellent beginning to the study of usury in early Christianity, and a fairly fair treatment of the three theologians who devote an entire sermon to the topic of usury.

Stanislas Giet's 1941 publication, *Les idées et l'action sociales de saint Basile* includes partial translation of Basil's *Homilia in psalmum* 14 with minor commentary. Giet's comments are concerned principally with Basil's use of the word τόκος[15] and with his position on lending at all, aside from lending with interest.[16] One interesting point unique to the Giet document is that he notes comparisons made almost a century earlier by E. Fialon between Basil's *Homilia in psalmum* 14 and Plutarch's *That One Ought Not to Borrow*;[17] however, Giet dismisses Fialon's claim that Basil depends on Plutarch.[18] Giet's article of three years later, "De Saint Basil à Saint Ambroise: La condamnation du prêt à intérêt au IV[19e] siècle," elaborates on his previous work and explores the texts in greater detail, detailing to what extent Basil influenced Ambrose[20] and who, in turn, influenced Basil.[21] Giet's secondary goal is an examination of the two documents as

---

still remain so today. The bishop eventually returned the borrowed money to the King, but Theudebert replied: 'I have no need to take this money. It is enough for me that, when you asked that I should make a loan, those who were poor and in dire distress were returned to prosperity.' By taking no payment Theudebert restored the citizens of Verdun to affluence" (Gregory of Tours, *History of the Franks*, 190–91).

14. "The statements of the popes to which reference has been have no definitive value; whilst the opinions of the Fathers seem, when sifted, to condemn usury, not as opposed to justice, but merely as opposed to charity in so far as it may be extortionate" (Cleary, *The Church and Usury*, 36).

15. "τόκος—birth, offspring, interest or oppression" (Liddell and Scott, *A Greek-English Lexicon*, 1803).

16. Giet claims that Basil—who in his travels had seen the benefits of lending in an agricultural setting—was not opposed to the practice of lending, but was opposed to lending with interest, or lending which had as its goal the impoverishment of an individual. Giet, *Les idées et l'action sociales*, 120–21.

17. Plutarch, *De vitando aere alieno*, 317–39.

18. Giet, *Les idées et l'action sociales*, 121.

19

20. Ibid., 106–19.

21. Ibid., 120–21. Giet condemns a second time the comments of Fialon and adds to this dismissal the work of M. Marconcini, who suggests a strong philosophical influence in Basil's position.

symptomatic of the difficulty of rapport between the churches of the East and the West.[22]

From 1971 to 1974, Robert P. Maloney produced articles focusing on usury from one of four different angles: philosophy of ancient societies, conciliar legislation, early Christianity and the ancient Near East. Based on his 1969 doctoral thesis, *The Background for the Early Christian Teaching on Usury*,[23] Maloney's articles together compile a large group of sources including ancient philosophers, Rabbinic and New Testament sources, ending with the figure of Pope Leo the Great (390–461). Maloney's Christian sources include Eastern and Western theologians, and are explored in historical sequence. Early Christian authors included in his articles mirror Seipel,[24] but they do not include Cyril of Jerusalem[25] or Theodoret of Cyrrhus,[26] whose brief mentions of usury will be considered in chapter 4 of this project. Among Maloney's many contributions is his notation of the influence of Philo of Alexandria's writings on Clement of Alexandria, Basil the Great and Ambrose. In reference to Clement of Alexandria's *Stromateis*, Maloney notes that Clement "borrows copiously" from Philo, sampling lines from Philo's *De virtutibus* almost word for word.[27] Maloney

22. Ibid., 95–96, 128.

23. Maloney, *The Background for the Early Christian Teaching on Usury.*

24. Clement of Alexandria, *Paedagogus* 1.10 (PG 8:364); *Stromateis* 2.19 (PG 8:1014); Tertullian, *Aduersus Marcionem* 4.17 (PL 2:398–99); Apollonius, in Jerome's *De viris illustribus*, 40 (PL 23:655); Cyprian, *De lapsis*, 6 (PL 4:470–71); Lactantius, *Institutiones divinae* 6:18 (PL 6:698–99); Athanasius, *Expositio in psalmum*, 14.2–5 (PG 27:100); Hilary of Poitiers, *Tractatus in psalmos* 14.15 (PL 9:307); Basil, *Homilia in psalmum* 14 (PG 29:264–65); *Epistula* 188 (PG 32:682); Gregory of Nyssa, *Contra usurarios* (PG 46:433–52); *Epistula ad Letoium* (PG 45:234); Gregory of Nazianzus, *Oratio* 16.18 (PG 35:957); Ambrose, *De Tobia* (PL 14:759–94); John Chrysostom, *Homilia* 56 *in MT.* (PG 58:558); *Homilia* 41 *in Gen.* (PG 53:376–77); *Homilia* 13 *in* 1 *Cor.* (PG 61.113–14); Jerome, *In Ezechielem Commentarii* 6.18 (PL 25:176–77); *Sifre on Deuteronomy;* Augustine, *Ennarationes in psalmos,* 36, *Sermo* 3.6 (PL 36:386); *Ennarationes in psalmos,* 126 (PL 37:1692); *Epistula* 154 (153) 25 (PL 33:665); *Sermo* 38 (PL 38.239–40); *Sermo* 86.5 (PL 38:525–26); *De baptismo contra Donatistas* 4.9 (PL 43.162); Leo the Great, *Nec hoc quoque* (PL 54.613); *Sermo* 17 (PL 54:180–82); Maloney, "Teaching of the Fathers on usury," 243–63.

25. Cyril of Jerusalem, *Catechesis 4: De Decem Dogmatibus*, PG 33:454–504.

26. Theodoret, 78: *To Eusebius, bishop of Persian Armenia*, PG 83:1252–56.

27. Maloney, "Teaching of the Fathers on Usury," 243. In all fairness, the same year as Maloney's article was published, Martin Hengel also noted the heavy influence of Jewish wisdom combined with Stoic and New Testament ethics in Clement of Alexandria. This, plus the situation in Alexandria resulted in a revaluation of the radical criticism of property, which was turned inward, rather than the open renunciation of wealth. Hengel, *Property and Riches in the Early Church,* 77–78. Further, Maloney does

comments also that Basil's closing statements in his *Homilia in psalmum* 14 resemble the same text,[28] and that Philo subsequently influenced the Western Ambrose through the Eastern Basil, as Ambrose relied heavily on Basil's texts for his *De Tobia*.[29] In addition to noting passages of scripture Basil heaped up in defense of his position,[30] and that Basil chided both rich and poor for their greed—the rich for wanting more at the expense of another and the poor for wanting money for things that they do not need, such as fancy clothes and rich foods[31]—Maloney observes Basil's debt to Philo of Alexandria and Aristotle, whose play on the word τόκος enters into the works of both. Gregory's position on usury is given almost equal attention by Maloney, who notes Gregory's argument against lending from nature (fecundity and sterility), the way by which the evil of debt pervades society, and the paradox that borrowing increases need, rather than diminishing it.[32] Of all the early Christian authors on whom he writes, Maloney devotes his attention primarily to Ambrose's *De Tobia*,[33] which he claims is "comprehensive," but "far from original."[34] Maloney's contribution to the study of usury cannot be over-emphasized, as his four

---

not, however, quote the lines from Philo which Clement allegedly copiously borrows.

28. Maloney, "Teaching of the Fathers on Usury," 249.

29. Ibid., 251.

30. Ezekiel 22:12; Deuteronomy 23:19; Jeremiah 9:6; Psalm 54:12; and Matthew 5:42.

31. Maloney, "Teaching of the Fathers on Usury," 247–48.

32. Ibid., 249–51.

33. Ibid., 251–56.

34. Ambrose, *De Tobia*, 28.29 (PL 14:769); 36 (PL 14:771–72), in Maloney, "Teaching of the Fathers on Usury," 253. In addition to rebuking the greedy lender, Ambrose provides anecdotes which demonstrate the ravages of interest on society; some borrowed from Basil and some his own Ambrose, *De Tobia*, 42 (PL 14:792), in Maloney, "Teaching of the Fathers on Usury," 254. In addition to abuses such as the pledging of one's family or own body against a loan, there was *anatocism*, which was the scandalous practice of the accumulation of additional interest capitalised on the original interest. Ambrose attacks an abuse of usury known as *anatocism* (PL 14:778) and condemns any type of usury, whether it is in the form of money or less obvious payments such as food or clothing. Maloney briefly addresses Ambrose's belief—fairly unique among early Christian authors—that the New Testament does not necessarily abolish the right to take interest, pointing out that Ambrose saw the "foreigner" as the enemy of Israel. Ambrose, *De Tobia*, 54, 85 (PL 14:780–81 and 791), in Maloney, "Teaching of the Fathers on Usury." 254. Maloney raises the problem of Ambrose's commentary Deuteronomy 23:19–20—the "irritating text"—but fails to address it satisfactorily; at length he dramatically casts the understanding of it to "the course of later history." Maloney, "Teaching of the Fathers on Usury," 264–65.

articles pull together a huge variety of primary sources and provide an additional abundance of secondary source material to consult for further study. Though a few primary sources are omitted, together the articles cover much of the necessary groundwork needed for further projects on usury in the early Christian world.

According to Homer and Sylla, interest rates in Latin America have traditionally been higher than those in North America and Europe; consequently, while the United States experienced double-digit inflation in the 1980s, by the 1990s, Latin America had experienced triple- or even quadruple-digit inflation.[35] As a result of the injustices that occur under such stressful economic conditions, United Methodist Minister, liberation theologian Justo L. González felt compelled to explore texts from the early Christian era that dealt specifically with economic issues. González states in the introduction to his 1990 publication, *Faith and Wealth: A History of Early Christian Ideas On the Origin, Significance, and Use of Money,*[36] that one of his goals was to make known such materials because in light of the protests of Catholics and Protestants against papal or Church involvement in or opinions on the US economy,[37] economics was from the earliest times—and still should be today—a theological concern. In his section on the Cappadocians,[38] González cites both *Contra usurarios*[39] by Gregory of Nyssa, and *Homilia in psalmum* 14[40] by Basil of Caesarea; his examination of both texts is general, but he focuses primarily on Basil, as Evelyne Patlagean does briefly in *Pauvreté économique et pauvreté sociale à Byzance, 4e-7e siecles.*[41] González suggests that Gregory of Nyssa's text is based on that of his brother Basil's and addresses only one minor difference in the brothers' works, specifically their audiences.[42] To demonstrate consistency between Basil's *Homilia in psalmum* 14 and some of Basil's other works, González quotes from an additional homily of St. Basil's in

---

35. Homer and Sylla, *History of Interest Rates,* 619.

36. Norman Jones's *God and the Moneylenders: Usury and Law in Early Modern England,* the publication of which preceded González by one year, was exclusively the "biography of the Act of Usury of 1571," and confines his history of usury from the Old Testament to the mid-sixteenth century to one paragraph.

37. González, *Faith and Wealth,* xiii.

38. Ibid., 173–86.

39. Gregory of Nyssa, *Contra usurarios,* in ibid., 175.

40. Basil, *Homilia in psalmum* 14, in ibid., 175.

41. Patlagean, *Pauvreté économique et pauvreté sociale,* 177–78.

42. González, *Faith and Wealth,* 175–76.

which he blames the drought of 382 on the greed of the community.[43] As Maloney did before him, González mentions the influence that Basil's *Homilia in psalmum* 14 had on Ambrose, pointing out that passages in Ambrose's aforementioned *De Tobia* quote the Cappadocian saint "almost word for word."[44] González concludes in his "Retrospect"[45] that usury is soundly condemned by the early Christian authors, with perhaps the sole exception being a passage by Clement of Alexandria, who may have believed that the prohibition against interest could be applied only to loans to fellow believers.[46] Although only a small portion of his text touches on the subject of usury, still González its the highlights of the patristic position, citing—if not quoting—from the most important primary sources.

The following year, Casimir McCambley translated Gregory of Nyssa's *Contra usurarios*, which was published in the *Greek Orthodox Theological Review*. Prior to the translated text he provides introductory material on Gregory of Nyssa's text,[47] in which he references Maloney's "The Teaching of the Fathers on Usury." McCambley begins by discussing usury in general and how the two brothers stand in a long line of tradition of denunciation of the practice. Unlike any other author, McCambley claims that early Christians authors used the phrase "Forgive us our debts, as we have forgiven our debtors," as justification for their position.[48] McCambley compares the works of the two brothers on what appears to be level ground: he mentions Gregory's deference to Basil's previously public statements on the evils of usury,[49] references Ezekiel and how they both maintain that usury debases an individual to the status of a slave.[50] McCambley cites Basil's use of the word τόκος, and he does not tie the word to Aristotle; rather, he observes how Gregory demonstrates the foulness of τόκος by comparing it to fertility in nature in his *Commentary*

43. Similar to Gregory of Nazianzus in his *Introduction to Oration*, 16. *On His Father's Silence, Because of The Plague of Hail,* Basil exhorts his community to "Destroy the contract with heavy interests so that the earth may bring forth its produce. Basil, *Homilia dicta tempore famis et siccitatis,* 4 (González, *Faith and Wealth,* 177).

44. Ibid., 190.

45. Ibid., 225–34.

46. Ibid., 225. It is interesting that González does not mention that this sounds very much like what Bishop Ambrose believed as well. Unfortunately, González does not quote or even cite the Clement of Alexandria text, which would be interesting to compare with Ambrose.

47. Basil, *Homilia in psalmum* 14, PG 29:263–80.

48. McCambley, "Against Those Who Practice Usury," 288.

49. Gregory of Nyssa, *Contra usurarios,* in ibid., 288–89.

50. Gregory of Nyssa, *Contra usurarios,* in ibid., 289.

on Ecclesiastes,[51] and McCambley devotes the remainder of the article to Gregory's understanding of conscience and human nature, influenced by both Plato and Scripture.[52] McCambley's article is helpful not only for the valuable translation he provides and his notation of other texts by Gregory that touch on the subject of usury—such as the aforementioned *Commentary on Ecclesiastes* and Gregory's fifth homily on *The Lord's Prayer*[53]—but also for his insightful reflection on Gregory's theological anthropology.

In 1997, Thomas Moser published his thesis on usury laws and history, *Die patristische Zinslehre und ihre Ursprünge: Vom Zinsgebot zum Wucherverbot*. An examination of pre- and post Christian usury theory, Moser follows in the footsteps of Maloney, organizing his text and modeling his thesis along the same lines as his predecessor. However, though their texts are similar in form, their theses differ: Moser's thesis is that the usury prohibition adopted by patristic authors is not dependent solely on Scripture, but comes to be formed by equal influences of Scripture, Hellenistic philosophy and Roman legislation hostile to interest taking.[54] Though Maloney would not likely disagree strongly with this—and though Maloney tied these same themes together in his thesis of thirty years prior—still, his claim is that the primary motivation against usury was a Christian concern for "practical charity among the brethren."[55] Moser's text is divided into two portions, with a lengthy first part dedicated to providing a thorough examination of interest in the ancient world and the Hebrew Bible (law and poetic books), demonstrating effectively continuity of condemnation. Again, like Maloney does before him, Moser emphasizes the role of Philo of Alexandria;[56] however unlike Maloney, Moser demonstrates the synthesis that Philo provides in his usury theory, combining the injunction of Deuteronomy with the Aristotelian ban against breeding money from money in his statement against usury in *De virtutibus*.[57] After providing

51. Gregory of Nyssa in ibid., 290; Gregory of Nyssa, *Fourth Homily*, in *Commentary on Ecclesiastes*; *In Ecclesiasten* (PG 44:615–754).

52. McCambley, "Against Those Who Practice Usury," 290–94.

53. Gregory of Nyssa, *De Oratione Dominica* (PG 44:1119–94).

54. Moser, *Die patristische Zinslehre*, 5.

55. Maloney, *The Background for the Early Christian Teaching on Usury*, 4.

56. Maloney concisely states that through "Clement, Basil and Ambrose, he [Philo] influences the development of Christian thought on the point" (Maloney, "The Teaching of the Fathers," 243).

57. "He forbids anyone to lend money on interest to a brother, meaning by this name not merely a child of the same parents, but anyone of the same citizenship or nation. For he does not think it just to amass money bred from money as their yearlings are from cattle." Philo, *De virtutibus*, 14. Also in Moser, *Die patristische Zinslehre*, 101.

additional sources from Philo on usury,[58] Moser concludes that Philo influences the future of the discussion on usury on three main counts: first, the taking of interest has dire consequences for the usurer;[59] second, the morally objectionable attitude of the financier; and third, the existence of interest is objectionable from a moral point of view because money is not capable of reproduction.[60] The second portion of Moser's text focuses its attention on the texts that concern usury. Although Moser generally includes the customary figures east and west, he incorporates authors not yet included in studies on usury, such as Johannes Mandakuni[61] and Aristides of Athens.[62] Yet, in his elucidation on the passages, Moser curiously neglects to include Gregory of Nyssa's *Contra usurarios*, choosing instead to cite passages from Gregory's *Fourth Homily* from his *Commentary on Ecclesiastes*. This omission, though mystifying, does not diminish his fine contribution to the study of usury in the letters, sermons and councils of the early Christian era.

The final consideration of Basil and Gregory's sermons on usury in this first chapter is from Susan R. Holman's *The Hungry Are Dying: Beggars and Bishops in Roman Cappadocia*[63] Holman's text considers how the Cappadocian bishops—Basil, Gregory Nazianzen and Gregory of Nyssa— depict "the poor" in sermons which deal specifically with poverty, and how in this particular portrayal they sought to incorporate the poor under the mantle of the Church by appealing to Christian philanthropy. Prior to examination of Basil's *Homilia in psalmum* 14 and Gregory of Nyssa's *Contra usurarios*, she provides a pithy history of usury, to provide the necessary cultural background against which the sermons were written.[64] Her examination of Basil's *Homilia in psalmum* 14 focuses on the way in which Basil's understanding of the debtor and "the poor" are reflected in

58. Philo of Alexandria, *De specialibus legibus*, 2:74–76.

59. See Ezekiel 22:6–13.

60. Moser, *Die patristische Zinslehre*, 104–5. This was Aristotle's concern and will be addressed by Basil and Gregory as well.

61. Ibid., 194–95.

62. Ibid., 131.

63. Holman, *The Hungry Are Dying*. Holman has published two additional articles on this subject. See Holman, "The Entitled Poor," 476–89; and Holman, "'You Speculate on the Misery of the Poor,'" 207–28.

64. Holman, *The Hungry Are Dying*, 115–20. In this section she refers to Maloney's "Teachings of the Fathers on Usury," and cites the known texts (Holman, *The Hungry Are Dying*, 119 n. 71).

his sermon. She notes that Basil's emphasis on redemptive alms[65] in no way suggests radical reconstruction of society to the benefit of the poor, but upholds the conventional Roman notion of civic patronage, and urges that the wealthy discontinue making a mockery of the patronage system by robbing the poor of their civic rights.[66] One is to "lend to God"—in this case meaning "the poor"—because God is the ultimate benefactor. At the conclusion of her section on Basil, Holman—as Cleary before her—claims that Basil's text provided immediate inspiration, the themes of which "are soon repeated by Gregory of Nyssa, Ambrose, and John Chrysostom."[67] Holman proceeds to draw fine comparisons, but privileges Basil and Ambrose's texts, demonstrating effective connections and comparative language; with Gregory's *Contra usurarios*, Holman notes that he emphasizes the role of the creditor and debtor while Basil the role of the lender,[68] that Gregory uses wilderness imagery in his sermon,[69] and that they are both in agreement that the relationship between creditor and debtor must be radically redefined "in both the cosmic and the civic realm"[70] in order to solve the problem of the financial enslavement of the poor.[71] In her thoughtful work on the responsibility of religion and famine dynamics, Holman comes closest to a balanced treatment of the two sermons.

Conclusion

Prior to the arrival of subprime lending in the early 1990s, scholars habitually wrote that usury in our day is a dead issue;[72] that Christians repeatedly pay out interest without thinking twice;[73] that society is numb to both the

65. I refer to redemptive alms as it specifically relates to usury as "heavenly usury."

66. By "civic rights" Holman means their patrimonies, inheritances, the inheritances of their children, personal freedom, human dignity, etc. (Holman, *The Hungry Are Dying*, 122).

67. Holman, *The Hungry Are Dying*, 123; see note 46. She is generous to Gregory in her article "Usury as Civic Injustice," stating that Gregory's "later sermon against usury was deliberately constructed as a supplement to Basil's *HP14b*" (Holman, "'You Speculate on the Misery of the Poor,'" 218).

68. Holman, *The Hungry Are Dying*, 123–24.

69. Ibid., 123–24.

70. Ibid., 124.

71. Ibid.

72. Ballard, "On the Sin of Usury," 210; Sutherland, "The Debate Concerning Usury in the Christian Church," 3.

73. Maloney, "Early Conciliar Legislation on Usury," 145; Maloney, "The Teaching

idea of moderate interest and dialogue on the subject altogether.[74] The financial crisis of the first decade of the twenty-first century reminded us of the importance of reflection on economic morality and responsibility, and provided evidence that it is time for re-evaluation of the role of debt in our lives and its effects on local and global communities. The distortion of the "American Dream" of a home and two cars financed by debt has instigated new conversation[75] on the topic between ethicists, economists, theologians and historians as well as the construction of legislation,[76] and a selection of texts devoted to the subject of economic justice and human resources have emerged, including Susan R. Holman's edited volume *Wealth and Poverty in Early Church and Society* and Leemans, Matz and Verstraeten's edited volume *Reading Patristic Texts on Social Ethics: Issues and Challenges for Twenty-first-century Christian Social Thought*, both of which emerged from scholarly conferences devoted current research on poverty, wealth, and social ethics.

This first chapter has considered a select twentieth- and twenty-first-century historiography of usury from the early Christian era, for the purpose of examining to what degree Gregory and Basil's sermons are being considered by poverty and social justice scholars of the early Christian era. This examination of usury scholarship suggests that the author most quoted, noted, translated and analyzed is Basil the Great; while Gregory of Nyssa is present in these treatments, still, Ambrose remains the comparable companion to Basil. Gregory sermon, though hardly derided, remains consistently to be considered the text of lesser import. The sole exception to this is within McCambley, whose analysis offered before the translation focused, naturally, on Gregory.

Though the topic of usury does not burn in the breasts of most theologians, historians or religion scholars of the past century, still, the subject is intriguing enough that by the 1970s interest in interest elevated

---

of the Fathers on Usury," 241; Maloney, "Against Those Who Practice Usury by Gregory of Nyssa," 287; Buckley comes to the rescue of the subject, writing that "Usury today, however, is not the dead issue that might be imagined" (Buckley, *Teachings on Usury in Judaism, Christianity, and Islam*, xv).

74. Sutherland, "Usury: God's Forgotten Doctrine," 14; Sutherland, "The Debate Concerning Usury in the Christian Church," 3; Mills, "The Ban on Interest," 1; Mills, "Interest in Interest," summary.

75. Geisst, *Collateral Damaged*. See also Deconto, "The People's Interest."

76. *Credit Card Accountability Responsibility and Disclosure Act of* 2009, HR 627, 111th Cong. Online: http: http://www.gpo.gov/fdsys/pkg/PLAW-111publ24/pdf/PLAW-111publ24.pdf/.

alongside the economy, and modern writers desired to fill in the empty centuries passed over by historians who concentrated their efforts in the Middle Ages. In the 1980s, the world poverty situation made usury a convenient topic for theologians who chose to segue from the denunciations and condemnations in Jewish and Christian scriptures to contemporary economic disasters brought about by usury. When capitalism began to subordinate human progress to economic ends, Christians stepped up to address economic life in the capitalistic world and the damage in its wake.[77] As thoughtful citizens of the world are becoming increasingly outraged by the wholesale destruction wrought upon human bodies due to poverty, the subject of usury will continue to be addressed. Usury as a topic might not be provocative, but the circumstances of dire poverty are. Usury, credit, debt—however you want to name it—has for too long subordinated human health and dignity to economic ends,[78] and despite the advances of science and technology, people yet live in the same circumstances as the original recipients of laws against it.[79] Those whose eyes glaze over by the notion of usury would do well to clear their sight.

77. Jones, *Capitalism and Christians*, 8.

78. Ibid.

79. Sutherland, "Usury: God's Forgotten Doctrine," 14.

2

Usury in Greek and Roman Society

In a fictitious letter, the Greek sophist Alciphron writes in the voice of a citizen who has come to the city to borrow money, and who regrets having not made use of his friends in a time of financial hardship:

> The usurers in this city, kind friend, are a great nuisance. I do not know what was the matter with men when I ought to have gone to you or some other of my country neighbors at the time I was in need of money for purchasing a farm at Colonus. On that occasion a man of the city went with me to the house of Byrtius to introduce me to him. There I found an old man, looking wrinkled and with brows contracted, holding in his hands an antique paper, rotted by time and half eaten by moths and insects. Forthwith he spoke to me in brusquest fashion, as though he consider talking loss of time. But when my voucher said I wanted money, he asked me how many talents. Then when I expressed surprise at his mention of so large a sum, he forthwith spat and showed ill-temper. Nevertheless he gave the money, demanded a note, required a heavy interest on the principal, and placed a mortgage on my house. A great nuisance these men who reckon with pebbles and crooked fingers. Never, ye Spirits, who watch over farmers, never may it again be my lot to behold a wolf or a usurer.[1]

Though contrived, this account of the proud small landowner who wishes *not* to be a burden on his friends reflects a reality of ancient economic life. As individuals have always depended on small sums lent for short terms to "tide one over," the non-intrusive nature of small loans has left

1. Alciphron, 1.26.

relatively little impact on economic history as a whole;[2] on the other hand, one can trace the history of larger loans that led people to the usurer in Greco-Roman society through—in addition to laws that attempted to curb it—the language of letters, philosophy and religion.[3] As stated in the previous chapter, there are many texts devoted to the subject of usury from an economic perspective, but far fewer address solely the subject of usury from either an historical or theological perspective. Therefore, to provide a suitable foundation for theological reflection on usury as it is considered by early Christian authors, this chapter provides analysis of the subject of usury as it developed in the laws and philosophy of Greek and Roman society. Because laws concerning usury appeared prior to philo-sophical reflection on the problem, this chapter shall consider attitudes towards and outcomes of lending in Greece and Rome centuries before and up until the fifth century CE; general practices, laws, and abuses shall be considered. The second section shall consider philosophical reflection on the problems of usury, and shall distil the thoughts of specific Aristote-lian, Stoic and Neoplatonic authors concerning usury, for the purpose of later addressing how heavily early Christian authors were influenced by these opinions in addition to—or perhaps more than—the prescripts of the Hebrew Bible against usury.

2. Millett, *Lending and Borrowing in Ancient Athens*, 187. Millett points out that the general designation for usurer is *obolostatēs*, which translates to "lender of obols," which indicates small-scale transactions. Millett, *Lending and Borrowing*, 182.

3. There have been several unpublished theses written with usury as their topic, but focus on specific aspects of usury; titles of interest include: Donald M. Cox, "The History of Interest and Usury to the Nineteenth Century"; Charles Thomas Barlow's study of usury as it is confined to the Roman Republic, in his thesis "Bankers, Mon-eylenders and Interest Rates in the Roman Republic"; John R. Sutherland's treatment of Jewish usury laws in "Economic Development and Usury Laws"; and Mary Alice Stone's literary examination of the topic in "The Portrayal of Contemporary Usury in the Elizabethan Drama." An older German text which deals quite adequately with the rise and development of usury in Greece, Rome and the Roman Empire is Gustav Bil-leter's *Geschichte des Zinsfusses*. However in English, most texts on the history of usury or interest rates are concerned primarily with the Middle Ages and the Scholastic concerns with this subject, and so treat the Greek, Roman, and Jewish situation within the first few pages, but do not provide the subject with a thorough execution. The largest section devoted to the rise of usury in Greece and Rome is in Sidney Homer and Richard Sylla's *A History of Interest Rates*, but these authors draw primarily from Gustave Glotz's *The Aegean Civilization* and *Ancient Greece at Work*; A. M. Andreades's *A History of Greek Public Finance*; and Fritz M. Heichelheim's *Ancient Economic His-tory; From the Palaeolithic Age to the Migrations of the Germanic, Slavic, and Arabic Nations.*

The Development of Usury in the Roman Empire

In addition to the acquisition of religious culture, Rome inherited Hellenistic economic culture[4] when she conquered the Mediterranean; this included the fact that the lending of money or goods was a common and accepted practice in rural Greece among family and friends,[5] and no law bridled the rate of interest.[6] In agricultural communities, the whims of pastoral mischief could harm one homestead yet leave another intact; families deemed it necessary to strike a balance between dependence and advantage. Reciprocity was encouraged, and Hesiod's *Works and Days*[7] advocated fair lending practices without formal interest, but surely with motive: "Take good measure from a neighbour, and pay it back well, with the same measure, or better if you can, so that you may later find him reliable should you need him."[8]

Interest on loans was never universally endorsed, but it was a fact of life from the time of the maturing of the banking system in Greece in the seventh and sixth centuries BCE[9] and the growth of trade and industry. Prior to this era, the ancient economy did not largely support an investment economics, as the majority of the people lived at subsistence level, and thus dependency and obligation were integral to survival.[10] One of many social changes brought about by development of trade in Greece was that families were no longer content to satisfy their own needs. As

4. Cameron, *Concise Economic History of the World*, 37.

5. Glotz, *Ancient Greece at Work*, 240. See also Maloney, "Usury in Greek, Roman and Rabbinic Thought," 79.

6. Millett, *Lending and Borrowing*, 181.

7. Hesiod dedicated the text to his brother Perses who had lost his land because of too many debts. Hesiod, *Works and Days*, 349.

8. Hesiod, *Works and Days*, 348–51 and 477–78. Chester G. Starr writes that in a largely agricultural system that is not dependent upon coinage, it is difficult to understand how peasants came to be so heavily in debt. In such a world, usually one neighbor helps another. He cites French, with whom he disagrees, who wrote, "It is not difficult to imagine how the peasants had come to fall into debt" (French, *Growth of the Athenian Economy*, 12–14). French cites overpopulation as the reasons peasants were forced off the land. Starr disagrees, claiming that there was no increase in farm productivity and labor at this time, for had there been Solon of Athens would not have encouraged immigration. French does, however, explain the way in which advance sales on crops not yet harvested (futures) could add up over a period of time to great indebtedness. Starr, *The Economic and Social Growth of Early Greece*, 3–20.

9. Heichelheim, *An Ancient Economic History*, 135–36.

10. Millett, *Lending and Borrowing*, 72 n. 4; Meikle, "Modernism, Economics and the Ancient Economy," 242.

individuals saw the financial benefit of over-production,[11] large estates no longer limited production to the needs of the family on the estate but sold or loaned additional produce or animals to peasants living on the lands. Conveniently for the lord, peasant wives, children and land were used as security against loans[12] which held an interest rate of up to thirty-six percent or more.[13]

Peasants had the most difficult time with the loan system, and it is tempting to suspect that they were set up to fail; the price for natural products was low while interest rates for loans—which were based on sea-trade with short-term/high-risk/high-interest—were high. Rural debts were often contracted for consumption rather than production, and such debts mounted under the instability of crop production. A farmer who attempted to make up the difference by over-cultivation often found there was no guarantee that the land would yield a needed return. Despite kinship and community support, for one reason or another someone inevitably slipped through the net. If Hesiod's method was rejected,[14] then a peasant's only choice while in financial difficulty would be to turn to the nearest lord,[15] who loaned rather than gave to his dependent at a rate of interest which the peasant might not be able to repay.[16] Debtors lost

11. It was not simply the traders and aristocrats who sought wealth; Hesiod comments that even simple craftsmen and potters ran after profit. Starr cites Hesiod "IV" but does not indicate if this is from the *Works and Days* (which has no chapters), or from another text. Solon catalogues the many ways of acquiring wealth, and astutely notes that those who are wealthy "have twice the eagerness that others have." Solon, fr. 1, in Starr, *Economic and Social Growth of Early Greece*, 48.

12. Glotz, *Ancient Greece at Work*, 73–74. For more on this, see the chapter "Debt-Bondage and the Problem of Slavery," in Finley, *Economy and Society in Ancient Greece*, 150–66.

13. Homer and Sylla, *A History of Interest Rates*, 40.

14. "Take good measure from a neighbour, and pay it back well, with the same measure, or better if you can, so that you may later find him reliable should you need him" (Hesiod, *Works and Days*, 348–51).

15. The lord did not represent the highest political authority, nor did their way of life differ greatly than those beneath them, but they did represent stability and unity (Starr, *Economic and Social Growth of Early Greece*, 30).

16. The constricting contract produced by usury is evident in a remaining papyri from 273 BCE: "Dionysius son of Apollonius, Gazaean, in the service of Dinon, has lent to Isidorus, Thracian, of the troop of Lycophron, holder of the 40 arurae, 34 drachmae of silver, this being the price of the Crown corn, on interest at the rate of 2 drachmae each month on each mina. Isidorus shall repay the loan to Dionysius in the month Artemisius of the 13th year with the interest. If he fails to repay in the stated time, he shall forfeit one and a half times the amount of the loan, and Dionysius

wives and children, and entire families were sold into slavery; now known as "Dependants" or *Hektemors*,[17] peasants were left to farm land that was no longer theirs. This type of practice resulted in deep-seated misery and extreme hatred between the classes.[18]

Solon, archon of Athens in 594 BCE, had as his priority the liberation of the "dark earth" from indebtedness. In one of the first acts of legislation against usury and other crimes against the poor, Solon annulled many rural debts and reduced others, forbade "loans on the person"[19] and made this prescription retroactive. Aristotle especially wrote in glowing terms about Solon's reforms,[20] noting abuses that existed prior to his legislative actions as well as actions he took to relieve tensions of the situation:

> After that, there was civil strife for a long time between the nobility and the common people. For the whole political setup was oligarchical, and, in particular, the poor together with their

---

shall have the right of execution upon the property of Isidorus and that of his surety, making exaction in whatever way he chooses as in respect of debts to the Crown." "66. Loan of Money," *Select Papyri* 1:199.

17. There is disagreement about this term. Glotz claims that the peasant was only allowed to keep one-sixth of the production; other scholars, among them French, in *The Growth of the Athenian Economy*, write that the yield of one-sixth was for the landlord, which would mean that the peasant kept five-sixths. French quotes—but does not cite—a Greek historian who writes that the *Hektemors* "tilled the lands [of the rich] handing over one-sixth of the produce." French, *Growth of the Athenian Economy*, 12. Glotz, *Ancient Greece at Work*, 80–81. See also Glotz, *The Greek City and its Institutions*, 103–4. Woodhouse accuses Aristotle of confusing the situation by his ambiguous language on the subject. Woodhouse, *Solon the Liberator*, 31.

18. Consider the rural unrest of Miletus, where dissident peasants seized the children of the local rich and flung them onto the threshing floor, where they were trampled by oxen (Starr, *Economic and Social Growth of Early Greece*, 181). To be fair, it should be noted that not all were done in by their loans, and not all loans were life-threatening; temples, private cults and the *demes* also lent out small amounts for individuals who happened to need a small sum for a ceremonial banquet or sacrificial animal. Finley, *Economy and Society*, 259–60 n. 31.

19. "As soon as Solon had been entrusted with full powers to act, he liberated the people by prohibiting loans on the person of the debtor, both for the present and the future. He made laws and enacted a cancellation of debts both of private and public, a measure which is commonly called *seisachtheia* [the shaking-off of burdens], since in this way they shook off their burdens." Aristotle, *Constitution of Athens*, in Fritz and Kapp, 73. See also Plutarch's *Solon*, 43–76.

20. Aristotle's words in favor of Solon's reforms are curious, as both Plato and Aristotle spoke against the folly of attempting to discipline the wealthy by canceling the debts of the poor, which they did not consider to be the solution to the problem (Aristotle, *Politics*, 1305a; Plato, *The Laws of Plato*, 684e).

wives and children were serfs of the rich. They were called Pe-
latae and Hectemori ["sixth-parters"], for it was at this rent that
they cultivated the land of the wealthy. All the land was in the
hands of the few, and if the serfs did not pay their rent, they
and their children could be sold into slavery. All loans were
contracted upon the person of the debtor, until the time of Solon, who was to become a leader of the people. The hardest and
most hateful feature of the political situation as far as the many
were concerned was their serfdom. But they also nursed grievances in all other respects, for they had, so to speak, no share in
anything.[21]

As a result, Solon enacted the following legislation: "The three most dem-
ocratic features of his constitution appear to be the following: first, and
most important, the law that nobody could contract a loan secured on his
person . . ."[22]

Despite such strong sanction, the elimination of a few abuses was ineffective against the obstacle of usury, which remained a regular practice.
Besides pledging one's own family or one's own body, there were additional
offences associated with usury such as *anatocism*, a scandalous practice in
which the accumulation of interest was capitalized on the original interest. In addition to simply ignoring the laws, documents were occasionally
falsified so the debtor paid interest on a larger loan than was received.[23]

21. Aristotle, *Constitution of Athens*, 2.2.

22. Aristotle, *Constitution of Athens*, 9.1.

23. Holman cites an example of this contained in the second-century-CE Document II of the "Babatha" archive. According to Holman, Babatha's husband Judah
signed for a loan on a document that was later altered to read "forty denarii." Modern
editors of the text suggest that while Judah received his forty denarii, he paid interest
on sixty. *The Documents from the Bar Koch Period in the Cave of Letters*, 41–46, 58–64,
in Holman, *The Hungry Are Dying*, 118. This same woman had previously had trouble
with stolen interest, and sued her son's guardians for keeping one-half percent interest of his illegally invested patrimony (Holman, *The Hungry are Dying*, 116). This is
validated in the *Theodosian Code*: "Emperors Arcadias and Honorius Augustuses to
Eutychianus, Praetorian Prefect. The moment that they are instituted, tutors shall immediately appear before the judges, so that, in the presence of the chief decurions, the
defender, and public office staffs, and inventory shall be made with due formality, and
all the gold and silver found in the pupils' substance, as well as anything else that does
not suffer change with the lapse of time, shall be marked with the seals of the judges,
senators, and public office staffs, and placed in safest custody by the authorization of
a public order. There shall be no expectation of interest, nor shall any having become
an adult, attains legal age, when he does not so much begin to have time for lawsuits as
to rejoice that he has been restored so soon to his whole patrimony. Since a moderate
fortune, too, must be considered, if perchance movables alone, and no immovables,

There was one type of lender not detested by the public, and one type of non-interest loan not affected by the increase in usury: the ἔρανος.[24] The ἔρανος was an interest-free loan extended among family and friends, in a type of loan system known as "pooling."[25] The only interest paid was the gratitude of the debtor to the lender, and the lender hoped only to see a return of his capital. The risk involved in this type of loan was taken on the part of the lender rather than the debtor, and was greater than in the case of usury, for the lender stood to loose money as well as a friendship if the debt was not repaid.[26] The ἔρανος evolved into a loan from a social gathering among friends. Maloney, in "Usury in Greek, Roman and Rabbinic Thought," notes the evolution of the term from its mention in Homer's

---

are left to a person as an inheritance, and no income from landed estates can be reckoned upon, out of which the pupil's household or the pupil himself can be supported, either suitable estates shall be purchased with the aforesaid movables, or if perchance, as usually happens, suitable estates cannot be found, in accordance with the general rule of the ancient law, and income shall accrue from interest. Thus in this case also, in which there is no hope for income from landed estates, the needs of the minor shall be provided from the income of his movable property; and in the former case in interest shall by no means be sought without the risk of the tutor" (*Theodosian Code*, 3.30.6).

24. Glotz, *Ancient Greece at Work*, 240. The ἔρανος seems to anticipate how interest-free loans were supposed to take place among the Israelites, distinct from loans which they granted to those who lived removed from Hebrew communities. See also Millett, *Lending and Borrowing*, 153–59.

25. Sahlins, *Stone Age Economics*, 188. "Pooling" is a type of lending that is primarily a distribution among equals. This is a fairly important point, in that lending of this type among equals did not take place to assuage poverty, but to provide an individual with a financial advantage. Millett, *Lending and Borrowing*, 153. The ἔρανος did, however, sometimes cut across social boundaries, and a perfect example of this is found in Demosthenes, who writes of a prostitute who bought her freedom by raising ἔρανος contributions from her customers, including one Phrynion, who acted as an agent on her behalf: "When Phrynion came to her, she told him the proposal which Eucrates and Timanoridas [her Corinthians owners] had made to her, and gave him the money which she had collected from her other lovers as a contribution [ἔρανον] towards the price of her freedom, and added whatever she had gained for herself, and she begged him to advance the balance needed to make up the twenty minae, and to pay it to Eucrates and Timanoridas to secure her freedom. He listened gladly to these words of hers, and taking the money which had been paid in to her by her other lovers, added the balance himself and paid the twenty minae as the price of her freedom to Eucrates and Timanoridas on the condition that she should not ply her trade in Corinth" (Demosthenes, *Private Orations*, 59.30–32).

26. Starr writes that morality—like the aforementioned philosophy—was tied to practical actions; if one's friends were in trouble, one should help them. Hesiod and Solon both write about the strong ties in Greek society, which advocated collective assistance during times of distress. (Starr, *Economic and Social Growth of Early Greece*, 39).

Odyssey as a communal banquet among friends, to a general gathering among friends, and finally to a gathering of friends who come together to help another friend with a loan.[27] As he points out, the meal element eventually faded, but what remains central to the ἔρανος is the common base of friendship, to the extent that the ἔρανος can refer either to the loan itself, or to the group who have gathered in friendship. Information regarding any legal formalities of the ἔρανος is scant, and no evidence remains that provides a methodical explanation of the ἔρανος,[28] but what can be uncovered is that the lender often received his money back through an installment plan, and that the loan could be pressed for in court if necessary.[29]

Usury increased after the fourth century BCE; creative ways of using money were emerging[30] and the credit system was used extensively as individuals invested over fifty percent of their fortunes in land, houses and slaves.[31] Usury was regarded as useful for encouraging business and trade, with some businesses dependent entirely on the loan system.[32] Debtors were prosecuted, but many continued to borrow to maintain lavish lifestyles,[33] to fund a dowry,[34] or because they had pledged to a cause more than they could afford.[35] In addition, the seizure of hoards of Per-

27. Maloney, "Usury in Greek, Roman and Rabbinic Thought," 81. See also Finley, *Economy and Society,* 68; and Beauchet, *Histoire du droit prive de la republic athenienne.* See also Liddell and Scott: "ἔρανος, ὁ, meal to which each contributed his share. II. *loan,* raised by contributions for the benefit of an individual, bearing no interest, but recoverable at law, in instalments" (Liddell and Scott, *Greek-English Lexicon,* 680).

28. Millett, *Lending and Borrowing,* 153.

29. Aristotle mentions a system set up to prosecute men who accepted an ἔρανος loan but did not pay it back. "They also set up by lot five men as Introducers (*eisagogeis*), who introduce the law cases which are to be decided within a month, each one acting for two tribes . . . Furthermore, prosecution for assault, and cases arising out of friendly loans (*eranoi*), out of partnerships, in regard to slaves, draft animals, trierarchies, and transactions with banks are introduced." Aristotle, *Constitution of Athens,* 52.3–4. See also Millett, *Lending and Borrowing,* 153–54.

30. Glotz, *Ancient Greece at Work,* 364.

31. In 410 a certain Diodotos invested 48,000 of his 80,000 drachmas; another's fortune was composed of only 900 of ready cash while his investments totaled over 28,500. These are only two examples of how the Greeks of these times kept a sum of money for basic needs and invested the remainder. Glotz, *Ancient Greece at Work,* 238.

32. The expanding market system encouraged borrowing, to the extent that the businesses of some individuals were maintained specifically by loans. Glotz, *Ancient Greece at Work,* 240–41.

33. Finley, *Economy and Society,* 69.

34. Ibid., 70.

35. "In order that I might be thought better, by you and, should some misfortune

sian wealth by Alexander the Great inserted a huge cache of coinage into the Mediterranean world.[36] This, in addition to the expansion of trade, resulted in the interest rate falling in the third and second century down as low as seven percent, and it remained so until Roman conquest plundered the provinces first with soldiers, and then with publicans.

The Romans were originally an agricultural people with a high regard for private property. They had an appreciation for the soil but cared less for matters of exchange, and left such troubles to be handled by slaves and servants. Roman law—though suited for an agrarian society—strictly enforced business contracts and property privileges to the extent that one of Rome's greatest contributions to economic theory was its conviction of private property rights.[37] But Rome's single greatest contribution to the world of economics was the "peace" which it established in the Mediterranean in order for trade to develop under propitious conditions.[38]

Roman law was concerned primarily with enforcing the rights of the individual to use, enjoy and abuse their property,[39] and property rights were the foundation of Roman law. In addition to property rights, Roman law attempted to exert control over interest rates on loans. Like the Greeks, Roman moralists condemned lending at interest, but the laws consistently allowed for the practice.

The Romans banking system involved various financial transactions such as money-changing, mortgages on land, houses or slaves, or nautical loans.[40] Loans made to people who were short of funds or who found themselves in a financially awkward position were primarily from friends or family, and carried no interest.[41] In this respect, they were similar to the ἔρανος loan enjoyed among the Greeks. Individuals at a higher level of in-

---

overtake me (i.e. should I be brought before a court) I should have a better chance in court" (Lysias, *Subverting the Democracy* 25.13, in Adkins, *Merit and Responsibility*, 202).

36. Homer and Sylla, *A History of Interest Rates*, 38–39.

37. González, *Faith and Wealth*, 15. This is partly due to the sacred connection which the Romans had to the land, similar to the ancient Hebrews. Their farms contained altars to their ancestors, which lent a reverent quality to the homestead.

38. Cameron, *Concise Economic History of the World*, 37.

39. "jus utendi, jus fruendi, jus abutendi" (González, *Faith and Wealth*, 19).

40. This early commercial loan was high interest and high risk: the lender advanced money, essentially gambling that the voyage would be successful. If it was, the lender got the money back plus interest; if it was not, the money was lost (Jones, *The Roman Economy*, 187; Morley, "The Early Roman Empire: Distribution," 587).

41. Jones, *The Roman Economy*, 187.

come—nobles and aristocracy—lent money to client kings and provincial cities; this type of loan carried an uncommonly high interest considering that it was practically a no-risk loan, as the lender usually had access to the military forces to press payment if necessary.[42]

Evidence for a legal injunction against usury in Roman society is contained in the Law of the Twelve Tablets,[43] c. 451–449 BCE; the eighth tablet addressed rates of interest, stating that "No person shall practice usury at a rate of more than one-twelfth."[44] Any usurer who charged a rate higher would be required to restore the sum four times over.[45] Historians are not in agreement about fixed rates for interest prior to the fifth century, but it is most likely that until this time the rates were arbitrary.[46] Compounded interest was forbidden, although ways were found around this.[47] In 397 BCE the rate was restricted to twelve percent, which indicates that scant attention was given to the injunction of the eighth tablet,[48] an unfortunate fact that seems to be reflected consistently in the examination of the legislation.

Despite legislation that indicates otherwise, evidence remains to suggest that the Roman ideal was a loan without interest: Herienouphis son of Psemminis, one of those who have returned in consequence of the order, has lent to Eunous son of Patseous and to Patseous son of Orses, both of them Persians of the Epigone from Pathyris, five talents two thousand drachmae of copper money *without interest* for thirty days from the eleventh of Mesore of the aforesaid year.[49]

But despite the kindly terms of this first portion of the contract, the second portion—repayment—makes the terms of non-payment chillingly

42. Ibid.

43. The *Twelve Tablets* are sometimes referred to as the *Twelve Tables*.

44. According to Note 93 of *Table 8*, scholars have argued over the phrase *unciario faenore* (the *uncia*—from which we have the "ounce"—is the twelfth portion of an object), with suggested rates ranging from one percent to one hundred percent. It is a waste of time to point out that both of these extremes are useless numbers, so this paper will assume that the interest suggested was either ten or twelve percent, as one *uncia* of one hundred percent over the course of one year equals twelve percent yearly interest. (*Table* 8, 8.18a in *Ancient Roman Statutes*, 11).

45. *Table* 8, 8.18b (*Ancient Roman Statutes*).

46. Louis, *Ancient Rome at Work*, 86.

47. *Dig.* 3.5.37; 12.6.26.1; 26.7.7.8, in González, *Faith and Wealth*, 19, 26; Andreau, *Banking and Business in the Roman World*, 92.

48. Louis, *Ancient Rome at Work*, 87.

49. "106 BCE, P.Amph. 50," *Select Papyri*, 1:201 (italics added).

clear: "The borrowers themselves are sureties for each other for the payment of all the liabilities of this loan, and Herienouphis shall have *the right of execution* upon their persons together or singly or upon whichever he chooses and upon all their property as if by legal decision."[50] Solon's legislation freeing the debtor from enslavement—or in this case death—is forgotten.

Titus Livy provides a valuable resource for first century Roman attitudes about lending. Neither the injunction of the Twelve Tablets nor the restriction of rates has suppressed usury, for he writes that the *Lex Licinia Sestia* (375 BCE) attempted to deal with this economic cancer:

> An opportunity for innovation was presented by the enormous load of debt, which the plebs could have no hope of lightening but by placing their representatives in the highest offices ... For the present it was resolved that Gaius Licinius and Lucius Sextius should be elected tribunes of the plebs, a magistracy in which they might open for themselves a way to other distinctions. Once elected, they proposed only such measures as abated the influence of the patricians, while forwarding the interest of the plebs. One of these had to do with debt, providing that what had been paid as interest should be deducted from the original sum, and the remainder discharged in three annual installments of equal size.[51]

As other laws before, the *Lex Licina Sestia* appears to have done little to alleviate the situation, for Livy writes that the *Lex Duillia Menenia* (357 BCE) reaffirmed the code of the Twelve Tablets and sought to address the problem of usury more directly: "Less agreeable to the senate was a measure which came up the following year ... [it] fixed the rate of interest at one percent, and was carried through by Marcus Duillius and Lucius Menenius, tribunes of the plebs. The commons ratified it much more eagerly than they had done the other law." [52] Five years later, another attempt was made to deal with what Livy claimed was "the sole obstacle to harmony": "The tribunes continually vaunted their backing of the Licinian law: the plebs were more concerned with the distress they suffered from the increasing weight of usury, and their private worries broke out into public quarrels ... Now that the minds of men were once inclined

---

50. "106 BCE, P.Amph. 50," *Select Papyri*, 1:201–3 (italics added).

51. Livy, *History of Rome*, 6.35.

52. Livy, *History of Rome*, 7.16. Jean Andreau writes that the debt crisis of 340 and 350 instigated this legislation, with resultant reduction in penalties until 342 when interest loans were banned. (Andreau, *Banking and Business*, 91.

to concord, the new consuls set themselves to obtain relief in the matter of usury also, which appeared to be the sole obstacle to harmony. They made the discharge of debts a concern of the state, appointing five commissioners, whom they called bankers, from their having the disposition of the money.[53]" Again, Livy cites a usury law of 347 that reduced interest rates and spread out the payments in equal instalments: "The same peaceful conditions continued at home and abroad during the consulship of Titus Manlius Torquatus and Gaius Plautius. But the rate of interest was cut in half (*semiunciarium tantum ex unciario fenus factum*) and debts were made payable, one-fourth down and the remainder in three annual installments; even so some of the plebeians were distressed, but the public credit was of greater concern to the senate than were the hardships of single persons.[54]" While writing about a variety of financial transactions which took place a further five years later in 342, Livy claims that "I find in certain writers that Lucius Genucius, a tribune of the plebs, proposed to the plebs that it should be unlawful to lend at interest,"[55] a statement that seems to indicate that he is somewhat doubtful about the legalities of this measure.[56]

Litigation against usury appears to have ceased momentarily, as Romans busied themselves migrating and settling in new colonies after the Latin war.[57] In 326 BCE, legislation attempted again to restrain interest allowed by the original edicts of the Twelve Tablets after a young man named Gaius Publilius, who had given himself up for his father's debt to one Lucius Papirius, was stripped and beaten after the boy rebuffed Lucius's sexual advances. Gaius Publilius broke free and rushed into the street, cursing the violence and the usurer and inciting a mob to protest against multiple abuses:

53. Ibid., 7.21.5–8.

54. Ibid., 7.27.3.

55. Ibid., 7.42.1; Andreau, *Banking and Business*, 91.

56. Maloney and Andreau refer to this as a law, but Livy does not claim that it is a law, only that it is a proposition. Maloney points out that while the existence of this law has been contested, still there are other sources which attest to its existence. Maloney, "Usury in Greek, Roman and Rabbinic Thought," 90. See also Tacitus: "and at length usufruct was unconditionally banned." Tacitus, *Annals*, 6.16. Appian, *Bella civilia* 1.54, and, the *Lex Marcia*, which was possibly of the same age, also gave the debtor legal rights against the lender. The *Institutes* of Gaius, a revered Roman jurist during the reign of Hadrian (117–138 CE) includes a reference to the *Lex Marcia*: "also the *Lex Marcia* against money-lenders, so that if they collected interest, they could be compelled by this proceeding to refund it" (Gaius, *The Institutes*, 188).

57. Frank, *An Economic Survey of Ancient Rome*, 31.

and a great throng of people, burning with pity for his tender years, and with the rage for the shameful wrong he had undergone, and considering, too, their own condition and their children's, rushed down into the Forum, and from there in a sold throng to the Curia. The consuls were forced by the sudden tumult to convene the senate; and as the Fathers entered the Curia, the people threw themselves at the feet of each, and pointed to the young boy's mutilated back. On that day, owning to one man's outrageous injury, was broken a strong bond of credit, and the consuls were ordered to carry a proposal to the people that none should be confined in shackles or in the stocks, save those who, having been guilty of some crime, were waiting to pay the penalty; and that for money lent, the debtor's goods, but not his person, should be distrainable. So those in confinement were released, and it was forbidden that anyone should be confined thereafter.[58]

This Magna Charta of plebeian rights functioned in a similar way to the aforementioned measures taken by Solon; no longer could a lender seize possession of the debtor if the debtor defaulted on a loan. Now, only possessions could be taken as compensation for debt.[59]

Civil wars in the third century BCE of the Roman Empire coincided with a change in standards of living; nobility who had grown fat off usurious practices relegated the peasants to a deplorable condition. The growth of *latifundia*[60] increased at the expense of small land-holding farmers burdened by debt, and the Empire—heavy with empty wheat fields—was forced to begin to import grains from Egypt and Sicily.[61] Farmers had little or no capital to renovate their farms, learn new farming methods, and plant vineyards or aviaries for the favored delicacies of the upper class.[62]

---

58. Livy, *History of Rome*, 8.25. This law is also mentioned in Cicero, *de Rep.*, 2.59: "The bonds of citizens were released and thereafter binding for debts ceased." Frank, *An Economic Survey*, 32.

59. Creditors had personal rights over the body of the debtor; they had the right to sell into slavery, put to death, or tear the limbs from those who failed to meet financial obligations. There were examples of bondage slavery after this, but cases were rare, and the contracts did not hold up in court. Frank, *An Economic Survey*, 32.

60. *Latifundia* is a process whereby large estates absorb incorporate smaller farms into theirs. This has a twofold purpose: it increased one's property and enslaved the local population (González, *Faith and Wealth*, 29–33).

61. Louis, *Ancient Rome at Work*, 89–90. See also González, *Faith and Wealth*, 31.

62. The aristocracy hungered after rare or small birds (thrushes, peacocks, and the like), fish, oysters, vegetables, and exotic fruits, primarily imported from Asia.

Land lay fallow as farmers fled to cities and upset the social order with un-
employment and all the charms that poverty and boredom bring to a big
city. Hostile generals gathered them in, nurtured their dissatisfaction, and
used them to abolish security in the city and settle minor conflicts against
one another by means of blood and fire; the countryside, meanwhile, was
deflowered and left useless for agricultural production, had there been
anyone to make use of it.[63] At the same time, increased desire for luxury
products among the aristocracy resulted in a flourishing trade which be-
lied the economic chaos that reflected the reality of the majority of those
in the Empire. Financial prosperity was not, as Paul Louis writes, the result
of a unified nation working together and enjoying in all ranks the benefits
of affluence, but "it was that of an oligarchy of pillagers who exploited
tens of millions of men, subjected them to permanent and practically
unpaid labour, and, to crown all, confiscated by means of usury public
and private fortunes as they began to accumulate again."[64] In third-century
Rome, usury was salt on an open wound, but despite legislation, Romans
consistently found ways to get around legal prohibitions against it. The
amount of legislation indicates that it must have been fairly easy to evade
the laws altogether. Many simply lent through the Latins, who—like the
Metics in Greece earlier,[65] the Gentiles for the Jews, and then the Jews for
the Gentiles—were used to dodge interdictions against usury. An attempt
was made in 193 BCE to end this practice with legislation that required
Latins to declare their debts.[66]

A percentage of the debt problem that beset the Empire can be connected to taxation. Ever touchy over issues concerning personal rights,
Romans believed that taxation was incompatible with the rights of a free
person; the very act of being taxed implied oppression. Initially Romans
were only taxed during times of war, and the money was generously returned to them if the booty acquired was sufficient to allow for it. In addition to warfare taxation, provinces were required to pay both income

---

Another specialty food, cheese, rose in prominence as cereal foods declined (Louis,
Ancient Rome at Work, 163).

63. Ibid., 163.

64. Ibid., 91–92.

65. The Metics were individuals of foreign birth who lived and worked in Greek
cities; they were not citizens, and their rights were limited. After amassing a great deal
of wealth, a Metic might gain the respect of the citizen, as well as citizenship (Glotz,
Ancient Greece at Work, 163). Metics were used like the Latins and the Gentiles as in
intermediary in the loan process as a way of dodging interest restrictions.

66. Louis, *Ancient Rome at Work*, 210.

and poll taxes, while other taxes were dependent on the specific areas, such as temple taxes, sales, inheritance, crop and slave taxes and taxes. Tax farmers, or "publicans" collected the tariffs, and in the process inspired formidable hatred for their methods of exploitation.[67] They collected a fee along with the taxes, and often raised the taxes in order to raise their fees. Publicans also made profits by reselling goods collected in kind—which they often hoarded—and by taking advantage of the uneducated and rustic.[68] Their primary job, however, seemed to be the total annihilation of the land-owning free peasant, for if a farmer was unable to pay his taxes the publican might loan the farmer the money to do so at a rate which fluctuated between twelve and forty-eight percent.[69] Publicans contributed to the disorder of the Empire by financing whichever general seemed to offer them the best opportunity to continue in their nefarious ways. Their lending practices were not limited to individuals, for they formed syndicates which—as well as employing other methods to systematically exploit the land—granted loans at high interest for commercial or industrial purposes.[70] Laws against loan abuses of the publicans were largely ineffective because publicans were responsible for a great deal of revenue,[71] and

---

67. The equestrian order was another group in the Roman Empire that enriched itself by war, trade and usury. They rose to prominence in the land during the time of the civil wars, 264–30 BCE. Hostile to the senators—although barely distinguishable from them initially—they sought support from the *plebs*, until their riches grew too abundant for the *plebs* to support them, at which point they turned to gain support from their previous enemies. By 122 BCE they were masters of Rome, and maintained this position for eighty years until they were annihilated in 82 BCE by Sulla, along with a great many other citizens (Louis, *Ancient Rome at Work*, 105).

68. González, *Faith and Wealth*, 38.

69. Ibid. See also Jones, *The Roman Economy*, 119. Cicero writes that the publicans bargained for greater than 12 percent of the balance. Cicero, *Letters to Atticus*, 5.21.

70. When Sulla came to power he took from the publicans the grants they had extracted from Asia, which amounted to 26,000,000 [English] pounds (Louis, *Ancient Rome at Work*, 117. See also "Sulla" in Plutarch, *Plutarch's Lives*, 4.323–445).

71. Cicero writes about them in silvery terms: "To take part against the publicans is to alienate from the Republic and ourselves a body to whom we owe considerable obligations and which we have ourselves attached to the State," in Louis, *Ancient Rome at Work*, 116, who does not cite the source. Louis also mentions that Livy praises their patriotism, but again does not provide a citation. Louis notes that although these gentlemen praised the publicans, to do so "was to be wilfully blind to the abuses and misdeeds which history has recorded and which remains undeniable." Louis, *Ancient Rome at Work*, 117.

because those who were to enforce laws against the abuses often shared in the ill-gained profits.[72]

Legislation continued at a steady pace against usury, although running through the edicts it is clear that measures against the practice were largely ineffective: In 217 BCE the Lex Flaminia *minus solvendi* allowed debtors to pay their debts with reduced coinage;[73] in 193 BCE the Lex Sempronia made the Latins declare all debts;[74] in 89 *praetor* A. Sempronius Asellio resurrected a law that prohibited interest-bearing loans;[75] 88 BCE the *Lex Cornelia Pompeia* returned to the interest rates of the Twelve Tablets, which was one-twelfth;[76] in 86 BCE: the *Lex Valeria* allowed bankrupt debtors to satisfy their obligations by repaying only one-quarter of their debts to lenders.[77] In 72 BCE, Lucullus made one percent per month the maximum interest rate for Asia and Cilicia.[78] Cicero, a contemporary, provides valuable information about usurers: interest rates in Rome were officially set at twelve percent,[79] but moneylenders extended loans at six percent if the security was good.[80] A man whose name was in good standing could obtain a loan at four percent, but if his name were not, rates could be up to forty-eight percent if security was not good, or if the usurer was just plain Machiavellian.[81]

72. González, *Faith and Wealth*, 39. See also Louis, *Ancient Rome at Work*, 113.

73. Berger, "Lex Flaminia," in Maloney, "Usury in Greek, Roman and Rabbinic Thought," 91. Maloney writes that there is doubt about the details of this law.

74. Berger, "Leges Semproniae," in *Encyclopedic Dictionary of Roman Law*, 560.

75. Appian, *Bella civilia*, 1.134.232–39; Andreau, *Banking and Business*, 91.

76. Berger, "Leges Semproniae," in *Encyclopedic Dictionary of Roman Law*, 550; Andreau, *Banking and Business*, 91.

77. Berger, "Leges Semproniae," 560.

78. Maloney, "Usury in Greek, Roman and Rabbinic Thought," 91; Andreau, *Banking and Business*, 93.

79. Cicero, *Letters to Atticus*, 5.21.

80. Ibid., see also Pliny *Letters and Panegyrics*, vol. 1:7.18: "I had promised a capital sum of 500,000 sesterces for the maintenance of free-born boys and girls, but instead of paying this over I transferred some of my landed property (which was worth considerably more) to the municipal agent, and then had it reconveyed back to me charged with an annual rent payable of 30,000 sesterces" (six percent). See also Pliny the Elder: "Assuming that by the valuation of that period their cost may be put at 100 sesterces per amphora, but that the interest on this sum has been adding up at 6 per cent" (Pliny, *Natural History*, 4:16.56).

81. In *Letters to Atticus*, Cicero writes of a debt situation that he attempts to handle for a community. The people of Salamis request that Cicero intervene when the lender wanted to take 48 percent rather than the traditional 12 percent represented in the

Tacitus, a senator, consul and governor whose career took place during the reigns of Emperors Domitian (81–96 CE) and Trajan (98–117 CE), briefly traces in his *Annals* attempts to suppress usury in the period prior to the death of Augustus (14 CE) to the death of Nero (68 CE). Tacitus summarizes the chaos brought about by corrupt lending practices in Rome:

> Meanwhile, an army of accusers now broke loose on the persons who habitually increased their riches by usury, in contravention of a law of the dictator Caesar,[82] regulating the conditions of lending money and holding property within the boundaries of Italy: a measure dropped long ago, since the public good ranks second to private utility. The curse of usury, it must be owned, is inveterate in Rome, a constant source of sedition and discord; and attempts were made to repress it even in an older and less corrupt society. First came the provision of the Twelve Tables that the rate of interest, previously governed by the fancy of the rich, should not exceed one-twelfth percent for the month; later, a tribunician rogation lowered it to one-half of that amount; and at length usufruct was unconditionally banned.[83]

Romans continued to be very vocal in their dissatisfaction with the system.[84] As a result of the debt owed to the Roman *negotiatores*, Tacitus writes of uprisings in 21 CE in Northern Gaul, instigated by Julius Flo-

---

edict which Cicero had inherited from the previous governor, and which he had also ratified. Cicero became the middleman in a difficult dispute between the money-lender—who believed that he is owed nearly 50,000 (English) pounds—and the townspeople—who believed that they owed Salamis closer to 25,000 (English) pounds: "The bystanders all declared that the conduct of Scaptius was outrageous in refusing 12 percent with compound interest. Others said that he was a fool. He seemed to me to be more of a knave than a fool; for either he was not content with 12 percent on good security, or he hoped for 48 percent on very doubtful security" (Cicero, *Letters to Atticus*, 5.21). Cicero is wearied by this exchange, and the letter does not indicate who received what in the end. In a rather interesting twist, his later indifference to the plight of the townspeople of Salamis when Scaptius attempts to collect on this large sum is strange, as he initially shows alarm at the interest rate which, if pressed, "spelled ruin to the community." Cicero, *Letters to Atticus*, 5.21. He adds to this tale that he has received a letter that there is the possibility of the repudiation of debts, and he hopes that this does not come to pass, for he believes that such measures do more harm than good to public finance.

82. Jackson writes that there is nothing known of this law. Tacitus, *The Annals*, 180 n. 1.

83. Tacitus, *The Annals*, 6.16.

84. Finley, *Economy and Society*, 92.

rus among the Treviri and Julius Sacrovir among the Aedui: "And so in assemblies and conventicles they made their seditious pronouncements on the continuous tributes, the grinding rates of interest, the cruelty and pride of the governors. . . . There was hardly a community into which the seeds of the movement had not fallen."[85] Roman citizens praised the rebels, claiming that "war itself was a welcome exchange for the horrors of peace."[86] But facing defeat, the rebellions ended when both instigators killed themselves.

Problems in the Roman Empire brought on by usury were crucial to the failure of the economic situation. The confiscation of lands by the nobility coincided with the rise in poverty of huge numbers of people; this, combined with threats to their physical being created feelings of hatred and revolution, and one can hardly be blamed for refusing to fight for a country which would allow one's liberties to be counted so cheap.[87] Only when wrathful masses were on the verge of insurrection did the aristocracy respond with the cancellation of debts.

One famous usurer in the first-century Roman Empire was the imperial tutor, advisor and speech-writer for Nero, Roman aristocrat and Stoic philosopher Seneca, who once lent ten million *denarii* at high rates to the Britons.[88] Much hated for his huge interest rates by which "Italy and the provinces were sucked dry by his usury,"[89] he was condemned by the Emperor's later advisors for his wealth, property, and desire for public popularity. Seneca was dismissed by Nero, subsequently handed over much of his property and wealth, and retired to a life of philosophy.[90]

85. Tacitus, *The Annals*, 3.40.

86. Ibid., 3.44.

87. In addition to the two Gaul revolts mentioned above, the secessions of 495 of the Sacred Mount and 286 of the Janiculum are two of the best known—of the many— revolts. Louis, *Ancient Rome at Work*, 87–88. After these revolts, the government responded by the repudiation of debts. See also Maloney, "Usury in Greek, Roman and Rabbinic Thought," 91, and Louis, *Ancient Rome at Work*, 87–88.

88. According to Cassius Dio (62.2), Seneca called in a loan of forty million *sesterces* in order to hasten the British revolution of 61 CE. See also Jones, *The Roman Economy*, 124; and Tacitus, *The Annals*, 13.42 n. 3, 74.

89. Tacitus, *The Annals*, 13.42.

90. Tacitus, *The Annals*, 14.54. Seneca's enemies were such and his fear of poisoning so great that he had to survive on fresh fruit and running water. He attempted suicide with his wife, but they both botched it, lingering on in pain. He even attempted to drink poison, but that failed him. He finally suffocated in a vapor bath. Tacitus, *The Annals*, 15. Dio Chrysostom, a contemporary of Plutarch, was also attacked for his expansive wealth. During a time when the price of grain was rising and a bread riot

There is improvement after the beginning of the Common Era, but even with interest set at twelve percent citizens were too skittish to borrow public funds and were borrowing amongst themselves, privately. Pliny the Younger wrote to Trajan in 112 CE, requesting that he lower the interest rate to encourage people within his province to borrow: "Would you then consider, Sir, whether you think that the rate of interest should be lowered to attract suitable borrowers, and, if they are still not forthcoming, whether the money might be loaned out among the town councillors upon their giving the State proper security? They may be unwilling to accept it, but it will be less of a burden to them if the rate of interest is reduced.[91]" Trajan wrote back hopeful words, agreeing that the only solution was to lower the interest rate, and that he trusted that Pliny could lower this in accordance to the amount of potential borrowers of public funds. In addition to this advice Trajan noted the potential danger, for he cautioned Pliny against taking aggressive measures, for "to force a loan on unwilling persons, who may perhaps have no means of making use of it themselves, is not in accordance with the justice of our times."[92] Despite this enlightened and just approach, abuses took place and restrictions were established, only to be largely ignored. Fewer borrowed than had before, and for different reasons; there was a lesser quantity a small farms, and therefore fewer farmers trying to "get by" with a minor loan that could bring major woes. Nobles,

---

had occurred, a mob made an attempt of vandalism on his properties. The following day he addressed them, protected by the local authorities, protesting that he has performed many "liturgies" [beneficent works] for the community, and refuting the claim of being a common money-lender for minor purchases such as food, although he does engaging in money-lending for business purposes. He begs the community to stop thinking about trivial needs—like food—and to reflect on his problems: "But consider my own claims too, gentlemen, not unsympathetically. For my father left us an estate which, while reputed to be large, was small in value, yes, much less than that of others; for no less than four hundred thousand drachmas were in bills receivable, besides foreign business ventures of such nature that they were far more troublesome than the bills. For we had no security, I might say, for any part of our assets, but my father had acquired all his wealth through trusting to his own influence, believe that no one would contest his claims. Yet, left as I was in such a situation, while I have not even now succeeded in securing a settlement of that part of the loans that fell to me, I have performed for you the greatest liturgies, in fact no one in the city has more of them to his credit than I have...Nay but, someone may claim, though I lend money, I am unwilling to supply it for the purchase of grain. There is no need for me to say anything on that score either, for you know both those who lend money in our city and those who borrow" (Dio Chrysostom, *The Forty-Sixth Discourse*, 231–35).

91. Pliny, *Letters and Panegyricus*, 2.10.54.
92. Pliny, *Letters and Panegyricus*, 2.10.55.

on the other hand, continued to borrow not out of necessity but to satiate a fondness for luxury products.[93]

Roman Emperors were unrelenting in issuing legislation against usury. Alexander Severus (222–235 CE) prohibited senators from taking interest, but he allowed them to accept gratuities, which—in the end—added up to the very same thing. Soon after this edict was overturned, senators were allowed to accept six percent interest on a loan.[94] An interesting law appeared in the reign of Diocletian (284–305 CE), who struck at usurers not with legal restrictions, but with a shameful identity and an ethical stigma: in 284 CE he called for the fine of "infamy" on lenders who accepted illegal interest.[95]

The first Roman Emperor to openly favor the Christians—Constantine I—issued a decree against usury to limit disfavor shown to farmers and to control interest rates:

> If a person should lend farm products, either liquid or dry, to those who need them, he shall receive a third additional part as interest; that is, if the sum credited should be two measures, he shall gain a third additional measure. 1. But if, on account of the advantage of the interest, a creditor should refuse to accept payment of the debt when he is formally notified, he shall be deprived not only of the interest but also of the principal of the debt. 2. This law shall pertain to farm produce only, for a creditor is forbidden to receive more than one per cent for money lent on interest.[96]

The one-percent interest rate is meant monthly, or twelve-percent interest rate per year. Although Constantine fixed the lending rates at twelve percent, with the possibility of increase to thirty-three percent in exceptional cases, still lenders were able to demand thirty percent in Egypt and up to thirty-three percent in Greece.[97] Nevertheless, debts that were incurred in kind continued to be administered at a rate of fifty percent, a Hellenistic habit known as the *hemiolion*.[98]

---

93. Louis, *Ancient Rome at Work*, 317. It was against this latter type of lending that Basil the Great would speak most vehemently.

94. In 397 CE, senators were once again forbidden to take interest. *Theodosian Code*, 2.33.3.

95. *Codex Justinianus* 2.12.20.

96. *The Theodosian Code and Novels*, 2.33.1.

97. Louis, *Ancient Rome at Work*, 318.

98. Mitteis, *Reichsrecht und Volksrecht in den östlichen Provinzen des römischen Kaiserreichs* 513–14; Ernst Levy, *Weströmisches Vulgarrecht: das Obligationenrecht*; in Gofas, "The Byzantine Law of Interest," 1087.

Like the early history of the Empire, laws continued to be passed against fraudulent practices of usurers, which indicate that there must have been endless ways by which they evaded the law, to the frustration of those caught in their financial snares. In addition to this law, the Council of Nicaea 325 CE, under the leadership of Constantine, established in Canon 17 that no clergy should be tainted by the foul practice of usury:

> Forasmuch as many enrolled among the Clergy, following covetousness and lust of gain, have forgotten the divine Scripture, which says, "Those who do not lend money at interest," and in lending money ask the hundredth of the sum [as monthly interest], the holy and great Synod thinks it just that if after this decree any one be found to receive usury, whether he accomplish it by secret transaction or otherwise, as by demanding the whole and one half, or by using any other contrivance, whatever for filthy lucre's sake, he shall be deposed from the clergy and his name stricken from the list.[99]

This canon stated the conditions for Christian clergy, but individual Christians continued to entangle themselves in usurious loans, sometimes at their own financial peril. A fourth-century letter—contemporary to that of the Council of Nicaea—written from one Meletian[100] Christian to another on behalf of a member of their community states the dire consequences of usury which were still in place, and which could still plague one's household if one were unable to make good on a loan:

> Since therefore our brother Pamonthius has met with no ordinary reverses and has suffered most shameful treatment from pitiless and godless men, so that, one might say, he has perforce been bereft of our blessed hope, it behoved us to make application to your brotherliness by this present letter, exposing all his circumstances, in order that you being informed may help him, remembering the blessed apostle who tells us not to neglect those who are weak, not only in the faith but also in the affairs of this world. For this brother of ours was once a wine-dealer, and having for long been importuned by the magistrates in his

99. Canon 12, *The Seven Ecumenical Councils of the Undivided Church*, 36. Louis writes that while the Nicene Council forbade the clergy to practice usury, these decisions do not seem to have been regarded as the law (Louis, *Ancient Rome at Work*, 318).

100. Melitians were Egyptian Christians who were followers of Melitius, a bishop of Lycopolis who objected over the return to community by those who had fallen away from the faith during times of persecution.

native place with exactions beyond his means he consequently borrowed a great sum of money and being summoned to repay it and failing to meet his liabilities he was compelled by his creditors to sell his possessions down to the very garments that cloaked his shame; and even when these were sold, barely half the money could he scrap together for his creditors, who, those pitiless and godless men, carried off all his children, mere infants as they were. Wherefore we direct to you this letter, requesting you help him as far as your means allow, in order that he may recover his children from him . . . by all means help him since . . . they carried his children into slavery.[101]

While the tone of this letter is compassionate, still, one cannot help but note the clever way in which the author indicates his displeasure that Pamonthius has allowed this to happen, he who is "weak . . . in the affairs of this world."[102] There is a subtle suggestion that Pamonthius has brought this misfortune upon his household through his lack of business acumen, who—though he might have been a reputable and talented wine-maker—perhaps neglected to heed advice offered by Jesus to those who walk in the secular world: "See, I am sending you out like sheep into the midst of wolves; so be wise as serpents and innocent as doves."[103] Further, this document attests to the fact that the actual termination of debt bondage does not necessarily follow from its abolition.[104]

Compassion for the victim of usury was not limited to Christianity; thirty years later, due to whole-scale destruction of the Vandals, Emperor Valentinian (364–75 CE) halted the collection of interest in Africa. He too, disliked intensely the greedy lender, and forbade the collection of interest on what appear to be mainly moral grounds:

Certainly it is customary to assist debtors even when their property is safe, if some disaster should happen to them. But here, where there is the destruction of all fortunes, where even that which could be concealed through the ignorance of the owners was extorted by the intolerable tortures of the inquisitions, could anyone doubt that a man would surpass the atrocities of

101. "160. From a Meletian," *Select Papyri,* I: 379–81.

102. Perhaps the author is here making reference to Paul's first letter to the Thessalonians, in which he writes: "And we urge you, beloved, to admonish the idlers, encourage the faint hearted, help the weak, be patient with all of them" (1 Thessalonians, 5:14).

103. Matthew 10:16.

104. Millett, *Lending and Borrowing,* 78.

the enemy if he should now attempt to recover from persons who are despoiled, needy and exiled from their own country, that money which he had delivered to them when they were in safe and flourishing times should not scruple to exact payment of those persons whom he ought to be ashamed not to help, O Albinus, dearest and most beloved Father?

For this reason Your Illustrious and Excellent Magnitude in compliance with the regulation of Our pragmatic sanction shall know that in consideration of Our pity toward the Africans, Our Clemency has established that none of them shall be held liable for money that has been lent them, in the name of written instruments or of sureties, until the recovery of their own property, no matter who should sue them.[105]

The language of this law seems melancholy; Valentinian observes that while he could not protect the communities from all types of calamities from without, still it is fitting for an Emperor to protect his people from evils which can harm the community from within.

Emperor Theodosius I the Great, like Valentinian before him, held the greedy in contempt. On June 17, 380 CE he passed a law protecting debtors who were still unable to pay even after legal judgment had been passed against them. After a judgment against the debtor, one-half of the loan was required in immediate payment. If, however, three months after the judgment the debtor still had not paid, the lender was then allowed double interest on the loan. As a result, Theodosius I had to provide legislation to counter the measures of those who would try to ensure that their debtor would *not* pay, as it would be in the lender's best financial interest to postpone payment: "Of course, provision must be made on the other hand also against the notoriously fraudulent trickery of creditors, lest when the person condemned should delay payment, they should begin to hang over him with the hope of double the one percent [per month] interest."[106] Six years later Theodosius I ruled that usurers must pay a penalty in the amount of fourfold of the illegal interest they had extracted: "If any person, taking advantage of the necessity of the debtor, should extort anything beyond the one percent [per month] allowed by law, he shall immediately, without delay, restore what was rapaciously taken, and he shall be obligated to pay fourfold the amount as a penalty. But those persons who are detected as guilty of having acted with equal madness by making excessive demands in any transaction before the insurance of this law

105. *Novella* 12, in *Theodosian Code*, 526.
106. *Theodosian Code*, 4.19.1.

shall restore twofold the extorted sum."[107] At the same time, Theodosius I decreed that if, over the course of years, the interest were to accrue to being equal to the original loan, that double interest was only allowed to accrue on the principal, but that simple interest was allowed to accrue on the interest itself.[108]

Almost two hundred years after Emperor Severus allowed for senators to collect six percent interest, in 397 CE Theodosius I—along with his son the Eastern Co-Emperor Arcadius (395–408 CE) and Western Emperor Honorius (395–406 CE)—decreed that senators were once again forbidden to take interest, and chastised greedy debtors who wished to shirk their responsibilities by claiming that it was unlawful for them to pay interest to those born of the senatorial rank.[109] This did not end the argument, for in 405 CE Emperors Arcadius and Honorius permitted senators anew to extract the previously acceptable six percent interest; it was a losing battle, for they circumnavigated prohibitions by making loans in the names of their minor sons.[110]

It is appropriate to complete this section with extensive laws against usury with Emperor Justinian I (527–65 CE); continuing what by now had become a regal tradition, Justinian I had contempt for the greedy lender. An Emperor with a passion for the codification of Roman law, his *Codex Justinianus*—a complete collection of all imperial edicts since the days of Hadrian—contained previous injunctions against creditors as well as his own additions.[111] In 528 CE he reduced interest rates to four percent if the lender was an "illustrious" person or of higher rank, and six or six and one-quarter percent for ordinary loans;[112] he limited the rate of interest for farmers to four percent and churches and pious foundations to three

---

107. Ibid., 2.33.2. This returns to the original law of the *Twelve Tablets*, which claimed that the usurer who charged greater than the legal twelve percent would have to return the sum times four to the debtor.

108. Ibid., 4.19.2.

109. "Debtors contend in vain that they do not have to pay interest to their creditors who are minors, because, as they testify, such creditors are possessed of the Senatorial rank. Therefore debtors shall repay the principal with the interest as set forth in their stipulations" (ibid., 2.33.3).

110. Ibid., 2.33.3.

111. For more on Justinian the lawmaker, see Ostrogorsky, *History of the Byzantine State*, 75.

112. *The Code of Justinian*, 4.32.26.

percent;[113] commercial transactions could ask eight percent;[114] maritime and produces loans, which carried greater risk, could ask up to twelve and one-half percent, and likewise farm produce was limited at twelve and one half percent.[115] In addition, Justinian I forbade that interest could mount higher than double,[116] reinforced the laws against *anatocism*,[117] and set the rates of the return of a dowry at four percent if the dowry had not been returned within two years of the termination of the engagement or marriage.[118] Justinian I, a highly pious Emperor and champion of just social causes, has damning words to say about the practice of usury:

> We have considered it advisable to correct a most atrocious and inhuman abuse which is far worse than any act of impiety or avarice, and administer a remedy applicable to all persons, not only in this present time of necessity, but throughout all future ages; for it has come to Our ears that certain persons, in the province in which you govern [i.e., Thrace], being induced by avarice to take advantage of public distress, and, having drawn up agreements bearing interest, by which they loaned a small amount of grain, have seized the lands of the debtors, and that, for this reason, some farmers have fled and concealed themselves, others have died of starvation, and pestilence, not less terrible than a barbarian invasion, has, in consequence of the failure of the crops, afflicted the people. Hence we order that all creditors of this kind, no matter what may be the value of the articles which they have loaned . . . shall hereafter be entitled to receive annual interest on such articles at the rate of the eighth part of a measure for each measure furnished, and must return to the farmers the lands which they have taken in pledge . . . This law shall apply to all Our subjects, for it is humane and just, it relieves the poor, and affords adequate compensation to creditors.[119]

113. *Novel of Justinian*, 120.

114. Ibid., 4.32.26.

115. *Novel of Justinian*, 32.

116. Ibid., 121, *The Code of Justinian*, 4.32.27.

117. *The Code of Justinian*, 4.32.28.

118. Ibid., 5.12.31.5.

119. *Novel of Justinian*, 32. Justinian I's *Institutes* also contain a brief passage about usury, but it primarily reiterated the information found in the *Codex*. Essentially it states that if an individual defaults on a loan, then it is only right that the person pay interest, but only if this has been agreed upon among the parties. The interest rates, which had formerly been abolished by the *lex Genucia*, were set by Justinian I to

Justinian I's legislation had economic as well as moral concerns, for his ordinances fixed lending rates according to the status of the lender, not necessarily the need of the borrower. They must have been influential to a great degree, for subsequent Isaurian emperors issue no legislation on usury in their *Eclogia*, and no other legislation appears until the time of Emperor Nikephorus I (802–11), who abolished the charging of interest altogether.[120]

In sum, laws which attempted to address the problems of usury in the Roman Empire were no more successful than legislation put in place against usury in the Greek world. Condemned legally, usury existed as part of a growing economy, flourishing despite attempts to control the perimeters of the practice by way of limiting rates, establishing interest-ceilings, and censuring additional abuses that accompany the economic disease.

Philosophical Deliberation of Usury

According to H. Michell, Plato's *Republic* and Aristotle's *Politics* examination of the problems of scarcity and state fiscal management are largely ethical, rather than economic.[121] Yet the writings of Greek philosophers testify that a great deal of consideration and reflection was devoted to the subject of economy and how it affected the ethical character of an individual and, further, the ethical character of the city-state.[122] Unfortunately,

---

fluctuate between four percent and twelve percent (Justinian, *The Institutes of Justinian*, 325). Gofas also cites additional laws passed against usury and modifications set by Justinian I with regards to maritime loans, but the details of these are not pertinent to the discussion. Gofas, "The Byzantine Law of Interest," 1091.

120. Theophanes, *The Chronicle of Theophanes*, 168.

121. Michell, *The Economics of Ancient Greece*, 25. Michell's tone suggests that he sees this as a deficiency. In fact, a great many economic historians seem to feel this way. Eric Roll dismisses economic historians who feel that the subject of economic history owes little to the Greeks and other ancient writers: "It is perfectly true that the total volume of economic theory, in any modern sense, to be found in the writings of, for example, the Greek philosophers is very small; but we can only expect statements of an economic character to the extent to which certain of the material conditions of a commodity-producing society were already present in ancient Greek society." Roll, *A History of Economic Thought*, 10–11.

122. Sir Ernest Barker writes that each city was believed to set a moral tone, have a character and a code of comportment that was specific to itself. These particular "types" of city tone would naturally be discussed, for the purpose of discovering which type was superior, or what would be the superior type. As the city was understood to

moneylending was such a normal and widespread practice in Greece that the opinions of philosophers were not heeded with respect to this particular problem,[123] except by early Christian authors years later.

It is possible to detect in Plato's works the connection between usury and other forms of economic advancement because usury—or interest—owes its existence to the same vice which ultimately resulted in the rise of the city: greed. In his *Republic*, Plato writes that the development and creation of a city is brought about primarily via selfish desires; because humans have a variety of desires[124] that can only be met by other individuals, those who produce the goods and those who purchase the goods wish to be in close proximity to one another with the end result that they bond together in a mercantile society:

> "The origin of the city, then," said I, "in my opinion, is to be found in the fact that we do not severally suffice in our own needs, but each of us lacks many things . . . As a result of this, then, one man calling in another for one service and another for another, we, being in need of many things, gather many into one place of abode as associates and helpers, and to this dwelling together we give the name city or state . . . And between one man and another there is an interchange of giving, if it so happens, and taking, because each supposes this to be better for himself . . . Come, then, let us create a city from the beginning, in our theory. Its real creator, as it appears, will be our needs."[125]

---

contain individuals who both lived by and contributed to the city's tone, this created an ethical society as well as established that any type of political science would need to take into consideration the "ethical" nature of the city. The result is that Greek political theory is profoundly "ethical" at its core. "It is more than a legal structure," writes Barker, "it is also a moral spirit. This is indeed its inward essence and its vital meaning" (5–6). See also 81. See also Barker, "The Greek Theory of the State," 1–18. Individuals were aware of these differences, as is noted in the funeral speech of Pericles: "Our government is not copied from our neighbours . . . So too, with our education . . . We differ from other states in regarding the man who holds aloof from public life not as 'quiet' but as useless . . . In doing good, too, we are the exact opposite of mankind. We secure our friends not by accepting favours but by doing them" (Thucydides, 2.37). Therefore, while each state had a constitution, the constitution was not simply a set of laws, but was the suggestion for a "manner of life." See also Barker, *Greek Political Theory*, 6; Starr, *Economic and Social Growth of Early Greece*, 31–32.

123. Glotz, *Ancient Greece at Work*, 240; Maloney, "Usury in Greek, Roman and Rabbinic Thought," 85.

124. See "Needs and Desires," in Sayers, *Plato's Republic: An Introduction*, 28–30.

125. Plato, *Republic*, 369b.

Aristotle's notion about the beginning of economy is similar, but is based on a family-based structure[126] which branches out, rather than a need-based structure that gathers fairly autonomous individuals into it. For Aristotle, the family provides the basic needs for the human, but as humans are social—or, as he declares, political creatures—the state exists to make life acceptable for each person, and the essence of the human evolves most perfectly within this created community, the *polis*: "Hence it is evident that the state is a creation of nature, and that man is by nature a political animal. And he who by nature and not by mere accident is without a state, is either above humanity, or below it; he is the 'Tribeless, lawless, heartless one,' whom Homer denounces—the outcast who is a lover of war . . . And it is a characteristic of man that he alone has any sense of good and evil, of just and unjust, and the association of living beings who have this sense makes a family and a state."[127]

Although each point to a city-state[128] which is considered one organic whole, they are still describing a society which is essentially divided. For both philosophers, there are social differences among humans including divisions of free persons and slaves or servants, divisions of wealthy and poor, and divisions of labor for the purpose of producing the needs of society (food, shelter, clothing, etc.). According to Michell, the "keynote of all Greek philosophic theory in the political and social sphere"[129] is found in the acceptance by the individual of their role in this divided society; it is in the subordination of the individual to the state that a person can contribute most effectively to the welfare of the community, because it was believed that the state would only seek the advantage for its citizens.[130]

126. Starr writes that Greek life was primarily occupied with the family, which, when gathered into larger groups, was defined primarily by their shared religious experiences and beliefs (Starr, *Economic and Social Growth of Early Greece*, 35).

127. Aristotle, *Politics*, 1253a.

128. This is not to propose that either of these writers are suggesting the bustling metropolis that the modern person envisions by the word *city*, or *polis*. In fact, during their age most individuals still lived together in a group known as an ἔθνος, which is little more than a small clan of people.

129. Michell, *Economics of Ancient Greece*, 25–26.

130. When discussing the grammatical choices of the Greeks in their musings on state and society, Barker writes that it is logical that the aims of the State would be written in the imperative, for a State "*ought* to pursue the well-being of its citizens in the fullest and truest sense of the word: it *ought not* to make wealth, or power, or equality, its aim. A State *ought* to give honour and office to those who have given to it the virtue which furthers its aim: it *ought not* to put in authority the wealthy, merely because they are wealthy, or the poor, merely because they are poor." Barker, *Greek Political Theory*, 11–12.

How would the state—or those who ran it—seek the advantage for its citizens? Primarily the answer is found within a proper attitude towards property and wealth; Plato, who distrusted profit motive and who was suspicious of Athenian democracy,[131] advocates in his *Republic* an abandonment of private property and ownership among the upper ruling classes.[132] Political power would then be based within this special elite corps of individuals who were free of petty wants and the covetousness of their fellow human beings. In general Plato's *Laws* and *Republic* contain very practical measures[133] which Plato believed would eliminate the problem of scarcity for the greater population.[134] According to Plato, in such an environment, the only ones fit to rule were those not corrupted by the very things which the state produced, for the rulers will be from among those "who are really rich, not in gold, but in the wealth that makes happiness—a good and wise life."[135] True wealth was evident by right manner of life.[136]

In addition to other means whereby humans might create utopia, and eager to eliminate any evils that might result in the aforementioned

131. Roll, *A History of Economic Thought*, 20.

132. Plato, *Republic*, 7.521b. Roll writes that this is the misunderstood "communism" of Plato. (Roll, *A History of Economic Thought*, 20). Freed from the pursuit of filthy lucre, leaders would be able to devote themselves to the needs of their community. Basil of Caesarea's record of his conversion will reflect this spirit. He will write: "Reading the Gospel and realizing that the basic prerequisites for human completion are the renunciation of one's fortune, the giving to the poor, and also the retiring from all worldly cares and affections, I searched to find someone else who felt the way I did, so that together we could overcome the adversities of human life" (Basil, *Adversus Eustathium Sebastenum*, 2).

133. Because the State was considered to be a moral/ethical society, philosophers approached the subject from an ethical point of view. Consequently, they considered their works to be more practical then hypothetical; even if it was impossible to put their ideas into practice for an entire society, still an individual could incorporate much of it into their daily life (Barker, *Greek Political Theory*, 12).

134. Societies were to be limited in size (Plato, *Laws*, 737e) and age (*Republic*, 540E–1.a-c); further, a level of poverty was set beneath which no one could sink (*Laws*, 744e), individuals could horde only a set amount of wealth before the state bore down with an excessive special tax (*Laws*, 745a), international exchange was to be avoided by the purchase of all foods from within the community (*Laws*, 842c), and separate currency would be created for international exchange and domestic exchange (*Laws*, 742b).

135. Plato, *Republic*, 7.521b.

136. Right manner of life is evident in actions later taken by Basil of Caesarea, who perhaps will be influenced by Plato during his education under Libanius. During times of famine and economic strife in his community, Basil will advocate in both behavior and words subordination of the individual to the welfare of the community.

morally bereft behavior such as idleness or the creation of inferior products—only serving to bring down the quality and effectiveness of the city-state—Plato, in his *Laws*, advocates the eradication of taking interest. Included within a section devoted to a daughter's dowry, he champions the ἔρανος and adds an additional twist when he writes, "Moreover, no one should give money to someone he can't trust, and no money should be lent at interest. Anyone who has received a loan will be permitted to refuse to pay it back, both interest and principal."[137] For Plato, the ἔρανος— or "gift" credit—strengthened citizen solidarity; it was bad for friends to force one another to judge their relationships in crude monetary terms, and one friend taking another to court over money was contrary to the public well-being.[138] Clearly, it is not the plight of the poor with which Plato is concerned; rather, his concern is that those who are very rich are unlikely also to be very good, and therefore it is unlikely that they will be happy.[139] Plato asserts that those who are very wealthy can only become so by unjust means, and as a consequence they cannot be good, and so therefore they cannot be happy. This would be the reason why someone should not lend money at interest, for someone who engages in unjust actions cannot be happy, and taking interest from someone who does not even have the capital cannot possibly be considered just.[140] What is not considered in this passage is that someone might want to be unjust, or that someone might gain pleasure from taking part in unjust actions; the happiness of the wealthy seems here to be Plato's concern, rather than the unjustness of the lending practice, or any concern over the needs of the poor.[141] Considering always the benefit of the whole against the benefit of

137. Plato, *Republic*, 742c.

138. Millett writes that Plato believed strongly that ἔρανος loans were not to be recovered, as they were raised among and for friends, and among such company it is inappropriate to resort to the court system to settle concerns. Millett, *Lending and Borrowing*, 42. See also Plato, *Laws*, 915e, and *Republic*, 549e.

139. Plato, *Republic*, 742d–744a.

140. Prior to the development of the relationship between banking and production, loans were made primarily to individuals in distress; under these circumstances, taking interest from someone in distress was condemned (Michell, *Economics of Ancient Greece*, 30).

141. Plato writes that "in all such situations" (meaning in either good fortune or bad, in times of prosperity or "in the experiences brought by diseases and wars and poverty"), that "what is noble and what is ignoble in each case must be taught and defined." Plato, *Laws*, 632a. Plato seems to be suggesting that individuals must always react properly in all circumstances, and that poverty must be borne with dignity rather than outrage when the few have in abundance during times when the many have little

the individual—be they wealthy *or* poor[142]—Plato states that the underlying motive of having a law against usury is for the purpose of "making the people as happy and friendly to one another as possible. Now citizens don't ever become friends where they have many lawsuits among themselves, and where there are many injustices, but rather where such affairs are as minor and rare as possible."[143] From this one can easily conclude the following: corruption upsets the balance of society, corruption is the result of usury, and therefore, usury upsets the balance of society. As a result of this conclusion, the practice of usury must be eliminated, for peaceful is the man, Plato writes, who does not take to court another who owes him money.[144] He reiterates this opinion in Book 11, in a section concerning

---

or nothing at all. This is an ideal suggestion, but dignity has never yet satisfied a stomach, only pride.

142. Plato addresses specifically "the poor" as a class in Book 4 of his *Republic*, "Wealth, Poverty, and Virtue," but he does not appear to be concerned with exploitation or issues of inequality in a society in which slavery was common. Despite the title, "Wealth, Poverty, and Virtue" focuses little on either the wealthy or the poor, and is concerned primarily with war, education, law making, and the virtues of a perfect State: wisdom, valiant behavior, temperance and justice. Socrates responds to a question put forth by Adeimantus, who wants to know how does one address the incongruity that exists when the poor are no better off for living in a city filled with men of great wealth? Socrates [Plato] replies that the aim of the foundation of a State is the greatest happiness of the whole, rather than the happiness of one class; however, if all individuals are granted all benefits, then they will cease to perform their function in society, and merely live off their benefits: "But urge us not to do this, since, if we yield, the farmer will not be a farmer nor the potter a potter, nor will any other of the types that constitute state keep its form." Plato, *Republic*, 420e–421b. Those who do enjoy the benefits of society (the guardians) must perform their work so that the State will evolve in proper order. The result will be that the poorer members of society will receive the happiness "that its nature comports" (Plato, *Republic*, 421c). To put this in crude terms, in Plato's society you get what you deserve. Demonstrating how Christianity sought to rectify this view of the poor, Holman addresses how Basil's poverty sermons attempted to raise society's level of understanding about humanity in a society that did not traditionally consider the needs of those who lived on the financial fringes of civil society: "Basil in fact seems to seek to raise them *to* humanity in a society that did not traditionally view them in this way" (Holman, *The Hungry Are Dying*, 107; Holman's emphasis). Fuks's *Social Conflict in Ancient Greece* provides an enlightened and expert consideration on Plato and poverty.

143. Plato, *Laws*, 743c.

144. Plato, *Republic*, 549e–550a. However, there is another type of retribution here: "'You are aware,' said I, 'that the very house-slaves of such men, if they are loyal and friendly, privately say the same sort of things to the sons, and if they observe a debtor or any other wrongdoer whom the father does not prosecute, they urge the boy to punish all such when he grows to manhood, and prove himself more of a man than his father, and when the lad goes out he hears and sees the same sort of thing.'"

the orders of business and trade, where he pronounces quite simply, "No one is to make a sale or purchase on credit."[145]

Plato writes with increased venom on the evils of interest and greed in his *Republic*, claiming that an oligarchic system only advances those who are unfit to rule, the end result of which can be nothing other than civil unrest and finally revolution:

> Why, since its rulers owe their offices to their wealth, they are not willing to prohibit by law the prodigals who arise among the youth from spending and wasting their substance. Their object is, by lending money on the property of such men, and buying it in, to become still richer and more esteemed . . . And is it not at once apparent in a state that this honouring of wealth is incompatible with a sober and temperate citizenship, but that one or the other of these two ideals is inevitably neglected . . . And such negligence and encouragement of licentiousness in oligarchies not infrequently has reduced to poverty men of no ignoble quality . . . And there they sit, I fancy, within the city, furnished with stings, that is, arms, some burdened with debt, others disenfranchised, others both, hating and conspiring against the acquirers of their estates and the rest of the citizens, eager for revolution.[146]

Plato further asserts that the taking of interest is incompatible with proper citizenship, for the money-lenders only continue to insert "the sting of their money"[147] into the remnant of the population previously not affected, hastening the decline of the city-state.[148] Finally, Plato claims that not only do money-lenders infect their generation, but they poison the souls of their children, raising them to be useless, spoilt, and indifferent to all but the pursuit of money.[149]

In summary, Plato believed that usury was an evil practice that must be eradicated for the following reasons: first, usury was a barrier to the happiness of the individual whose unjust lending practices made the lender unhappy (the happiness of the one in debt is not mentioned). Second, as a result of the unhappiness engendered by usury, this foul practice disrupted the peace of the city-state. Third, the advancement in the

145. Plato, *Republic*, 915e.

146. Ibid., 8.555c–e.

147. Ibid., 556a.

148. Maloney, "Usury in Greek, Roman and Rabbinic Thought," 86.

149. Plato, *Republic*, 8.556c.

political system of men who engaged in usury resulted in civil unrest and not simply one but two generations of incompetent leaders and citizens; the practice of such an evil must not continue, for it served only to undermine the moral order of society.

Aristotle, on the other hand, was more resigned to economic growth than was his teacher.[150] As well, Aristotle had a more generous attitude towards private property than did Plato, and he maintains that possessions should remain in the hands of the owners if for no other reason than for the delight one feels when loaning something to someone else:[151] "It is clearly better that property should be private, but the use of it common; and the special business of the legislator is to create in men this benevolent disposition. Again, how immeasurably greater is the pleasure, when a man feels a thing to be his own . . . And further, there is the greatest pleasure in doing a kindness or service to friends or guests or companions, which can only be rendered when a man has private property."[152]

Aristotle saw money primarily as a medium of exchange that served a purpose but had no intrinsic value, unlike the object in demand.[153] Referring to Midas,[154] Aristotle affirms that there is no guarantee that one who has a bounty of coins is wealthy, for that person might still die of hunger.[155] After down-playing the acquisition of money, he describes the

150. Roll, *A History of Economic Thought*, 22.

151. This was not his sole reason for defense of private property, merely one. The subject of property is a large one for Aristotle, and one of his main defenses for private property is that if one is in possession of an object then one will treat that object with better care than if it belongs to both no one and everyone at the same time. "For that which is common to the greatest number has the least care bestowed upon it" (Aristotle, *Politics*, 2.1261). What Aristotle argues for is not more liberal ownership, but more liberal, trusting, and enlightened uses of the objects that individuals own.

152. Aristotle, *Politics*, 1263a-1263b.

153. Glotz, *The Greek City*, 69.

154. Ibid.

155 Aristotle, *Politics*, 1257. Gregory of Nyssa will make this same point in his *Fourth Homily* from his *Commentary on Ecclesiastes*, providing even more examples about the ways in which wealth can fail to provide for a person's life. He will claim that wealth is no guarantee of any benefits at all, including that an individual "will thereby become wise, sagacious, reflective, learned, a friend of God, prudent, pure, passion-free, detached and aloof from all that draws him towards evil"; in addition, there is no security that wealth will make someone "physically strong, pleasant to look at, extending life for many centuries, free from ageing, disease and pain, and all the things sought for in the life of the flesh." At the conclusion of this list, one is rightly left questioning what benefits wealth *does* extend (Gregory of Nyssa, *In Ecclesiasten*, 76–77).

two types of money-making: household management and retail trade. But there is a third, he writes, that is "the most hated sort."[156]

> Of the two sorts of money-making one, as I have just said, is a part of household management, the other is retail trade: the former necessary and honourable, the latter a kind of exchange which is justly censured; for it is unnatural, and a mode by which men gain from one another. The most hated sort, and with the greatest reason, is usury, which makes a gain out of money itself, and not from the natural use of it. For money was intended to be used in exchange, but not to increase at interest. And this term usury [τόκος] which means the birth of money from money, is applied to the breeding of money because the offspring resembles the parent. Wherefore of all modes of making money this is the most unnatural.[157]

While Aristotle's discussion of money is fairly limited, the larger discussion moves from theory of value to a brief treatise on the function of currency: money is for exchange, in a manner which is significantly different than barter. He barely tolerates trade, which he calls "unnatural," and considers usury a perversion of the function of money.[158] Aristotle, perhaps seeing the damning effects of any level of usury on the life of the debtor and soul of the lender, places money-making and money transactions within ethical limits; this cannot be done unless the various ways of employing money are judged as acceptable or unacceptable. Interest rates are irrelevant, for Aristotle's theory on exchange value is simple: the objects must be proportional in order to be exchanged, and exchanging one dollar now for two dollars later is not a fair exchange. Roll defends Aristotle's discussion, noting that Aristotle's theory of money distinguishes between the purchase/sale transaction—in which the desire for monetary or property gain is limited to one transaction that takes place in the natural world—and

---

156. Aristotle, *Politics*, 1258a.

157. Aristotle, *Politics*, 1258b.

158. Michell claims that the modern mind would have difficulty accepting the notion of condemning the taking of interest under any circumstances (Michell, *Economics of Ancient Greece*, 30). This is a fairly reasonable statement, for in the last seventy years western society has grown increasingly dependent on the credit system and so accepting of its nature that it is unlikely that many people even know what are acceptable interest rates and what are excessive. However, this statement alone proves that he himself is insensitive to the situation, for "any interest at all" could still bury a peasant.

lending with interest—in which the desire for monetary gain seems to be unlimited, and takes place in a theoretical realm.[159]

Aristotle's claim that money is a dead object can be addressed by looking at the key word in question, τόκος, Greek for "usury." Τόκος like many Greek words has additional denotations; the first definition is "childbirth," "parturition," or the "bringing forth" by women or by animal. Included within this definition, τόκος can also mean the very thing that is brought forth, as in "offspring," a human or animal baby. A second definition of τόκος is "the produce of money." The produce—offspring or child—of money would be its own offspring, which one would rightly call "interest." The third definition of τόκος is simply "interest," and the fourth—and perhaps the most interesting of all—is "oppression."[160]

The idea of money being either fertile or infertile comes up many times in the discussion of usury; essentially the question is, can money breed? According to Aristotle, the answer is no, money cannot breed, and to attempt to do so is perverse, for "of all modes of making money this is the most unnatural."[161] The word τόκος—birth, offspring, interest or oppression—is used in multiple ways in the previous passage. Before even mentioning the word τόκος, Aristotle first writes that money is to be used in exchange, not to increase at interest (third definition). Next, he writes that τόκος means that money gives birth to money (first definition), and that this is unnatural.[162] Further, he writes that τόκος is used because that which money breeds—more money—is the child of the parent (second definition). He ends this argument by asserting that of all of the ways of making money, this is the most deviant. He leaves the fourth definition of τόκος, oppression, for another discussion. For Aristotle money it is not a living object, and therefore cannot work any more than it can breed; unlike a human or an animal, money does not work, rather humans and animals work *for* money. At best, it can stand for the potential of work and the value of goods that exist, but if either of those are destroyed or fail to be realized, then money itself will lose value.[163]

---

159. Roll, *A History of Economic Thought*, 25–27.

160. Liddell and Scott, *A Greek-English Lexicon*, 1803.

161. Aristotle, *Politics*, 1258b.

162. The unnatural copulation and subsequent birth of money from money is later referred to by Gregory of Nyssa, whose understanding of fertility will be limited by dimensions of gender. Gregory will claim that objects which cannot be defined as either male or female cannot produce acceptable offspring, as they cannot be properly ordered. Gregory of Nyssa, *In Ecclesiasten*, 79.

163. Desmond, *The Greek Praise of Poverty*, 43–44.

Aristotle reveals his full feeling of the "meanness" of usury in a text that has been assigned to the later part of his life, his *Nicomachean Ethics*,[164] a series of documents exploring behaviors which might make for an enviable life: pleasure, politics, money-making and contemplation.[165] Usurers are mentioned in Book 4, in the course of an on-going discussion of moral virtue. Aristotle divides the "Virtues Concerned with Money" into two sections: the first section is "Liberality," in which he discusses liberal giving, meanness, and prodigality. The second section is devoted to "Magnificence," which surpasses liberality, as it involves giving on a grander scale.

In the section devoted to meanness, Aristotle claims that unfortunately "most men are fonder of getting money than of giving,"[166] and that there appear to be "many kinds of meanness."[167] After an amusing paragraph devoted to various names given to the stingy, he writes that among those who succeed "by taking anything from any source,"[168] are "those who ply sordid trades, pimps and all such people, and those who lend small sums and at high rates. For all of these take more than they ought and from wrong sources. What is common to them is evidently sordid love of gain; they all put up with a bad name for the sake of gain, and little gain at that."[169] Such meanness is, Aristotle claims, a greater evil than being a prodigal, for more people have erred by being stingy than by being a prodigal.[170] It is through various behaviors which fall under the category of "meanness" that an individual oppresses another by gaining "from his friends, to whom he ought to be giving."[171] As well, note that the usurer is cast alongside other such undesirable professions: the aforementioned pimp, as well as highwaymen, gamesters, and "the footpad";[172]

---

164. Aristotle, *Nicomachean Ethics*, v.

165. Ibid., vi–vii.

166. Ibid., 84.

167. Ibid.

168. Ibid., 85.

169. Ibid.

170. Aristotle defines a "prodigal" as "one who is being ruined by his own fault" (*Nicomachean Ethics*, 79), but not necessarily a bad or evil person. "This is why he is thought to have not a bad character; it is not the mark of a wicked or ignoble man to go to excess in giving and not taking, but only of a foolish one" (Aristotle, *Nicomachean Ethics*, 83).

171. Aristotle, *Nicomachean Ethics*, 85.

172. Ibid. Surely this attitude infected Aristotle's own student, Theophrastus, who described the "penny-pincher" as a miserable man who counts the glasses of wine his

such individuals are like canker sores in a healthy mouth. Aristotle here confirms the general description given to usurers, who are consistently portrayed in literature and dramatic works throughout the centuries with the same base characteristics, including that they are "old, gouty, miserly, suffer from dropsy and are prey to suicide."[173] Unfortunately, the usurer will continue to find himself in such company in lists of "sordid trades" or undesirable persons, and shall continue to be described in such unflattering terms in lists contained in the Hebrew Bible, the Mishnah and the writings of the early Christian authors.

In summary, Aristotle believed that usury was a hateful practice for the following reasons: first, the acquisition of interest was counterproductive to market equality; a seller should not expect to sell an object by expecting that over a period of time the buyer would have to keep paying for it. Aristotle saw usury in the same way; if one were to borrow one dollar, then one dollar should be returned, not two. To believe otherwise would go against his belief that money has a value independent of its fiscal function.[174] Second, Aristotle did not share the ancient eastern idea that dead matter was capable of reproduction;[175] money is not a living organism, and since an object that is not alive cannot be fertile therefore money—which is neither alive nor fertile—cannot produce offspring. Third, usury was evidence of "meanness," which is, in Aristotle's opinion, not an effective way to lead an ethical life. The position of usurer is shameful and degrading, hurting the very people who should be helped. Finally, Aristotle's writings contain an early uniting of the economic with the ethical; within this system, living and developing an ethical life is neither the pleasant contemplation of abstract notions of goodness and beauty nor selfish individualism, but is the acting out of one's own humanity within proper relationship to the other.

Plutarch, the neo-platonic philosopher, wrote with passion on the subject of usury. His *De vitando aere alieno*—"That We Ought Not to Borrow"—contains admonishments, anecdotes and advice associated with running oneself into debt. Writing about injustices perpetuated during the

---

guests have drunk, serves small cuts of meat, rejects bargain prices, tears up the house in search of a coin, will not let his wife lend out goods, and "is apt to charge a late fee and compound interest" (Theophrastus, *Characters*, 10).

173. Wright, in Millett, *Lending and Borrowing*, 185.

174. See "Graeco-Roman Economics" in Schumpeter, *History of Economic Analysis* (for more on Aristotle's theory of money.

175. Heichelheim, *An Ancient Economic History*, 104–5.

time of Solon, Plutarch questioned the overall effectiveness of his reforms, as money-lenders still controlled of market:

> For what good did Solon do the Athenians when he put an end
> to giving one's person as security for debt? For debtors are slaves
> to all the men who ruin them, or rather not to them either (for
> what would be so terrible in that?), but to outrageous, barba-
> rous, and savage slaves, like those who Plato says stand in Hades
> as fiery avengers and executioners over those who have been
> impious in life. For these money-lenders make the market-place
> a place of the damned for the wretched debtors; like vultures
> they devour and flay them, "entering into their entrails," or in
> other instances they stand over them and inflict on them the
> tortures of Tantalus by preventing them from tasting their own
> produce which they reap and harvest. And as Darius sent Datis
> and Artaphernes against Athens with chains and fetters in their
> hands for their captives, in similar fashion these men, bring
> against Greece jars full of signatures and notes as fetters, march
> against and through the cities, not . . . sowing beneficent grain,
> but planting roots of debts, roots productive of much toil and
> much interest and hard to escape from, which, as they sprout
> and shoot up round about, press down and strangle the cities.[176]

A second abuse Plutarch notes is discounting interest from a loan at the time of lending; as a result the debtor never actually received the full amount loaned. Disgusted, he writes, "While they are giving they immediately demand payment, while they lay money down they take it up, and they lend what they receive for money lent."[177] Side by side with the abuses perpetuated by usurers, Plutarch chastises those who borrow: the rich because they do not need it, the poor because they cannot pay it back:

> I am pointing out to those who are too ready to become borrow-
> ers that borrowing is an act of extreme folly and weakness. Have
> you money? Do not borrow, for you are not in need. Have you
> no money? Do not borrow, for you will not be able to pay . . .
> Being unable to carry the burden of poverty you put the money-
> lender on your back, a burden difficult for even the rich to bear
> . . . Live by teaching letters, by leading children to school, by
> being a doorkeeper, by working as a sailor or a boatman; none

176. Plutarch, *De vitando aere alieno*, 828–29.
177. Ibid., 829.

of these is so disgraceful or disagreeable as hearing the order "Pay up."[178]

Plutarch's major source of concern is repayment of money owed; if a debtor's income remains static there is little hope for repayment. This is, of course, a universal problem tied to debt: those who most need money can least afford repayment, and place themselves in servitude to the lender.

Not all spoke out against usury. Greek orator Demosthenes refused to put all money-lenders into the same category, himself having loaned money. He writes in his defense against himself and the practice that "I, for my part, do not regard a moneylender as a wrongdoer, although certain of the class may justly be detested by you, seeing that they make a trade of it, and have no thought or pity of anything else, except gain."[179] Demosthenes regards as wrongdoers those who seek nothing but gain, which would include not only a money-lender but any greedy trader. He makes the case that all who seek to keep their money active are not necessarily selfish, and should not all be put into the same class as the worst of usurers, unless, that is, "you mean this, that anyone who lends money to you ought to be detested by the public."[180] As well, Isocrates sees lending as a "good" in society, for it provided an opportunity for the righteous elite to profit in ways other than monetary: "the wealthy were better pleased to see men borrowing money than paying it back; for they thus experienced the double-satisfaction—which should appeal to all right-minded men— of helping their fellow-citizens and at the same time making their own property productive for themselves."[181] Sadly, evidence suggests that not all lenders of money were "right-minded."

Except in large cities, during times of famine or revolt, or when the situation of the distressed might lead to civil unrest, the Romans appear relatively unconcerned with the plight of the poor.[182] In general, writings which spoke harsh words against those who hungered after wealth were

---

178. Ibid., 829–30.

179. Demosthenes, "Against Pantaenetus," 53.

180. Ibid., 53. Lending was an accepted and common business practice, in spite of verbal tirades against it. The casual way in which individuals considered lending alongside business transactions is demonstrated in one of Pliny's letters. He writes, when inquiring about some property for sale: "You will want to know if I can easily raise this three million. It is true that nearly all my capital is in land, but I have some outstanding loans, and it will not be difficult to borrow." Pliny, *Epistle* 3.19.

181. Isocrates, *Areopagiticus*, VII, 35.

182. González, *Faith and Wealth*, 19 and 63.

written by men who had little to do other than be wealthy;[183] it is a grand tradition that poor people have scant time to devote to philosophy.

After the decline of imperial splendor in post–Punic War years (264–201 BCE) there were concerns about various economic problems, including the rise of *latifundia*, certain forms of moneymaking; at the same time, a return to a high regard of farming[184] emerges in the sources. This is reflected in Cato's second-century-BCE prose on agriculture, *De Agricultura*, which begins its random directions for the care of the farm with praise for the farmer and condemnation of other forms of money-making: "It is true that to obtain money by trade is sometimes more profitable, were it not so hazardous; and likewise money-lending, if it were as honourable. Our ancestors held this view and embodied it in their laws, which is required that the thief be mulcted double and the usurer fourfold; how much less desirable a citizen they considered the usurer than the thief, one may judge from this."[185]

The attitude directed towards usurers and others of mean professions comes from the Roman view of labor: labor is degrading, and the very need to work for a living is degrading—unless of course one happens to be an artist, architect or lawyer, as the somewhat Stoic Marcus Tullias Cicero happily happened to be. A wealthy man who owned at least fourteen grand estates, Cicero believed that those who sought great fortunes should be free to do so, as long as they harmed no one in the process: "Now riches are sought after, both for the necessary purposes of life and for the enjoyment of pleasure. But in men of greater minds the coveting of money is with a view to power and to the means of giving gratification . . . Magnificent equipages, likewise, and a style of living made up of elegance and abundance give delight, and hence the desire for money becomes boundless. Nor indeed is the mere desire to improve one's private fortune, without injury to another, deserving of blame; but injustice must ever be avoided."[186]

This is a common theme among the Romans: individuals may seek independent wealth for themselves as long as they do nothing to encroach

---

183. Roll has harsh words to say about the Roman thinkers, writing that "The great empire, by the side of which the Greek city state looks a very limited political unit, was incapable of producing great social thinkers," and that there was a "paucity of philosophical speculation in ancient Rome" (Roll, *A History of Economic Thought*, 29).

184. Roll, *A History of Economic Thought*, 29.

185. Cato, *De Agricultura*, 1.1.

186. Cicero, *De Officiis*, 1.8.

upon the rights of others.[187] The optimistic goal of such a view is that conflicts arising due to individual choices—such as seeking wealth—would
be resolved because the individual would recognize the self as function-
ing within a community; as such, harming another in the pursuit of one's
happiness upsets the balance of the community, and will ultimately harm
the self. So to seek wealth at no expense to another and for the purpose
of enjoying that wealth is acceptable, perhaps even commendable; conversely, individuals who seek wealth by hindering someone else's financial
situation, or merely because they desire *more* money, harms the public
well-being and is despicable. Cicero, who slanders close to all available
professions except for the ones in which he engaged,[188] begins his list of
infamy with the two most well known and despised: "Now with regard to
what arts and means of acquiring wealth are to be regarded as worthy and
what disreputable, we have been taught as follows. In the first place, those
sources of emolument are condemned that incur the public hatred; such
as those of tax-gatherers and usurers."[189] Like Aristotle, Cicero condemns
the role of the usurer, but not for the same reason; while Aristotle believed
that the practice of usury was perverse and unnatural, for Cicero there was
only a social condemnation, not a moral one. But like Plato and Aristotle,
Cicero's works express concern for the general health of society, and a society cannot be healthy if one gains at the expense of the other. Such actions
do more than just tip economic scales; injustices create hostility, hostility
among a large group precede social unrest, and social unrest means that
someone's house is about to be burned.

The lending practices of the aforementioned Seneca, Stoic philosopher and advisor to Emperor Nero, created plenty of hostility and social
unrest on its own. But actions aside, Seneca's writings largely consist of
variations on the acquisition, defense of, use of, and the abandonment of
wealth. To mention briefly a few of his literary achievements relating specifically to the subject of usury or lending, Seneca's *On Benefits* contains a
remarkable examination of the concept of true ownership and the delicate
balance of obligation that is often tipped when one friend owes another
a "benefit." Different from this, writes Seneca, is the experience of the

187. According to González, this is echoed in the *Corpus Juris Civilis*. See Dig.
1.8.2, in *Corpus Juris Civilis* in González, *Faith and Wealth*, 26.

188. To be fair, in addition to his condemnation of tax-gatherers and usurers,
Cicero wrote that all hired workmen and merchants, "fishmongers, butchers, cooks,
poulterers, and fisherman" are vulgar as well. Cicero, *De Officiis*, 1.42.

189. Cicero, *De Officiis*, 1.42.

debtor, whose good intentions mean nothing against a harsh creditor.[190] In either instance he counsels return, but for different reasons: "Return to one because he demands repayment, to another because he releases you from debt; to the former, because he is bad, to the latter, because he is good."[191] Further, he offers sagacious counsel to the debtor not to shirk any obligations but to return what is owed to the lender no matter the lender's social status: "Let no man make you bad because he is."[192]

Seneca expostulated on the subject of wealth at length in his *On the Happy Life* and in other essays, counseling individuals to "see clearly for yourself what is necessary and what is superfluous."[193] In the words of a man who has long been exposed to—and perhaps wearied of—the heavy and rich luxury foods so enjoyed by the Romans, Seneca wrote to encourage the abandonment of dainties, vanities, and snares of modern life brought on by possession of excessive funds, and quotes Attalus to make his point: "Freedom comes, not to him over whom Fortune has slight power, but to him over whom she has no power at all."[194] Finally, in Seneca's "On The Reasons for Withdrawing from the World," he counsels individuals to "possess nothing that can be snatched from us to the great profits of a plotting foe,"[195] and concludes with the following advice that—although it is not specifically mentioned—is uncannily appropriate to the usurer: "He who craves riches feels fear on their account. No man, however, enjoys a blessing that brings anxiety; he is always trying to add a little more. While he puzzles over increasing his wealth, he forgets how to use it. He collects his accounts, he wears out the pavement in the forum, he turns over his ledger,—in short, he ceases to be a master and becomes a steward."[196] This will be a claim later reiterated by Christian writings on the topic.[197]

190. Seneca, *De Beneficiis*, 7.14.

191. Ibid., 7.16.

192. Ibid., 7.17.

193. Seneca, *Ad Lucilium Epistulae Morales*, 110.

194. Ibid. If Seneca had been able to read Basil's *Homilia in psalmum* 14, he would have been given an alternative to the same idea of freedom and finances. Basil encourages those in need of funds to refrain from borrowing because as an individual contracts debt, simultaneously they place themselves into physical and spiritual bondage, an unnatural state before God: "You behold the sun as a free person. Why do you begrudge the liberty you now enjoy?" Basil, *Homilia in psalmum* 14.4.

195. Ibid., 14.

196. Ibid.

197. Gregory of Nyssa's will write: "Why do you harm yourself with anxiety by calculating days, months, the sum of money, dreaming of profit, and fearing the

In general, Roman authors chastised the greedy usurer, but did not necessarily condemn the practice of lending at interest, about which they made few judgments. Perhaps the strongest statement against the practice of usury is found in Cicero's *Offices* when he quotes Cato the Elder; after being asked "What do you think of lending at usury?" Cato the Elder replied, "What do you think of killing a man?"[198]

For the Roman gentleman, land was the preferred form of wealth over all others; the prosperous and dignified Roman gentleman owned land and sought more land, not liquid assets, as did the usurer. A usurer sought only money, not status, a position that would be suspect among the elite. Spectacularly moneyed, aristocratic Romans had leisure to devote to penning eloquent prose which defended private property and the folly of chasing wealth, for only one as resplendently wealthy as Seneca could write such a melancholy statement as "we must reflect how much lighter is the sorrow of not having money than of losing it."[199]

Conclusion

This chapter has provided a legal and philosophical foundation for the theological reflection on writings by early Christian authors Basil of Caesarea and Gregory of Nyssa by presenting a summary of the attitudes about lending in Greece and Rome in the centuries before and up until the fifth century CE, and including general practices, laws and their abuses. This second chapter concludes with a summary of the various attitudes towards usury between the Greeks and Romans that have been uncovered throughout this chapter.

Greek and Roman citizens actively engaged in casual lending practices in simple agrarian situations and by the worldlier ἔρανος; but while the same citizens were protesting loans with interest, the business community recognized the economic value and benefits of such loans. Among the philosophers, deliberation on the practice of usury evolved over time from a discussion which focused on the effects of the practice on society to the activity of the individual usurer. Plato was concerned primarily with how usury effected the overall health of society: he addressed the

---

appointed day whose fruitful harvest brings hail? . . . Such an impatient disposition results in obsession" (Gregory of Nyssa, *Contra usurarios*, 297).

198. Cicero, *De Officiis*, 2.25. That one can murder through financial snares is also found in the Hebrew Bible, as well as in the writings of the early Christian authors.

199 Seneca, *De trang. anim.* 8, LCL, in González, *Faith and Wealth*, 17.

state of unhappiness of the lender who engaged in unjust practices, he was concerned that the unhappiness of the individuals in debt could lead to social unrest and he despised the fact that wealth concentrated in the hands of unjust individuals resulted in an inferior government. Aristotle introduced ethical considerations to the commentary by claiming that usury was an unfair trading practice which denied that there are acceptable and unacceptable methods of monetary exchange, by asserting that money lacks fecundity and therefore cannot reproduce and by including usurers among others in lists of shameless occupations—a practice later repeated in the Hebrew Scriptures and among the early Christian authors. Plutarch severely condemned the activity of borrowing and equally chastised both borrowers and lenders, perhaps even more so than usury itself. Later Stoic philosophers, Cicero and Seneca, took a milder approach to the problem: Cicero saw no harm in the acquisition of wealth as long as it did no harm to one's neighbor; and while Seneca focused on borrowers and encouraged debtors to repay what they owed, he had few strong words to say about lending. While the attitude among philosophers toward usury abated somewhat over the centuries, the usurer as an individual continued to be despised.

Throughout this chapter, supplementary comments have been included in the notes to demonstrate parity between Greek and Roman writers and early Christian authors, including the influence of Plato, Plutarch and Seneca on Basil, Aristotle and Seneca on Gregory, and Cicero on John Chrysostom. Certainly methods employed in their sermons were drawn from the works of those whom they studied in their youth. We cannot know to the complete extent how the philosophers influenced early Christian authors on the subject of usury, but prominent similarities suggest that there is no reason to believe that they did not influence them, for early Christian authors claimed this rich history as they composed their sermons on usury, while attempting to offset the devastating effects of a system that was as equaling damning for the temporal present as it was for a spiritual future.

3

Usury in Jewish and Christian Scripture

The Hebrew Bible: Usury and Jewish Economic Wisdom

PROVISIONS AGAINST MISMANAGEMENT OF funds have always been written into law codes of past civilizations, primarily for the protection of the poor and unlettered but also for the purpose of protecting those who live in conditions of constant near-poverty. Prior to usury regulations of the Israelites, clauses addressing concerns over interest rates were a common feature in eastern legislation, and can be found in ancient law codes, agreements and contracts; only the nation of Israel did not allow for interest among her own people. The Code of Hammurabi (c. 1700 BCE) contains the most complete legal treatment concerning interest in the ancient Near East, allowing for profit on a monetary loan of up to twenty percent, and profit on a loan of grain of up to thirty-three and one-third percent.[1] The code also provided protection for the debtor in the case of crop failure and other problems, such as avarice of the money-lender, and fraud.[2] The Babylonians, however, were not the first to attempt to regulate interest or its potential abuses; Old Assyrian documents that antedate Hammurabi by more than one hundred years

1. The injunctions on usury are provided in Maloney's "Usury and Restrictions on Interest-Taking," 1–20. See also Ryan, who notes that the Babylonians had no word for usury, and loans both with and without interest were prevalent in their society, with rates from five and one-half to twenty-five percent. Ryan, *Usury and Usury Laws*, 38–39. See also Moser, *Die patristische Zinslehre*, 28–40.

2. Maloney, "Usury and Restrictions on Interest-Taking," 10.

provide evidence of loans carrying interest.[3] Although there is a lack of original records of Hebrew loans during the biblical period,[4] consistency can be found among these and other ancient civilizations which testify to the need for local relief among farming communities prior to harvesting.[5] Like peasants in all ages, subsistence living carried with it a moral dimension, as the family and close-knit community placed pressures on one-another for the purpose of avoiding starvation. Loans of food and necessities were short term and usually carried no interest, generally following along the lines of Hesiod's aforementioned advice to "take good measure from a neighbor, and pay it back well, with the same measure, or better if you can, so that you may later find him reliable should you need him."[6] But interest was a component of lending, as the following law attests: "If a man incurs a debt and Abad[7] inundates his field so a flood has carried away (the soil) or else (if) corn is not raised on the field through lack of water, in that year he shall not render (any) corn to <his> creditor; he shall blot out (the terms inscribed on) his tablet and shall not pay interest for that year."[8] This indicates that loans with interest played an active role in the economy, as this decree suggests a loan that is extended year to year, possibly in conjunction with the agricultural year. Note that the farmer's debt is not forgiven, merely that he is allowed to continue to maintain his debt without interest for another year. But while the laws of people in adjacent lands to the Hebrews had greater variety,[9] their laws do not reflect the same nuance of compassion or mercy.[10]

A consistent theme which runs throughout the codes of the Torah is that of God's concern for and protection of the distressed and downtrodden; in other words, the God of the Israelites does not tolerate oppression of the poor. This is distinct in provisions concerning the needs

---

3. Meislin and Cohen, "Background of the Biblical Law against Usury," 257.

4. Ibid., 255.

5. Ibid.

6. Hesiod, *Works and Days*, 348–51.

7. [Ed.] Abad is the god of rain and storms; Driver and Miles, *The Babylonian Laws*, Vol. 2, 29.

8. Driver and Miles, *The Babylonian Laws*, 2:29.

9. Stein, "The Laws on Interest in the Old Testament," 18–19.

10. Driver and Miles, *The Babylonian Laws*, vols. 1 and 2.

of the land[11] and the needs of the impoverished.[12] Unlike the Greeks but similar to the Romans, for the Israelites there was a strong and inviolable connection between acreage and its bounty and the metaphysical God who granted them. The earth was sacred because it belonged to God, and divine ownership extended to the agricultural by-products as well.[13] Thoughtful management would be needed to prevent decay. Once the land had been claimed by the Israelites, it was not distributed most liberally to those who had demonstrated great military prowess, but quite sensibly, larger portions were given to larger families:[14] "The Lord spoke to Moses, saying: to these the land shall be apportioned for inheritance according to the number of names. To a large tribe you shall give a large inheritance, and to a small tribe you shall give a small inheritance; every tribe shall be given its inheritance according to its enrolment."[15] In this passage there is acknowledgement that inequalities in the distribution of wealth (or in this case, land) can lead to grievances. The problem of scarcity is commonly accepted, specifically in the passages in Joshua regarding required land to suit the needs of large families. Relatively equal distribution of land should contribute to some degree of economic prosperity and help to reduce the problem of scarcity. Along with possession of the land comes an understanding that the individual is to live on that land in accordance with God's codes for proper relationship. In exchange for righteous living, God promises to deliver all that one needs for economic success:

> If you follow my statutes and keep my commandments and observe them faithfully, I will give you your rains in their season, and the land shall yield its produce, and the trees of the field

11. Exodus 23:10–11: "For six years you shall sow your land and gather in its yield; but the seventh year you shall let it rest and life fallow, so that the poor of your people may eat; and what they leave the wild animals may eat. You shall do the same with your vineyard, and with your olive orchard." See also Leviticus 19:9–10; 23:22; 25:2–4; Deuteronomy 24:19–21.

12. Deuteronomy 14:28–29: "Every third year you shall bring out the full tithe of your produce for that year, and store it within your towns; the Levites, because they have no allotment or inheritance with you, as well as the resident aliens, the orphans, and the widows in your towns, may come and eat their fill so that the Lord your God may bless you in all the work that you undertake." Note that this passage mentions the Levites, who could not own land. Soss, "Old Testament Law and Economic Society," 330.

13. Tamari, *Jewish Ethics and Economic Life*, 36–28; see also González, *Faith and Wealth*, 20.

14. Gordon, *The Economic Problem*, 16.

15. Numbers 26:52–54; see also Numbers 33:54.

shall yield their fruit. Your threshings shall overtake the vintage, and the vintage shall overtake the sowing; you shall eat your bread to the full, and live securely in you land. And I will grant peace in the land, and you shall lie down, and no one shall make you afraid; I will remove dangerous animals from the land, and no sword shall go through your land . . . I will look with favour upon you and make you fruitful and multiply you; and I will maintain my covenant with you. You shall eat old grain long stored, and you shall have to clear out the old to make way for the new.[16]

Reminiscent of the promise to Abraham,[17] this passage tells of God's promise to provide an abundant and fruitful life for those who live a righteous life; their need for food will be met with bumper crops, their animals and their families shall be protected from enemies and wild animals, and the very air will be scented with fecundity. But despite the benefits of land, still all did not prosper;[18] village stores from fallow and tithe years were not always enough to tide over those who suffered.[19] Hence, along with the blessings of land, possessions and money the Israelites also received an obligation to help those who, for whatever reason, suffered want. Charity and compassion were encouraged as primary deterrents to theft, which was considered an abhorrent crime primarily because theft can lead to other sins in addition to the breakdown of the fabric of society.[20] Those who were desperate enough to steal were understood not as merely stealing just the possession itself, but also stealing opportunity for life, the equivalent

---

16. Leviticus 26:3–10.

17. Genesis 12:1–3; 15:5–6; and 17:1–22.

18. "Since there will never cease to be some in need on the earth, I therefore command you, 'Open your hand to the poor and needy neighbor in your land'" (Deuteronomy 15:11).

19. Horsley, *Covenant Economics*, 41.

20. "Over and above the economic loss involved in theft and the moral effect on the individuals concerned, the rabbis were aware of its effect on the social and moral fabric of society. Judaism has always maintained that evil actions and wrongdoing, such as theft and robbery . . . are not only the problem of the parties concerned. Rather, by perverting concepts of what is permitted and what is forbidden, they eventually undermine the whole basis of society. Permissiveness in regard to theft sooner or later affects man's religious behavior, his sexual mores, and even his regard for the sanctity of human life." Tamari, *Jewish Ethics and Economic Life*, 41. See also chapter 4 for John Chrysostom's opinion on the matter of murder via financial indiscretions, and chapter 5 for Gregory of Nyssa's. Basil also makes the same parallel; see Basil, *Homilia dicta tempore famis et siccitatis*, in Holman, *The Hungry Are Dying*, 190.

of murder. Here usury is understood as the unjust extraction of money from one who is least likely able to pay; thus, usury is equated with theft.

Theft was considered a double crime by the Israelites; a sin against God, the owner of all, and against the individual from whom the thief stole.[21] The injunction against theft was far-reaching and covered a multitude of possibilities, ranging from the general command that one should not steal to more specific mandates involving everyday behaviors;[22] there is an injunction against the wealthy not to deny their workers their wages or to defraud them;[23] further, to deny a blessing of thanks to God prior to eating or drinking is a form of theft.[24] Theft, fraud, and misrepresentation are especially wicked if they are inflicted upon the ignorant or weak members of society,[25] and all of these behaviors and actions are inconsistent with living a Godly or righteous life. The intimate relationship between God and the people of Israel demanded that all activities in which they engaged—whether household, market or farm—should be subordinate to the ethical standards of the Torah in order for their people to achieve a collective sanctified state. One who is busy defrauding a neighbor is hardly engaging in sanctified behavior. This is based on the understanding that all that exists belongs first to God. Meir Tamari refers to this as the "divine origin of wealth," in which God has given possessions to individuals for them to use in the spirit of good stewardship.[26] To be wasteful or greedy is a clear mismanagement of God's money.

Before looking at specific examples of usury within the Hebrew Scriptures it would be beneficial to define "usury" and "interest" as the Israelites understood them.[27] There are various interpretations of the Hebraic words

21. Tamari, *Jewish Ethics and Economic Life*, 41.

22. Exodus 20:25: "You shall not steal." See also Leviticus 19:11: "You shall not steal; you shall not deal falsely; and you shall not lie to one another"; and Deuteronomy 23:24: "If you go into your neighbor's vineyard, you may eat your fill of grapes, as many as you wish, but you shall not put any in a container."

23. Leviticus 19:13: "You shall not defraud your neighbor; you shall not steal; and you shall not keep for yourself the wages of a laborer until morning."

24. This comes from a Talmud discussion concerning the blessing which one should make prior to eating: "No one should taste anything without first reciting a blessing over it, as it is said, 'The earth is the Lord's and the fullness thereof [Psalm 24].' Whoever enjoys the goods of this world without reciting a blessing is like a thief." From the *Talmud Bavli*, *B'rakhot* 35a, in Tamari, *Jewish Ethics and Economic Life*, 41.

25. Tamari, *Jewish Ethics and Economic Life*, 48.

26. Ibid., 36.

27. In our day usury is an antiquated term which suggests excessive interest, a term often accompanied by cliché caricatures such as Shakespeare's Shylock or Charles

translated "usury," and Edward Neufeld, in "Prohibitions against Loans at Interest in Ancient Hebrew Laws" explores in great depth the etymology of the terms. According to Neufeld, the Hebrew word for "usury" in Exodus and Deuteronomy is *nèsèk*, which means literally a "bite," as in a "bite" taken by the lender from the debtor.[28] The same author writes that the Hebrew word for "usury" in Leviticus is *tărbît*, which means "increase."[29] Seigfried Stein defines these terms differently, claiming that *nèsèk* is long-term yearly interest, whereas *tărbît* (or *tărbîth* as he writes) is a fixed rate of money or grain which is paid to the lender after the harvest along with the capital lent.[30] Rava, a fourth-century Babylonian *amora*,[31] believed that there was no difference really between the two terms, but that the Torah used the two synonymously; the *Jewish Religion: A Companion* agrees with this in its own definition of usury, claiming that the "Talmudic Rabbis held that the terms 'usury' and 'interest' are synonymous and they extended the biblical laws so as to prohibit any benefit the borrower extends on the usurer, even to greet him if it was not his usual practice to greet him, or even to thank him for the loan."[32] According to the *Encyclopaedia Judaica*, a more etymologically correct way of defining the two terms is that *nèsèk*—which means "bite"—is how the debtor defined usury, and *tărbît*—or increase— was how the lender defined usury.[33] Meir Tamari's explanations are the most poetic, for he claims that the two terms were used to make sure that a lender was held doubly accountable if he took interest; the lender literally "bites" the one to whom money was lent by increasing the poverty of the debtor, as the lender increased the debtor's woes by interest.[34] For the

---

Dickens's Ebenezer Scrooge. The acquisition of interest in the twentieth and twenty-first centuries does not constitute usury as it is defined in the modern world, and usury—or interest—plays a generally accepted and unquestioned role in modern business transactions. This is not the case for the Torah.

28. Neufeld, "Prohibitions against Loans," 355.

29. Ibid., 356.

30. Stein, "Laws on interest in the Old Testament," 163.

31. An "amora," otherwise known as a "sayer" or "spokesperson," originally was an interpreter of the rabbinic teacher for the students. The amora stood near the teacher, and after the teacher spoke to the amora, the amora spoke to the students. It is not known if the purpose of the amora was to translate the teachings from Hebrew into the vernacular, or to make the teachings audible to the audience. Later the term itself referred to a rabbi whose work was focused on the interpretation of the Mishnah (*Encyclopaedia Judaica* 2:863).

32. Jacobs, *Jewish Religion: A Companion*, 573–74.

33. *Encyclopaedia Judaica*, 16:28.

34. Tamari, *Jewish Ethics and Economic Life*, 176. In this section Tamari paraphrases

purpose of this project, it is best if we follow the precedent of the Talmudic Rabbis and understand "interest" and "usury" to be synonymous.

According to the *Halakah*[35] there are two types of forbidden interest: interest that is forbidden by the Torah, and interest that is forbidden by rabbinic law.[36] The sum of interest makes no difference, for a loan which demands a return of one percent interest is equally as prohibited as a loan which demands a return of forty-eight percent interest. Regardless, the Torah explicitly forbids loans whereby the debtor must pay a fixed sum above and beyond the amount of money that is loaned. Further, as was defined in the introduction, an understanding of interest must include two additional elements: time and risk. The individual who loans the money is unable to use that money while the money is in loan, therefore, the interest is essentially a payment made to the lender, who spends time waiting to receive the money back. Risk enters into the picture when one considers that the lender has lent money to an individual *who has none*, whose poverty automatically makes that person a bad risk. Therefore, the lender is risking that the money will be returned, rather than that the debtor will default on the loan. The interest, therefore, compensates for the risk the lender is willing to take, and the greater the risk, the higher the compensation.[37]

While Tamari writes that "All Jewish sources, however, show that Judaism does not see anything intrinsically wrong with lending money at interest,"[38] nevertheless passages in the Hebrew Bible indicate that this potentially lethal economic activity was regarded with suspicion. The excerpts in the Hebrew Bible which concern usury or interest are found in the books of Exodus, Leviticus, Deuteronomy, Psalms, Nehemiah, Habakkuk and Proverbs. The foremost to be considered is found in Exodus 22:25, at the end of an independent portion of laws referred to as the Book of the

---

Rashi on Exodus, and the use of the word *nèshèkh*: "A snake bite is at first only slightly uncomfortable, but later increases in pain and severity. So, too, interest (*nèshèkh*) is at first bearable, but as the debt mounts, the debtor's suffering increases."

35. The *Halakah* (from the verb *hālak*, or "to walk") is a collection of oral and written Rabbinic rulings on Jewish law, covering both collective and individual behavior. Since the codes were compiled c. 200 CE, those of Moses Maimonides (twelfth century) and Joseph Care (sixteenth century) are most successful (Krinsky, "Halakah," in *New Catholic Encyclopedia* 6:624.

36. Tamari, *Jewish Ethics and Economic Life*, 177.

37. Ibid., 178–79.

38. Ibid., 167.

Covenant.[39] The first segment of this combined causal/apodictic[40] law forbids the taking of interest from a fellow Israelite: "If you lend money to my people, to the poor among you, you shall not deal with them as a creditor; you shall not exact interest from them."[41] The second part of the passage deals with pledges taken in loan, or the holding by the lender of a personal object of the debtor until the debt is repaid. "If you take your neighbor's cloak in pawn,[42] you shall return it before the sun goes down; for it may be your neighbor's only clothing to use as cover; in what else shall that person sleep? And if your neighbor cries out to me, I will listen, for I am compassionate."[43] The Hebrew *im* (אם) is most often translated as "if"—as

39. Exodus 20:22–23, 33. While the date of composition of the Book of the Covenant is not determined, according to Whybray what can be determined is that it cannot be dated earlier than Israel's acceptance of the religion of Yahweh. In addition, it is likely that the Book of the Covenant can be dated as earlier than those of Deuteronomy, as those of Deuteronomy show dependence upon it. Whybray, *Introduction to the Pentateuch*, 118–120.

40. Despite disagreement with the formal classification of Albrect Alt, there is common agreement about the types of laws (Whybray, *Introduction to the Pentateuch*, 111). This particular law has a causal protasis ("If you lend money . . .") and an apodictic apodosis ("you shall not extract interest from them.") By way of helpful reminders, there are casuistic ("*If* you are caught eating ice cream, then you must share it.") and apodictic ("*You shall not* eat ice cream unless you share.") injunctions in the Scriptures. There are also laws that are a combination of the two ("*If* you eat ice cream and share it with your neighbor, *then you shall* be blessed"), and the curse ("*Cursed be* anyone who does not share ice cream with a neighbor. I am the LORD your God.").

41. Exodus 22:25. It is believed that this is the eldest of the prohibitions against usury, dated no later than the eighth century BCE (Meislin and Cohen, "Background of the Biblical Law against Usury," 253).

42. Pledges are a type of interest, for the debtor relinquishes a personal possession in lieu of the money loaned. The pledge then remains the possession of the lender if the debtor forfeits the loan. The Old Testament takes a very strong stand against pledges being used unjustly. See Deuteronomy 24:6, 10–13 and Job 22:6; 24:3–9. Certain assets—such as cloaks or a millstone—are not to be taken in pledge, for in the case of something as a millstone or perhaps tools, they are the only way for the debtor to earn a living, so to take them in pledge would mean that the debtor's family could neither eat nor could the debtor make money (either for life necessities *or* to pay back the loan). The purpose of this injunction was to prevent essentials from being pledged, which placed the debtor in an even more economically precarious situation. The commentator Maimonides later ruled that absolutely no pledges were to be taken from either rich or poor widows, for two reasons: first, having a pledge held over a widow might result in the creditor using his power for immoral purposes. Second, if the widow had to enter the house of the creditor to check on the security of her pledge, this might compromise her good name. *Mishnah Torah, Hilkhot Malveh u Loveh*, chap. 3, *halakah* 1, in Tamari, *Jewish Ethics and Economic Life*, 175.

43. Exodus 22:26–27.

in "If you lend money to my people . . ."—but according to Tamari, sages consider the word to mean "when," as in the more obligatory "*When* you lend money to my people . . ."[44] In other words, it is God's expectation that those who need help will receive help from those whom they—and God—consider to be family. The Israelites are cautioned to keep in mind that those who have fallen into difficult times are just as much beloved of God as are those who have maintained their standard of life. This is shown in two ways: first, the phrase "the poor among you" is anticipated by the affirmation of them being "my people"; second, in the latter half of the passage the "compassionate" God will hear the cry of one who has been wronged. This veiled threat claims that if the wronged individual informs God of the situation—as if God did not already know—then God will listen, for God is "compassionate," a word which is used in the Hebrew Scriptures only to describe God, and usually in conjunction with the term "caring."[45]

According to Meislin and Cohen, the lifestyle of the Hebrews at the time of the writing of the Exodus text corresponds roughly with that of the "pre-Hammurabic" period in Babylon,[46] and that at this point the Hebrews had not yet undergone the transformation from a tribal society to that of a nation in the more formal sense. Maloney, who dates the Covenant Code c. 1000 BCE, along with Meislin and Cohen, who date the text no later than the eighth century BCE,[47] notes that although the statements on interest in Exodus have less variety and flexibility than interest laws of other ancient societies, the need for the law against interest arose among the Hebrews for reasons similar to laws which arose among the Assyrians, Hittites and Babylonians: the need to relieve momentary economic distress.[48]

The next passage to consider is found in the book formerly referred to as "the Priest's Manual," as Leviticus was originally a continuation of the book of Exodus. Reinforcing the Exodus text, this passage involves an intimate family situation that can be considered fairly common: the arrival of the financially destitute family member: "If any of your kin fall into difficulties and become dependent on you, you shall support them;

44. Tamari, *Jewish Ethics and Economic Life*, 53.

45. Durham, *Exodus*, 329.

46. Meislin and Cohen, "Background of the Biblical Law against Usury," 259.

47. Ibid., 260.

48. Maloney, *Background for the Early Christian Teaching on Usury*, 53–80. Whether or not the Hebrew people engaged in agricultural pursuits or were largely still pastoral at the time of Exodus injunction is almost irrelevant; the reason for the law reflects immediate aid to those who need it, and that could be the case among either an ancient tribal society, or a more urban society.

they shall live with you as though resident aliens. Do not take interest in advance or otherwise make a profit from them, but fear your God; let them live with you. You shall not lend them money at interest taken in advance, or provide them with food at a profit."[49] One is not to be compassionate to foreigners—from whom interest can be charged—and yet ignore the needs of one's own family. Rather than turning them away or using them as a debt-slave,[50] the individual is counseled to refrain from profiting from their family member's misfortune . . . at least for the time being. As stated above in reference to Hesiod, in an agrarian society many relied on the open-hands of their neighbors to tide them over if the crop was ruined; here, the situation is similar, but it is specifically geared towards the family member. The phrase "do not take interest *in advance*" indicates the future possibility that the individual who is bestowing charity might call in a favor, but during the time of distress they are to make no such attempt to profit. This could also be referring to the aforementioned practice of subtracting the interest from the amount lent, prior to turning over the loan.[51] The lender who gives an interest-bearing loan to kin is guilty also of having transgressed the order that all "shall love your neighbor as yourself."[52] As well, charging interest on another who is needy is in defiance of an ordinance which God gave to Moses, when telling Moses exactly *how* the people of Israel will show that they are holy: "You shall not steal,[53] you shall not deal falsely; and you shall not lie to one another. And you shall not swear falsely by my name, profaning the name of your God: I am the Lord. You shall not defraud your neighbor, you shall not steal, and you shall not keep for yourself the wages of a laborer until morning. You shall not revile the deaf, or place a stumbling block before the blind; you shall fear your God: I am the Lord."[54] The latter is not an injunction against treating badly those who are handicapped, but has been interpreted by sages to mean that one is not to defraud another who does not understand, or is incapable of understanding; quite simply, not taking

49. Leviticus 25:35–37.

50. Horsley, *Covenant Economics*, 44.

51. Plutarch writes against this practice in *Moralia*; in Plutarch in Fowler, "That We Ought not to Borrow," 829.

52. Leviticus 19:18.

53. Here "usury" can be defined as stealing, for usury is unjust gain, and unjust gain is theft.

54. Leviticus 19:11–14.

unfair advantage, or giving to someone something that will bring harm upon them.[55] As well, three forms of "secret trickery" are listed: stealing, tricking, and lying. Those who had witnessed such transactions were liable under the law as well, for without their witness such a transaction would not have taken place. A similar passage is found in Deuteronomy; in the passage below the speaker is Moses who, anticipating that they will harden their hearts against one another as the time of the remission of debts draws near, states that no one is to wrest their debts from another member of the community:

> Every seventh year you should grant a remission of debts. And this is the manner of the remission: every creditor shall remit the claim that is held against a neighbor, not exacting it of a neighbor who is a member of the community, because the Lord's remission has been proclaimed. Of a foreigner you many exact it, but you must remit your claim on any member of the community who owes you . . . If there is among you anyone in need, a member of your community in any of your towns within the land that the Lord your God is giving you, do not be hardhearted or tight-fisted toward your needy neighbor. You should rather open your hand, willingly lending enough to meet the need, whatever it may be. Be careful that you do not entertain a mean thought, thinking, "The seventh year, the year of remission, is near,"[56] and therefore view your neighbor with hostility and give nothing; your neighbor might cry to the Lord against

---

55. Tamari, *Jewish Ethics and Economic Life*, 176.

56. The seventh year was a time when all debts within the community were cancelled, but all debts to foreigners were demanded, a very important year in an agrarian community: "Every seventh year you shall grant a remission of debts. And this is the manner of the remission: every creditor shall remit the claim that is held against a neighbor, not exacting it of a neighbor who is a member of the community, because the Lord's remission has been proclaimed. Of a foreigner you may exact it, but you must remit your claim on whatever any member of your community owes you." This is the most important economic law in the Hebrew code, but it is uncertain to what extent it was followed, as many scholars claim that codes such as those of the year of jubilee and the release of debts were instituted to suppress the development of city life, limit income growth and foster the old agrarian forms of living. See Soss, "Old Testament Law and Economic Society," 343. See also Neufeld, "Socio-Economic Background of Yobel and Semitta," 118. According to Crüsemann, the seventh-year remission was a device created by the ancient Babylonian kings who would release their communities from staggering debts created over the course of seven years (Crüsemann, *The Torah*, 227). See also Olivier, "The Effectiveness of the Old Babylonian Mesarum Decree," 107–13. It is not known if the ancient Israelites adapted this process, or invented it for themselves (Crüsemann, *The Torah*, 228.

you, and you would incur guilt. Give liberally and be ungrudging when you do so, for on this account the Lord you God will bless you in all your work and in all that you undertake. Since there will never cease to be some in need on the earth, I therefore command you, "Open your hand to the poor and needy neighbor in your land.[57]

Just who the "member of your community" or who the "needy neighbor" might be is not precisely stated; they would most likely be family, but there is ambiguity since the passage refers both to "the earth" (the land outside of Israel) and "your land" (Israel). Regardless, this passage shows that reality does not always live up to the ideal, for in an ideal society, there would be no poor. Concerning this reality, J. M. Hamilton writes, "Should reality not attain the heights of the ideal, there is a specific attitude which one should have toward the poor (unbegrudging charity) and a certain act which one should do (freely give)."[58] On a more practical level, this injunction keeps the greedy from getting everything into their hands, for they would lose both land and people[59] ever seven years. But a seventh year of freedom created lending problems, for as the seventh year drew near, lenders would be hesitant to extend their wealth if they thought that they might be forced to forgive the debt. Knowing this, the clause maintains that those who "cry to the Lord against you" will incur guilt upon the heads of the stingy kinsman. Within this same section is a promise of God's blessing on a nation who treats its poor justly: "When the Lord your God has blessed you, as he promised you, you will lend to many nations, but you will not borrow."[60] The righteous will form a nation of powerful lenders, not powerless borrowers. In addition, like the Exodus clause, "if" can be translated in this Deuteronomy passage as "when," as these are binding covenants. This is how the Lord your God wants you to treat your neighbors, *when* they fall into difficulty, as people do; this type of behavior is requisite, rather than voluntary, but it is still righteous behavior. This method of giving is perhaps best described by the word *chesed*,[61] or "loving kindness," which under the law is to be shown to people in need, even though they

---

57. Deuteronomy 15:1–3, 7–11.

58. Hamilton, "*HĀʾĀRES* In the Smemitta Law," 222.

59. Deuteronomy 15:12–15 addresses the remission of debt-slaves, and they are not to be sent out "empty-handed" but are to return to their ancestral property (Horsley, *Covenant Economics*, 46).

60. Deuteronomy 15:6a.

61. Buckley, *Teachings on Usury*, 37; Tamari, *Jewish Ethics and Economic Life*, 50, and 248.

may or may not deserve such treatment. In times of need *chesed* could be given to rich and poor alike. This type of behavior—and this type of non-interest loan—is very similar to the type of loan extended by the Greeks to their friends, the previously aforementioned ἔρανος. However, *chesed* is not identical to ἔρανος in that *chesed* is distinct from an act of charity, as *chesed* could be given to someone who did not necessarily deserve such treatment, whereas the ἔρανος was extended solely to a friend. *Chesed* is an expression of Levitical and Deuteronomic commands to give support to the needy.[62] For the poor, *chesed* represented an opportunity at a new life; for the wealthy, *chesed* represented an opportunity to maintain a way of life.

The passage against which Christianity would struggle is in Deuteronomy. This passage is not casuistic but is apodictic, reflecting that the Israelites have passed from a village situation to an organized political state, and clarifies the position of usury among the Israelites, who may now extract interest from foreigners but not from each other: "You shall not charge interest on loans to another Israelite, interest on money, interest on provisions, interest on anything that is lent. On loans to a foreigner you may charge interest, but on loans to another Israelite you may not charge interest, so that the Lord your God may bless you in all your undertakings in the land you are about to enter and possess."[63] The conundrum introduced in this passage—referred to by Nelson as the "Deuteronomic Double-Standard"[64]—must be addressed. While today it seems xenophobic, the goal at that time was economic self-preservation rather than a conscious attempt to promote the "brother" at the expense of the "other." This type of code reflects a new understanding of Israel, wherein it is no longer strictly the Israelite who is considered part of the community. Israel has to reconcile how it will live in relation to the many who are residing within their land.[65] The solution is to incorporate outsiders into the

62. Leviticus 25:35–37; Deuteronomy 15:7–11; see also Tamari, *Jewish Ethics and Economic Life*, 170.

63. Deuteronomy 23:19–20e. This passage is dated the latest among the three main usury passages, dated sometime in the seventh century BCE (Meislin and Cohen, "Background of the Biblical Law against Usury," 253).

64. Nelson, *The Idea of Usury*, 3–28.

65. Gordon, *The Economic Problem*, 26. See also Meislin and Cohen, who write: "After 722 the north was simply a province of the Assyrian Empire, ruled and dominated exclusively by foreigners . . . It would be unreasonable, in such an environment, to bind Israelites to obligations which would result in great advantage to non-Israelites, who in turn did not recognize any obligation to make non-interest bearing loans" (Meislin and Cohen, "Background of the Biblical Law against Usury," 265).

community while at the same time remaining above them by virtue of a personal relationship with God. It is important also to note that this injunction did not exist for the purpose of oppressing the "other." As Maloney pointed out in his article "Usury and Restriction on Interest-Taking in the Ancient Near East," usury was an accepted part of all societies in the east; therefore, if the Israelites were not to take usury from those outside their community—those who were taking usury from them—then the Israelites risked being economically gouged by their neighbors, a situation which does not make good financial sense.

The commercial result is that now there are two types of loans strictly defined: business loans to the foreigner with a quest for gain, and consumption loans to the "relation," with no quest for gain. The fiscal result is that two distinct types of gainful pursuit simultaneously emerge: welfare socialism and exploitative capitalism.[66] Further, this type of promotion is given religious sanctification, but not without excessive discussion on the problems about which this command brings. According to Tamari, Maimonides interpreted Deuteronomy 23:20—"On loans to a foreigner *you may* charge interest"—as "you shall" rather than "you may," so that it is understood that it is not up to the individual to decide if interest will form a part of the loan process, but it is a command.[67] Other commentators argued that taking interest from Gentiles was legal, but not required,[68] and the eleventh-century Rabbi Ishmael argued that the loving-kindness [*chesed*] which Israelites extended to one another—with regard to money—should extend to Gentiles as well, "for the sake of peace."[69] However one must respect the rights and care for the alien among the group,[70] still

66. Buckley, *Teachings on Usury*, 28.

67. Stein writes that oppression under Roman rule led to the interpretation which leaned towards the imperative translation of this passage rather than the permissive. He also notes that all modern Christian and Jewish interpreters—although he does not state what he means by "modern," nor does he name names—interpret this as a possibility, not as a command (Stein, "The Laws on Interest in the Old Testament," 162).

68. According to Tamari, Ramban (Nachmanides) argued that it was not a requirement to take interest from Gentiles. Tamari does not provide a citation for this. He also states that Raivad claims that the Torah grants permission to take interest from Gentiles, but does not require that Jews do so. As well, all of the commentators whom Tamari cites are in agreement that a Jew should not be making loans with a Gentile anyway, unless there are not other business transactions available as options. Tamari, *Jewish Ethics and Economic Life*, 180–81.

69. Tamari, *Jewish Ethics and Economic Life*, 181.

70. "When an alien resides with you in your land, you shall not oppress the alien. The alien who resides with you shall be to you as the citizen among you; you shall

the foreigner can be exploited for three reasons: first, they are pagan idolaters; second, charging interest to a pagan idolater binds the Israelites more closely to one another through mutual self-interest, and third, charging interest to a pagan idolater connects the Israelites more closely with their God.[71]

The Israelites desired to create a code which would bind them to one another as well as to their God, both for self-preservation and the protection of the poor.[72] Susan Buckley points out that the passages on usury in the Pentateuch are located in books in which the Israelites are formulating the religious law which will serve to order their moral life.[73] As the law code was evolving into a covenant code, their socio-economic position was affected by the "theological development of their relationship with God."[74] This type of economic arrangement results in security for socially depressed groups within the Hebrew nation, including widows, orphans, distant but dependent members of families, slaves, aliens, and those suffering from temporary financial problems. The direct result of helping such groups of people is a "blessing as a consequence," which ensures the economic success of those who open their hands to the aforementioned distressed group.[75] While passages in the code books demonstrate what was to be done for these people, additional passages in the Hebrew Bible[76] demonstrate the results of having done nothing.[77]

This particular mandate leads naturally to the following question: "With regard to usury, who is righteous?" The answer is not a pleasant one.

---

love the alien as yourself, for you were aliens in the land of Egypt: I am the LORD your God." For a New Testament statement on loving the stranger, see Matthew 25:31–46. Williams, *Understanding the Old Testament*, 137.

71. Buckley, *Teachings on Usury*, 13.

72. Johnson, in *A History of the Jews*, writes that this provision in Deuteronomy was created to bind them together during a time when their single goal was the survival of their community. "Lending therefore became philanthropy—but you were not obliged to be charitable towards those you did not know or care for. Interest was thus synonymous with hostility (Johnson, *A History of the Jews*, 173).

73. Exodus, Leviticus, and Deuteronomy (Buckley, *Teachings on Usury*, 2).

74. Ibid., 9.

75. Crüsemann, *The Torah*, 225.

76. Ezekiel, 2 Kings, Nehemiah, Isaiah, Job, Psalms, Proverbs, Habakkuk.

77. Having done nothing, argues Moser, is the reason for the injunction. Moser argues that the passage in Deuteronomy 23:20–21 is the oldest prohibition on interest, and was the foundational injunction upon which the others are expanded. He claims also that it was a law which was never enforced, but represented an ideal condition promoted by social criticism (Moser, *Die patristische Zinslehre*, 67–68).

While Stein writes that there are not many references in the Bible which can direct us as to whether or not these laws were faithfully kept,[78] there is sufficient evidence to suggest that they were not.

Once Israel's position on usury and/or interest had been established, subsequent concern was to place usury within the context of righteous vs. non-righteous behavior. Tamari, who writes that money-lending is an economically and socially beneficial activity which any market needs to survive and thrive, claims that the Mosaic code cautioned against taking interest from one another as an attempt to place this necessary action "within a framework of righteousness."[79] The result of engaging in righteous behaviors is spelled out in Deuteronomy in material terms, and the following passage identifies the benefits which the people of Israel will receive, as well as their place in the greater economic world:

> If you will only obey the Lord your God, by diligently observing all his commandments that I am commanding you today, the Lord your God will set you high above all the nations of the earth; all these blessings will come upon you and overtake you, if you obey the Lord your God . . . The Lord will open for you his rich storehouse, the heavens, to give the rain of your land its in its season and to bless all your undertakings. You will lend to many nations, but you will not borrow. The Lord will make you the head, and not the tail; you shall be only at the top and not at the bottom—if you obey the commandments of the Lord your God, which I am commanding you today, by diligently observing them, and if you do not turn aside from any of the words that I am commanding you today, either to the right or to the left, following other gods to serve them.[80]

Conversely, those who will not obey are faced with a grim list of curses which shall result in "disaster, panic, and frustration in everything that you do," including aliens, who, "residing among you shall ascend about you higher and higher, while you shall descend lower and lower. They shall lend to you but you shall not lend to them; they shall be the head and you

---

78. Stein, "The Laws on Interest in the Old Testament," 168. There is abundant extra-biblical evidence as well which indicates that the laws were not kept. Stein notes: the "Elephantini Papyri," numbers 10 and 11 in Cowley, *Aramaic Papyri of the 5th Century B.C.,* 169. See also the "Tebtunis Papyri," in *The Tebtunis Papyri,* vol. 3.; Baron, *A Social and Religious History of the Jews,* 1:261. See also Tscherikower and Heichelheim, "Jewish Religious Influence in the Adler Papyri," 25–44.

79. Tamari, *Jewish Ethics and Economic Life,* 167.

80. Deuteronomy 28:1–14.

shall be the tail."[81] Unlike the previous passage which placed Israel in the dominant lending position, this passage is a grim reminder that there is an alternative: poverty and submission to the foreigner.

Evidence that usurious practices took place among the Israelites despite ordinances against this behavior is found in several other books in the Hebrew Scriptures. In the book of Ezekiel usury comes to be connected with the most heinous crimes, and becomes connected with other sins. This is a particularly crucial passage in the history of usury in the Hebrew Bible, and indicates a definite change in tolerance towards the usurer. Previously the usurer did not receive punishment for such actions, but the giver of free loans received the blessings of God. However, the Ezekiel passage identifies one who takes nothing in usury as righteous and worthy of life, but conversely, the usurer as evil and worthy of death:

> If a man is righteous and does what is lawful and right—if he does not eat upon the mountains or lift up his eyes to the idols of the house of Israel, does not defile his neighbor's wife or approach a woman during her menstrual period, does not oppress anyone, but restores to the debtor his pledge, commits no robbery, gives his bread to the hungry and covers the naked with a garment, does not take advance or accrued interest, withholds his hand from iniquity, executes true justice between contending parties, follows my statutes, and is careful to observe my ordinances, acting faithfully—such a one is righteous; he shall surely live, says the Lord God. [82]

But the one who, in addition to various other wicked practices, "takes advance or accrued interest, shall he live? He shall not."[83] Even if a wicked man has a good son that cannot redeem the father for his iniquities: "As for his father, because he practiced extortion, robbed his brother and did what is not good among his people, he dies for his iniquity."[84]

In a further passage Ezekiel is told that he is to judge the city, bloodied by the sins of Israel. In this excerpt all of the sins that were previously listed are now being committed, including usury, which is judged alongside terribly violent crimes, including rape and incest:

> The princes of Israel in you, everyone according to his power, have been bent on shedding blood. Father and mother are

81. Deuteronomy 28:43–44.
82. Ezekiel 18:5–9.
83. Ezekiel 18:10–11.
84. Ezekiel 18:18.

treated with contempt in you; the alien residing within you suffers extortion; the orphan and the widows are wronged in you. You have despised my holy things, and profaned my sabbaths. In you are those who slander to shed blood, those in you who eat upon the mountains, who commit lewdness in your midst. In you they uncover their father's nakedness; in you they violate women in their menstrual periods. One commits abomination with his neighbor's wife; another lewdly defiles his daughter-in-law; another in you defiles his sister, his father's daughter. In you, they take bribes to shed blood; you take both advance interest and accrued interest, and make gain of your neighbors by extortion; and you have forgotten me, says the Lord God. See, I strike my hands together at the dishonest gain you have made, and at the blood that has been shed within you.[85]

In this disturbing inventory of sins being committed by Israel, usury is equated with other crimes representative of theft: rape, murder, and trickery. All of these crimes—violent or no—involve the defilement of an individual who has lost something to the thief: money, blood, dignity or life.

With the usurer in such company, it comes as no surprise that Psalm 15—the Psalm on which Basil and Gregory shall focus their sermons—mentions the usurer as one who is denied access to the shrine.[86] The Psalm begins with the questions "Lord who may abide in your tent? Who may dwell on your holy hill?" and answers with, among other things, those "who do not lend money at interest."[87] Proverbs 28:8, which lists the benefits of being poor but righteous, states: "One who augments wealth by exorbitant interest gathers it for another who is kind to the poor."[88] An enigmatic passage, it must be considered within its context, which is concerned generally with the poor and injustice. That being so, the author of Proverbs 28:8 points to the futility of the greedy gatherings of the usurer, whose gain will—in the end—be turned over to one who will distribute the wealth in a righteous way.[89] Apparently this does not include Job, who

---

85. Ezekiel 22:6–13.

86. Crüsemann, *The Torah*, 199. The Psalter, the ancient hymnal of Israel, was compiled for use in the temple of Zerubbabel (governor of Judah under the reign of Darius I, 521–485 BCE). See Ezra 5:2 and Haggai 1:1.

87. Psalm 15.

88. Proverbs 28:8.

89. Ballard recalls an infamous example of the redistribution of wealth, the "looting" of Egypt by the Hebrews, prior to their flight. Exodus 12:36: "and the Lord had given the people favor in the sight of the Egyptians, so that they let them have what they asked. And so they plundered the Egyptians." Ballard, "On the Sin of Usury," 218.

is accused by Eliphaz the Temanite as having extracted "pledges from your family for no reason,"[90] a previously mentioned type of usury.

Stories regarding unjust lending practices continue in the books of 2 Kings, Isaiah, and Nehemiah. In 2 Kings, a narrative concerning a victim of a moneylender lends itself to a miracle performed by Elisha. A woman is distraught because her husband is dead and a creditor is about to take her children due to her debt. She appeals to Elisha, who tells her to borrow as many vessels as she can from her neighbors and pour oil into them. Miraculously, her small jar of oil fills all the vessels which she borrows, and she sells the oil and pays off her debts.[91] Referred to disparagingly as a "fairy-tale,"[92] this narrative is one of four stories in the Elisha saga, which together illustrate just what the model prophet is capable of doing. While the moneylender certainly had committed no sin by lending money to the family prior to the death of the husband, unquestionably once the woman's husband died the moneylender had an obligation not to oppress the widow. A second infraction has occurred, for the moneylender is accused of attempting to take her family in lieu of the debt, violating the injunction against taking pledges. Thus the prophet steps in and aids the woman and her family.

Isaiah mentions usury once in a passage in which Israel is not divorced or sold into slavery arbitrarily, but because of their sins they have been pawned: "Thus says the Lord: Where is your mother's bill of divorce with which I put her away? Or which of my creditors is it to whom I have sold you? No, because of your sins you were sold, and for your transgressions your mother was put away."[93] Habakkuk, who lived possibly during the height of Babylonian power, hurls five "woes" against a wicked nation. The first of these laments is to those who gain by false methods: "Alas for you who heap up what is not your own! How long will you load yourselves with goods taken in pledges? Will not your creditors suddenly rise, and those who make you tremble wake up? Then you will be booty for them. Because you have plundered many nations, all that survive of the peoples shall plunder you—because of human bloodshed, and violence to the earth, to cities and all who live in them.[94]" Nehemiah contains a large passage which offers evidence that usury was being practiced within

90. Job 22:6.

91. 2 Kings 4:1–7.

92. Eissfeldt, *The Old Testament: An Introduction*, 46.

93. Isaiah 50:1.

94. Habakkuk 2:6–8.

Israel,[95] despite prohibitive codes of Exodus 22:25 and Deuteronomy 23:19–20. While repairing the walls of Jerusalem an assembly of people confront Nehemiah and claim that they have had to pledge their fields, vineyards and houses in order to obtain grain during a time of famine. Their children have been sold into slavery and they have lost their lands. Interrupting the construction of the wall,[96] Nehemiah, distressed by the tales of grief, brings his concerns before the nobles and officials, charging them to mend their ways:

> I said to them, "You are all taking interest from your own people." And I called a great assembly to deal with them, and said to them, "As far as we were able, we have bought back our Jewish kindred who had been sold to other nations; but now you are selling your own kin, who must then be bought back by us!" They were silent, and could not find a word to say. So I said, "The thing that you are doing is not good. Should you not walk in the fear of our God, to prevent the taunts of the nations our enemies? Moreover I and my brothers and my servants are lending them money and grain. Let us stop this taking of interest. Restore to them, this very day, their fields, their vineyards, their olive orchards, and their houses, and the interest on money, grain, wine, and oil that you have been extracting from them." Then they said, "We will restore everything and demand nothing more from them. We will do as you say."[97]

All of Nehemiah's criticisms to the officials point to the interconnection of the financial predicament and usurious practices: he accuses the officials of afflicting their own kin, acting like pawnbrokers rather than like brothers;[98] he points out the absurdity of seeking freedom with the end result being the enslavement of themselves to one another;[99] finally, he questions should they not fear God and obey God, in order to avoid being ridiculed

95. Nehemiah 5:1–13a.

96. There is disagreement that such an issue would have interrupted the construction, and scholars have suggested that Nehemiah inserted a later problem into the chronological period of the wall. However, H. G. M. Williamson, after citing various opinions, claims that the literary construction of the account does not suggest that this chapter had been inserted at a later date, and thus the confrontation must have occurred during the construction of the wall. Williamson, *Ezra, Nehemiah*, 235. His points are rational: had Nehemiah *not* dealt with the problem in a timely fashion, he would have faced at the very least a halt in construction, and at worst a civil war.

97. Nehemiah 5:7b–12.

98. Buckley, *Teachings on Usury*, 22; Kinder, *Ezra and Nehemiah*, 95.

99. Nehemiah 5:8b.

by enemy nations, which would occur because of the maltreatment of their own?[100] In the end he counsels the cancellation of the pledges—which essentially turns the loans into "gifts,"—and forces them to make formal pledges that they shall favor generosity to avaricious behavior.

To summarize, passages of unjust lending found in 2 Kings, Nehemiah, Proverbs, Psalms, Habakkuk and Isaiah are proof that in direct violation to the codes of Exodus 22:25 and Deuteronomy 23:19–20, creditors are charging interest, despite the fact that the religious leaders tried to enforce the ethical code and the literary and prophetic traditions warned against it. But there remains another side to borrowing: the payback. The individual who took a loan had a real obligation to repay the loan; their poverty did not exclude them from the responsibility of making good. Though the one who extends credit has a responsibility to aid the poor, still the lender is not to be burdened by the economic woes of the borrower. Tamari stresses this point, claiming that the "requirement of payment of the loan exists to reinforce the Jewish dictum that people have obligations as well as rights, a consideration often blurred in modern welfare economics." [101] According to Scripture, it was believed that those who did not repay their loans were wicked, and open to the possibility for divine punishment: Psalm 37 declares that the "wicked borrow, and do not pay back, but the righteous are generous and keep giving."[102] The succeeding statement in this passage assures that this will be evident materially, for "those blessed by the Lord shall inherit the land, but those cursed by him shall be cut off."[103] Implicit in this second passage is the understanding that poverty might be evidence of someone's secret wickedness, and

---

100. Nehemiah 5:9. The passage "Moreover I and my brothers and my servants are lending them money and grain. Let us stop this taking of interest"—Nehemiah 5:10—could be an indication that Nehemiah himself was involved in the extraction of interest on loans, but it is not clear to what extent he was involved in the practice, if at all (Williamson, *Ezra–Nehemiah*, 240). I would not press the point. Nehemiah states, "Moreover, I and my brothers and my servants are lending them money and grain," but he does *not* state: "Moreover I and my brothers and my servants are lending them money and grain *for a price*." He could have been lending them money and grain to make up for the fact that the others had driven them into debt and Nehemiah's personal resources were beginning to feel the strain. Leonard Johnston, in *A History of Israel*, writes that Nehemiah was revolted by the practice of usury and was "sharing freely anything he possessed with those in need" (Johnston, *A History of Israel*, 149).

101. Tamari, *Jewish Ethics and Economic Life*, 54.

102. Psalm 37:21.

103. Psalm 37:22.

therefore those who were poor were in that predicament as a punishment for their sins.

But whether borrowing or lending, each portion of the transaction is layered with religious meaning and the opportunity either for the demonstration of sinfulness or righteous behavior. Being only the steward of what God has given, the lender has only one obligation, and that is to lend. The borrower has two obligations: first, the righteous borrower has an obligation to put the loan to a virtuous cause, which could include buying a house, maintaining a house, paying bills, financing a business, or simply purchasing the necessities of life. The unrighteous borrower would mismanage the funds or squander the money on wanton activities such as evenings spent drunk, gambling, or engaged in other scandalous activities best left unmentioned. Second, whether or not the money has been invested virtuously, the borrower has an obligation to return the loan at the appointed time and failure to do so is equal to theft.

Both the Talmud and the Mishnah agree and support codes against usury of the Pentateuch, with the Talmud not allowing for even the "dust" of interest.[104] However, Talmudic commentators went to elaborate lengths to justify business dealings which would not transgress the Torah, including "increased price for repayment, business partnerships which paid the lender a salary, or gave him a share of the profits, or devices which allowed a lender to lend money to a non-Jew, who in turn leant it to a Jew."[105] In the Mishnah the definition of "usury" changes from "taking a bite" to "profit," and usury comes to mean the avoidance of enriching one at the expense of another during the course of rather ordinary market transactions. Thus, the definition of "usury" grows to include various forms of profit-making opportunities. Despite the attempts to engage in usury under the guise of harmless market transactions, usury is never considered to be a legitimate business activity among the Jewish people, and it remains listed in the Mishnah along with a collection of other despised trades, including gamblers, herdsmen, publicans, dung-collectors and pigeon-trainers, reminiscent of Aristotle's list of those "who ply sordid trades, pimps and all such people, and those who lend small sums and at high rates."[106] Those who engaged in these trades were deprived of their rights and shunned.[107] Conversely,

---

104. Roth, *The Standard Jewish Encyclopedia*, 1344–45. For a modern treatment of usury and Jewish law, see Zipperstein, *Business Ethics in Jewish Law*, 39–47.

105. Johnson, *A History of the Jews*, 173.

106. Aristotle, *Nicomachean Ethics*, 84.

107. Jeremias, *Jerusalem in the Time of Jesus*, 311.

the benefits of free charity were extolled: "He who lends without interest is regarded by God as if he had fulfilled all the commandments."[108]

The New Testament: Usury and Universality

That debt played a role in controlling populations in the Roman Empire is present in the language of the New Testament; if what Jesus taught expressed something of the social reality of first century Palestine, then his language represents a bold—and dangerous—critique of the Roman system, and thus it would be necessary for his words to be expressed in the language of parable.[109] Douglas Oakman's work on Jesus responses to poverty and debt suggests that Jesus's claims present a radical reconstruction of economic systems based on power and status, systems that reinforced dependency and duty.[110]

In the Sermon on the Mount[111] Jesus exhorts his listeners to "give to everyone who begs from you, and do not refuse anyone who wants to borrow from you."[112] In a passage that fails to distinguish between the Israelite and the foreigner, no longer is an individual to allow an "insider/outsider" mentality to direct their economic activity; rather, one is to contribute to the redistribution of goods and money by lending to everyone without discrimination and by not entertaining the thought of ever seeing that money again. Lending without expecting repayment is now encouraged as an act of charity, and even to desire a return of the money is evidence of misplaced concern: "If you lend to those from whom you hope to receive," Jesus asks, "what credit is that to you? Even sinners lend to sinners, to receive as much again. But love your enemies, do good, and lend, expecting nothing in return,"[113] a phrase that might be better translated, claims Paul Mills, as "lend, *hoping* nothing in return."[114] The result of this

108. *Exodus Rabbah*, Mishpatim, 31.13, in Holman, *The Hungry Are Dying*, 47.

109. Oakman, *Jesus and the Peasants*, 25.

110. Ibid., 32–33.

111. Matthew 5–7; Luke 6:17–49.

112. Matthew 5:42.

113. Luke 6:34–35. Consistent also with this passage is Jesus's social advice that "When you give a luncheon or a dinner, do not invite your friends or your brothers or your relatives or rich neighbors, in case they may invite you in return and you would be repaid. But when you give a banquet, invite the poor, the crippled, the lame and the blind. And you will be blessed, because they cannot repay you, for you will be repaid at the resurrection of the righteous." Luke 14:12b–14.

114. Mills, "Interest in Interest," 9.

interpretation, he maintains, is that the individual was to loan without hope that the principal would be returned, which turns the loan into a gift.[115] I.H. Marshall, on the other hand, asserts that "lend, expecting nothing in return" did not mean that the lender was to consider the loan as a "gift," but that the lender was not to expect that he could gain by way of "loan" from the same—or another—individual.[116] But the phrase "lend, expecting nothing in return,"[117] suggests that the lender is to release both the money and their concerns for it at the same time, a position that would be later partly supported by Clement of Alexandria, when he counsels against internal attachment to money in light of Jesus's comments to the wealthy young man.[118] As the money departs, so too is the despair that accompanies a loss of money to depart; the lender will not be forgotten by God if the lender were to fall into financial disrepair as a result of having giving away that sum. Regardless, Jesus is exhorting his community to change their attitudes about the departure of money from one's own purse. Whether the money is considered by them to be a free loan or as a gift, or even as a possibility of future credit, Jesus counsels his listeners to detach themselves from concern over the money once it has left their hands. This method suggests a shift in behavior *and* thinking which has at its core love for the neighbor and trust in God rather than justice.[119] As well, Jesus's appeal takes further the notion of lending to those who are not part of one's own community: "But love your enemies, do good, and lend, expecting nothing in return."[120] The Israelites are exhorted to lend not only to those who are their kin, and not only to those who are strangers in their land, but to those who would—under other circumstances—do them harm. For those who need incentive for such comportment, Jesus informs them many times that they shall get their laurel: "Your reward will be great, and you will be the children of the Most High; for he is kind to the ungrateful and the wicked. Be merciful, just as your Father is merciful."[121] Halvor Moxnes writes that what is created is a three-part exchange: the first party (the lender) gives to the second party (the debtor) without

---

115. Ibid.

116. Marshall, *The Gospel of Luke*, quoted in Mills, "Interest in Interest," 7.

117. "καὶ δανείζετε μηδὲν ἀπελπίζοντες." Literally, "and lend, despairing nothing (or not at all)." Luke 6:35.

118. Clement of Alexandria, PG 9:602–52.

119. Roll, *A History of Economic Thought*, 32.

120. Luke 6:35a.

121. Luke 6:35b–36. See also Luke 12:33 and 14:14.

thought of repayment, but the first party (the lender) is in fact repaid by the third party (God).[122] Indirectly, God continues as the benefactor of the poor, "my people . . . the poor among you."[123] The compensation, then, is not to be that of a crude monetary type, but a spiritual remuneration, a consistent theme throughout the writings on usury by the early Christian authors.[124] It is easy to assume that it is only money of which Jesus speaks; in a primarily agrarian community people would probably casually borrow an assortment of items such as tools, seeds or manual labor from one another with great frequency.[125] Situated immediately following the Beatitudes and the "Golden Rule," this is a passage which seems to support financial support of those to whom one might not necessarily wish to give,[126] with the end result not of monetary advantage, but spiritual advantage. But in addition, the purpose of the loan system in the Torah was to foster righteous living, the result of which is a healthy community spirit that reflects the relationship between the community and their God. Petty bickering over minor details can easily and quickly turn friend into foe, most especially when one feels cheated; in which case, when Jesus says to "love your enemies" his definition of "enemy" might very well have included "those with whom you are currently bickering over something stupid." The end result is that Jesus does not seem to be calling for an interest-free loan economy, but for a loan-free economy which—Oakman notes—is a radical and economically subversive suggestion.[127] In this case, loans are viewed by the lender as gifts and the return on such is to be

122. Moxnes, *The Economy of the Kingdom*, 156.

123. Exodus 22:25.

124. Basil, using this same theory, will exhort the wealthy to give, assuring them that "if you are seeking additional payment, be satisfied with that from the Lord. He will pay the interest for the poor." Basil, *Homilia in psalmum* 14, in Schroeder, *On Social Justice*, 98. Most boldly, Gregory will refer to God as the "Debtor." Gregory will beseech the lender to consider as their pledge the present bounty of the earth, and all which is inheritable from God: "Consider the sky's expanse, examine the boundless sea, learn from the earth's magnitude and count the living beings which it nourishes . . . Do not demand gain but give bountifully and without corruption (Prov 19.17). Then you will see God who abundantly dispenses his grace" (Gregory of Nyssa, *Contra usurarios*, in McCambley, "Against Those Who Practice Usury by Gregory of Nyssa." 296).

125. Buckley, *Teachings on Usury*, 90.

126. Ibid.

127. "Yet as we have seen, remission of debts was a revolutionary slogan in agrarian antiquity, and such tales on the lips of a Galilean prophet probably sounded subversive." Oakman, *Jesus and the Peasants*, 29.

regarded as secondary to the primary problem of helping one who needs help, even to the degree that one extends aid to one's own enemy. Bruce Ballard refers to this not as a command on Jesus's part, but as a "counsel of perfection," a "strengthening of the Old Testament morality."[128] More than that, however, it is a strengthening of an old world morality; one can find in this passage a parallel between Jesus's desire to foster community welfare and Plato's understanding of the ἔρανος loan, in which he believed that the repayment of loans among friends was both crude and unnecessary, and that legal actions against debtors should be discouraged.[129]

But if trade and business relationships are based on credit and hospitality, what is the effect of a free-loan system? If this type of lending were employed on a regular basis, it would break down the system of patronage in the traditional form, for even those who freely gave did so because of the obligations then owed to them as a result of their "gifts."[130] While this system might not be effective with regard to the economic health of a community, still the wholeness of the people would prosper; under the system introduced by Jesus the debtor is not in arrears to a benefactor either for the monetary gift or for the servitude or gratitude to which they would once have been held, for "God is the only patron; consequently, all people are his clients."[131] Not only is the debtor freed, but the notion of hospitality is freed, and hospitality can now be offered without the binding obligations which it previously placed on the guest.[132] Gifts are now to be truly gifts, not obligations, and all gratitude and rewards which were previously owed to the lender/host are now to be directed directly to God, patron of all.[133]

128. Ballard, "On the Sin of Usury," 222.

129. I am not suggesting that Jesus was inspired or influenced by Plato, but merely note that the two were of like mind in seeking the advantage of the community.

130. "Once it had been the glory of the great man to be for small men 'an acropolis and tower'; in the days when the only wealth known was that which was consumed, the rich man was glad to employ his surplus in extending his circle of dependants" (Glotz, *Ancient Greece at Work*, 80).

131. Moxnes, *The Economy of the Kingdom*, 157.

132. Luke 14:12–14: "He said also to the one who had invited him, 'When you give a luncheon or a dinner, do not invite your friends or your brothers or your relatives or rich neighbors, in case they may invite you in return, and you would be repaid. But when you give a banquet, invite the poor, the crippled, the lame, and the blind. And you will be blessed, because they cannot repay you, for you will be repaid at the resurrection of the righteous.'"

133. Moxnes, *The Economy of the Kingdom*, 157. "The esteem that accrues to the generous man all to one side, generosity is usefully enlisted as a starting mechanism

Jesus attitudes towards debt are further revealed in a parable which utilizes forgiveness of the debtor by the lender to illustrate the act of generosity. While dining at the house of a Pharisee, a woman who was known to be a sinner comes to the house with a jar of perfume; weeping, she kisses Jesus's feet, wipes them with her hair and anoints them with the perfume. The Pharisee thinks that if Jesus were truly a prophet, Jesus would know just what type of woman was touching him.[134] In response to these unspoken words, Jesus turns to his host, and says: "A certain creditor had two debtors; one owed five hundred denarii, and the other fifty. When they could not pay, he cancelled the debts for both of them. Now which of them will love him more?" Simon answered, "I suppose the one for whom he cancelled the greater debt." And Jesus said to him, "You have judged rightly."[135] Using her actions to shame the host for having neglected the duties of hospitality,[136] Jesus forgives the woman her sins and urges her to go in peace.[137] While a modern understanding of this passage offers a defense for the willingness of Christianity to welcome sinners as well as addresses the attitudes of those who would be in judgment of such sinners, the primary focus of this passage is on forgiveness of debt: those who have many debts will be forgiven much; no debt is too deep, no sin too grave. Applied to Jesus's contemporary situation, lenders should demonstrate charity by forgiving the grave debtor before the debtor is given a grave. The greater the debt, the greater the charity and the greater response for love or, as Oakman writes, the response is proportionate to the experience.[138]

The level to which debt permeated relations is revealed in the parable of the ungrateful servant in Matthew 18:23–35. The narrative is sparked by the ever impetuous Peter, who, thinking that he is being philanthropic

of leadership *because it creates followership*" (Sahlins, *Stone Age Economics*, 208; italics original). This image of the wealthy patron is seriously and consistently undercut by Jesus's message in the Lukan gospel.

134. Luke 7:36–39.

135. Luke 7:41–44.

136. "Then turning toward the woman, he said to Simon, 'Do you see this woman? I entered your house; you have me no water for my feet, but she has bathed my feet with her tears and dried them with her hair. You gave me no kiss, but from the time I came in she has not stopped kissing my feet. You did not anoint my head with oil, but she has anointed my feet with ointment.'" During the course of a traditional luxury meal of just such a type as a man of means would host, the first stage would include washing the hands and feet of the guests, and anointing them with oil to remove the odor of the day (See Malina and Rohrbaugh, *Social-Science Commentary*, 331).

137. Luke 7:48–50.

138. Oakman, *Jesus and the Economic Questions of His Day*, 150.

with his forgiveness, asks Jesus how many times should one forgive, and then answers his own question with the generous number seven. Jesus responds with the following tale: a king forgives a servant a remarkably massive monetary debt. Upon leaving, the servant sees another who owes him a paltry sum of money, and as the second servant cannot pay, he is thrown in jail by the first servant. Others hear of this and report to the king, who confronts the first servant with his appalling behavior and, in a rather macabre ending, orders the first servant is to be tortured "until he would pay his entire debt," which obviously he cannot do if he is being tortured rather than working. Therefore, the first servant has been cast into eternal damnation. Rich in the ability to forgive, the first servant was niggardly with his forgiveness, not half as willing to spend mercy as he was willing to spend money that was not his to begin with. Jesus ends the parable with chilling words: "So my heavenly Father will also do to every one of you, if you do not forgive your brother or sister from your heart."[139] On the bright side, one can consider that Jesus does intend some comfort, for the king does forgive an enormous debt for the first servant, a forgiveness which others are capable of receiving. If the first servant is to represent the common person in their relationship to God, then the first servant's forgiven debt represents the many sins for which an individual owes remuneration to God. In these accounts, grace "does not come without strings attached."[140]

The troubled relationships that result from debt and poverty are highlighted in a parable in the gospels of Luke and Matthew.[141] The parable of the harsh master is told immediately after Jesus has informed the chief tax collector Zacchaeus that he shall be staying with him that night. Stricken when the crowd begins to grumble that Jesus will be staying at the house of "one who is a sinner," Zacchaeus quickly repents of his past deeds: "Look, half of my possessions Lord, I will give to the poor; and if I have defrauded anyone of anything, I will pay back four times as much."[142] Zacchaeus has promised to pay back the amount that the Twelve Tablets required of any usurer who charged a rate higher than the legal limit; if convicted in court, that individual would be required to restore the sum four times over, which was twice the amount of a convicted thief.[143] If

139. Matthew 18:35.

140. Oakman, *Jesus and the Peasants*, 35.

141. Luke 19:11–27; Matthew 25:14–30.

142. Luke 19:8.

143. The Eighth Tablet—"Torts and Delicts" (damages, injuries, and legal offences)—addresses the offences of the usurer: "18a . . . No person shall practice usury

Zacchaeus is guilty of this offence, then Jesus has elected to spend his evening with a usurer, a man rated lower than a thief in the legal system and in the public eye; but by this choice he brings about the repentance of a wicked man, and justly rewards Zacchaeus for that repentance: "Then Jesus said to him, 'Today salvation has come to this house, because he too is a son of Abraham.'"[144] Jesus takes advantage of his audience—already angered because he has favored an alleged usurer—to relate the following parable: a nobleman/master entrusts his servants with different amounts of money, and after a period of time expects them to produce not only the original sum, but the interest or benefit gained by their investments. At the return of the master, the servants who have increased their sums are praised and are given great responsibilities, and the "lazy" and fearful servant who has gained nothing—having wrapped his talent and placed it in the ground for fear of losing the money of his harsh master—has even that single talent taken away from him. Naturally, the master is angered by this, especially when he hears the reason why the servant did not increase his talents:

> Then the one who had received the one talent also came forward, saying, "Master, I knew that you were a harsh man, reaping where you did not sow, and gathering where you did not scatter seed; so I was afraid, and I went and hid your talent in the ground. Here you have what is yours." But his master replied, "You wicked and lazy slave! You knew, did you, that I reap where I did not sow, and gather where I did not scatter? Then you ought to have invested my money with the bankers,[145] and on my return I would have received what was my own with interest."[146]

---

at a rate of more than one-twelfth." "18b . . . A thief shall be condemned for double damages and a usurer for quadruple damages." Johnson et al, *Ancient Roman Statutes*, Table 8, 11.

144. Luke 19:9.

145. The mention of the bank where the master's talent would gain interest was possibly a reference to the Temple, which functioned somewhat as a bank in the ancient Near East. Individuals who came to worship in Jerusalem bringing with them foreign money were forced to sell it to the money lenders for most likely a wicked price Note that Jesus's encounter with the money-changers in Matthew and Luke are the only places in the New Testament Scriptures where Jesus comes closest to having an authentic meltdown (Buckley, *Teachings on Usury*, 44; Maloney, "Usury and Restrictions on Interest-Taking in the Ancient Near East," 15).

146. Matthew 25:24–28; see also Luke 19:20–23.

Not a few have concluded from the statement "Then you ought to have invested my money with the bankers . . . I would have received what was my own with interest" to mean that usury was acceptable to Jesus as it is mentioned, but not explicitly condemned.[147] Ballard rejects this, and notes that G. S. Luttrell is one of few modern writers who write against the idea that Jesus is supporting usury in this passage.[148] Buckley, too, asserts that the Hebrew Scripture ban on usury is not being condoned by Jesus in this parable.[149] Conversely, Maloney, who claims that "there is no explicit judgment on the morality of usury"[150] in the New Testament, insists that as usury was a common practice in the ancient world, its incorporation into the parable makes no statement either for or against the practice.[151] I disagree with Maloney's comments in this case because the act of gaining interest on money is equated with the activity of a "wicked" master. Reading this text more literally, Halvor Moxnes might argue that this text reflects the dynamics of Palestinian society, and demonstrates the precarious situation in which managers were placed when they were left to govern estates and money in the place of an absentee landlord. While neither Buckley nor Ballard touch on the moral aspects of the relationship between the "lazy" servant and his master, Moxnes mentions briefly that this passage demonstrates that in this society one person's gain was understood as a direct consequence of another's loss;[152] one did not become wealthy independently, but as a result of the impoverishment of another.

Wealth gained at the expense of another is one of two themes that Malina and Rohrbaugh contest make up the different interpretations of this same parable.[153] They claim that the Matthew text is not concerned with profit or wealth, but uses economic language with which the peasant society of this day would be familiar: a rapacious master and dishonorable servants who increase his wealth by unjust means, and as a result

147. Ballard, "On the Sin of Usury," 222–23.

148. Ibid., 223. See Luttrell, "Usury," in the *Encyclopedia of Biblical and Christian Ethics*, 421.

149. Buckley, *Teachings on Usury*, 93.

150. Maloney, "The Teaching of the Fathers on Usury," 241.

151. I disagree with Maloney's claim because the act of gaining interest on money is equated with the wicked master. "The existence of the practice is acknowledged and castigated as reaping where one has not sown and gathering where one did not winnow" (Buckley, *Teachings on Usury*, 93).

152. Moxnes, *The Economy of the Kingdom*, 84.

153. Malina and Rohrbaugh, *Social-Science Commentary*, 149–150.

his honor as a freeman is not blemished.[154] Although Western society has read from this passage that Christians are to use their "talents" or "what they have been given" to increase the wealth of their master,[155] from the perspective of a first-century peasant the interpretation is different. First, one is not to seek to increase the wealth for an avaricious and dishonorable master; second, the wealthy are greedy and will reward those who cater to their behavior; third, one should expect to be treated badly by the wicked.[156]

Malina and Rohrbaugh assert that the same parable in Luke is used for a different purpose. Again, in the modern West this passage has been used to promote capitalistic behavior.[157] But Malina and Rohrbaugh point out that this parable comes after a section in which the author promotes the notion of discipleship involving the sharing of possessions, and so the author wanted to indicate that in fact nothing had yet changed.[158] Socially, economically and politically, the structures were still intact, despite measures taken by disciples to alter their lives to fit the new kingdom.[159] The individuals hearing this parable would still consider the two servants who aided their master's gain as was stated above: they are thieves seeking to increase their wicked master's unfairly large piece of the economic pie; further, they would be reminded not to jump to any conclusions about the forthcoming Kingdom of Heaven;[160] things have not changed for the better quite yet, the rich still take care of their own.

154. Malina and Rohrbaugh write of the "limited goods" theory of this period, in which it was believed that all wealth had already been distributed, and so the acquisition of anything was at the direct loss to someone else. An honorable freeman would not then seek to increase his wealth or he would be called a thief. As a result, masters would entrust investments with the servants, for it did not matter if they acted honorably or not, as they were not free persons and therefore had no honor (Malina and Rohrbaugh, *Social-Science Commentary*, 149). See also Rakover, *Unjust Enrichment in Jewish Law*.

155. Christians have interpreted this passage to read that like the servants who have increased the wealth of their master, they are to spread the good news of the gospel or create more members for the kingdom of heaven (Malina and Rohrbaugh, *Social-Science Commentary*, 150).

156. Malina and Rohrbaugh, *Social-Science Commentary on the Synoptic Gospels*, 150.

157. Ibid., 390.

158. Ibid., 389.

159. Prior to this parable is the controversial passage in which Jesus tells "a certain ruler" that in order to inherit eternal life he must "sell all that you own and distribute the money to the poor, and you will have treasure in heaven; the come, follow me" (Luke 18:22b).

160. Malina and Rohrbaugh, ibid., 389–90.

The remaining passages in the New Testament which mention interest or loans—or at least allude to them—are not, in my opinion, concerned with the same issue of usury as is raised here. One of the most obscure passages in the Gospels concerning loans is found in Luke 16:1–13, and forms half of a duet of parables about the squandering of money.[161] But while the Parable of the Unjust Steward has confounded scholars through literally hundreds of commentaries, it was probably not out of the intellectual reach of Jesus's listeners. The story concerns a steward who is exposed to his master as having acted unjustly. Fearful for his future, the steward ponders his fate. Calling his master's debtors to him, he encourages one to reduce his bill of debt by fifty percent and another by twenty percent. Rather than being enraged by this behavior, the master instead praises the "unjust steward" for having acted shrewdly. Several scholars[162] have suggested that the steward cut the usurious interest from the bill, and so the steward was "reducing" the bill to the original debt. Problems with this interpretation are summarized by David Landry, who suggests that usury cannot be in question here because the amounts of the loans forgiven do not correspond with the interest normally charged for such a loan.[163] As well, there is nothing else in the text to indicate that the steward is suddenly concerned with his master's observation of the laws against usury.[164]

The final passage in the gospels to be addressed is concerned with Jesus simple injunction: "Forgive us our debts, as we also have forgiven our debtors."[165] In Oakman's *Jesus and the Peasants*, he suggests that there is a direct link between the debt which God grants to humanity (a vertical relationship) and the debt which humans grant one another (horizontal); that which God grants is moral and vast in scope, while that which humans grant to one another is material and immediate. They differ greatly, and yet are inextricably linked.[166] In other words, the moral righteousness of an individual can aid in the distribution of the material needs of those

161. The parable of the Prodigal Son is the second in this set.

162. Including Derrett, "Fresh Light on St. Luke 16: The Parable of the Unjust Steward." 198–219; Fitzmyer, "The Story of the Dishonest Manager," 23–42.

163. Landry, "Honor Restored," 287–309. But can we be so sure that Jesus would have been either aware of or concerned with the interest rates of the day? He told a story, he did not present a fiscal review; it is likely that even without current interest rates his audience would have understood that this was a narrative about greed.

164. Landry, "Honor Restored," 290.

165. Matthew 6:12; literally, "as also we forgave (ἀφήκαναμεν)—[the assumption being made that the forgiveness to the debtors has *already* happened]—our debtors."

166. Oakman, *Jesus and the Peasants*, 38.

impoverished by an oppressive system. The removal of obligation from those suffering allows for them the possibility that they might get "their daily bread,"[167] a meal which might very well have been earned through begging or prostitution.

Additional texts in the New Testament which touch on "debts" do not further the discussion of usury.[168] I would conclude that the passages within the New Testament which contain direct references to loans that might be usurious are confined to Luke 6:34–35; 7:36–50; 19:11–27; Matthew 25:14–30; and 18:23–35. These statements of Jesus reflect a conscious attempt to shift the end result of loan-making from that of profit for the lender to gift to the debtor. This requires not only a fundamental change in the way a lender thinks about money before the money has left the lender's hands, but also a precise new way of *not* thinking about money after it has left the lender's hands. The end result of such an interpretation of the Torah is idealistic, but simple: Jesus exhorts his listeners time and again simply to lend money and be done with it. If a lender is encouraged never to hope to see the principal again, then it stands to reason that the lender should not hope to see any interest either.

Conclusion

While the Jewish understanding of usury was also partially formed by a desire for a benevolent society, the element of virtue is added to their understanding of that society, a society which makes exceptions for those within and without. They understood that usury was part of the general world system of business, but knowing this, they attempted to incorporate the enterprise of lending into the life of their community in ways which were morally acceptable and which demonstrated righteous behavior before God. Thus, two types of lending appeared within this system of ethical

---

167. Matthew 6:11.

168. Buckley cites Romans 13:7–8 as a practical admonition on behalf of Paul for Christians not to leave any accounts outstanding, but I am not convinced that this passage is particularly connected with the subject of usury (Buckley, *Teachings on Usury*, 94). As well, she cites 1 Thessalonians 4:10b–12 as relevant to the subject at hand. She considers this passage to be referring to the need for Christians to avoid being dependent on others who are outside of the Church, but as a similar passage in 2 Thessalonians suggests that there are individuals within this community who are living off of one another, there does not seem to be any indication that they are going outside of their community and borrowing money for their needs (Buckley, *Teachings on Usury*, 94).

monotheism: loans extended to the family without interest—the *chesed* loan, similar to the Greek ἔρανος—and loans extended to the foreigner with interest. Despite the several injunctions against usury, evidence that the practices took place is indicated by the many biblical passages which deal with the abuses of usury. A righteous person in that society would not make a loan to another with interest, and because of its association with theft and trickery, the usurer came to be equated in the Hebrew Scriptures with rapists and murders, in a way similar to the grouping of despicable professions by the philosophers. The effect of such activity is no longer mere condemnation by the community, but condemnation by God. The usurer is eventually included within a list of those whose actions brand them as nefarious, those who will die for their iniquity.

The New Testament makes little mention of usury, except within the context of a few statements and parables of Jesus, which indicates that it was a known practice. From Jesus's statements which deal with money one can safely draw the conclusion that the practice of usury is not consistent with the teachings of Jesus. Counseling for the renunciation of all debts, Jesus encouraged individuals to take the injunctions against interest from the Scriptures one step further and forswear the return of even the principal, fully forgetting the interest; at its most radical, it could be considered the very dismantling of the loan system. Chapters Four and Five will consider to what degree early Christian Greek theologians claimed the rich history of scripture, philosophy and law as they composed their sermons on usury, while attempting to offset the devastating effects of a system that was as equaling damning for the body present as it was for the soul in the future.

4

Early Greek Fathers and Usury[1]

ＡLTHOUGH SCRIPTURAL MANDATES AGAINST the practice of usury might lead one to assume that usury was universally condemned, the inconsistencies between the legal right to engage in usury and conciliar legislation against clergy who engaged in usurious activities created a curious situation, resulting in an uneasy tension between the practice of the secular laity and moral reproach of the clergy. As paganism subsided early Christian officials had fewer marginal peoples to blame for the ills of society, and as moneyed families converted, religious authorities began to target rich individuals whose gains subsequently oppressed others in the flock. While it might be assumed that the subject of usury would be brought up within sermons on wealth, this is in fact not the case; of the authors examined, the subject was often brought up in ways that seem utterly disconnected with the scriptural passages being analyzed or the heresies being refuted. This fourth chapter considers the ways in which references to usury are included in the various writings of a selection of early Greek Fathers, for the purpose of addressing the following questions: first, to whom does the term "usurer" apply? Does the term "usurer" refer only to a monetary "usurer," or does the term "usurer" come in time to refer simply to one among many wicked characteristics in a corrupt and sinful individual? Second, how is biblical scripture employed in the sermons that include condemnation of usury? Is the Deuteronomic injunction against usury within the community—while allowing for

---

1. Material in this chapter was foundational for a chapter I wrote titled "'That which has been wrung from tears': Usury, the Greek Fathers, and Catholic Social Teaching," in Leemans et al., *Reading Patristic Texts on Social Ethics*.

the practice outside the community (Deuteronomy 23:19–20)—found within the works of the early Christian authors, or is the practice simply forbidden altogether? If the practice of usury is simply forbidden, then what defense is given for its condemnation? The primary sources to be considered include several homilies, an oration, a letter, theological instruction, and one or two refutations. The chosen passages were all written within approximately 250 years of one another, from the end of the second century to not quite the middle of the fifth, a period of great transition both for Christianity and the Roman Empire. The authors have been grouped into two segments: the first considers select writings of Clement of Alexandria, Cyril of Jerusalem, Gregory of Nazianzus and Theodoret of Cyrrhus. Because of the bounty of references to usury in the sermons of John Chrysostom, a second section will be devoted exclusively to his contribution to the eastern early Christian response to the problems of usury. The conclusion will consider all authors together.

Clement, Cyril, Gregory, and Theodoret

During the rise of the banking system in Greece and the Roman Empire, there was not always a clear distinction between a banker and a money-lender; but what is clear is that while early Christian authors did not particularly condemn the role of the banker, they always condemned one who engaged in usury.[2]

2. Laiou, "Church, Economic Thought and Economic Practice," 440. It is possible to conclude that some bishops suggest that usury rates set within legal limits were acceptable; examples to support this position include Clement of Alexandria, who may have suggested that the prohibition against interest applied only to loans to fellow believers; Clement of Alexandria, *Stromata*, PG 8:1023. Similar to Clement, Ambrose allows for the same distinction, but in much less ambiguous language; Ambrose, *De Tobia* 15.51 (PL 14:779). Cleary notes that Bishop Sidonius Apollinaris of Clermont might have recognized the right of a cleric to demand usury, but I am not convinced that this is what the bishop is suggesting; Cleary, *The Church and Usury*, 57. Cleary also mentions St. Gregory of Tours, who relates the tale of Desideratus, Bishop of Verdun; see chapter 1, note 51. The bishop asked for a loan from King Theudebert and promised to repay it with interest: "If in your compassion you have any money to spare, I beg you to lend it to me, so that I may relieve the distress of those in my diocese. As soon as the men who are in charge of the commercial affairs in my city have reorganized their business, as has been done in other cities, I will repay your loan with interest," Gregory of Tours, *History of the Franks*, 190–91. However, I disagree also here with Cleary, who states that this tale indicates that neither "his lordship nor Gregory thought it unreasonable that usury should be paid in the case," Cleary, *The Church and Usury*, 57. I would point out that Gregory's text does not suggest any such

While there was sufficient ammunition against usury available in Hebrew scripture and Greek and Roman practice, Philo of Alexandria (c. 20 BCE—50 CE) is credited by authors Maloney and Moser as being a particularly influential figure for usury theory, and the individual upon whom later authors modeled their condemnations.[3] Without question, the interpretation of Scripture employed by the eclectic Philo influenced many early Christian authors, and through them many generations of Christian authorities. Philo addresses usury in two texts, *On the Virtues*[4] and *The Special Laws*,[5] and categorically rejects the taking of interest. The texts suggest that Philo sees the debtor as a poor person, not one who is living beyond one's means, and he questions the legitimacy of expecting one who has not the capital to provide more: ". . . for a person who borrows is not living on a superabundance of means, but is obviously in need."[6]

---

thing, as we have no indication about what any of the parties thought; the Bishop recognizes that interest is a part of the lending process, and includes it in his request to someone who might very well not have lent to him otherwise. Worth noting, in the end King Theudebert repudiated not just the interest, but the principle as well, which indicates to me that the King realized that taking usury from a bishop who borrowed money to get an *entire community* out of poverty seems inappropriate. Gregory of Tours, *History of the Franks*, 191. Finally, a passage translated differently by both Cleary and McCambley places Gregory of Nyssa in the position of recognizing that usury might be employed amongst the wealthy, but not those of lesser means. The following, from his *Contra usurarios*, "καὶ δανείζετε μηδὲν ἀπελπίζοντες," is translated in Cleary as "Do not force poverty to give what pertains to the rich alone to give," Cleary, *The Church and Usury*, 51. From this, Cleary concludes, Gregory is recognizing that the wealthy might extract interest from *one another* but not the poor. McCambley, however, translates the passage to read: "[do not] force poverty upon those who are rich," which does not result in the same conclusion, if one considers that Gregory is, in this passage, soundly condemning the practice. McCambley, *Against Those Who Practice Usury*, 298. I am not of the opinion that Gregory allows for a distinction to be made when usury is involved between the wealthy or poor, at least with respect to this sermon. And while some might conclude that bishops probably turned a blind eye to low rates extended among business partners, the explicit and consistent rejection of usury among the bishops are of such a tenor that it is more likely they would not have been shy to criticize the motives of anyone who thought even a small amount of interest would be appropriate.

3. Maloney, "The Teaching of the Fathers on Usury," 243; see also Moser, *Die patristische Zinslehre*, 96–108. I summarize Moser and Maloney's comments on Philo in Chapter One. My opinion about the influence of Philo on Basil of Caesarea will be discussed in Chapter Five.

4. Philo, *De virtutibus* 14.

5. Philo, *De specialibus legibus* 2.74–76.

6. Ibid., 2.74. See chapter 5: Basil also will question this judgment: "Tell me, do you really seek riches and financial gain from the destitute? If this person had the resources

In his passage on usury in *On the Virtues*, Philo combines[7] Israelite law with the wisdom of Aristotle: "He forbids anyone to lend money on interest to a brother, meaning by this name not merely a child of the same parents, but anyone of the same citizenship or nation. For he does not think it just to amass money bred from money as their yearlings are from cattle."[8] Maloney notes the passage and its influence on authors Clement of Alexandria, Origen, and later authors,[9] and Moser lauds the cleverness of one who has efficiently combined the law of Deuteronomy with the Greek argument against usury.[10] Like his predecessors, Philo employs similar rhetorical devices when writing about usury and usurers, such as casting the lender in the role of one who has been overtaken by a savage character, taking on the "nature of wild beasts."[11] Both Gregory and Basil will make use of this method, inconsistently shifting the lender from engaging in a manner like a beast, and then as a hunter of innocents.[12] But perhaps the most influential passage on usury is found in Philo's *The Special Laws*, where he elaborates on the above idea of charity among citizens or even among a nation. Philo confirms that the alien is not allowed the same special treatment as the resident, a statement that will be highly influential in the Christian analysis of usury. According to Philo—here upholding the Deuteronomic code—one should not expect to profit off one's kinsman:

> Human vicissitudes are manifold, and life is not always on the same anchorage, but is like an unsteady wind, ever veering round to the opposite quarter. Now the best course would be that the creditors liberality should be extended to all debtors. But since they are not capable of showing magnanimity, some being under the domination of their money or not very well

---

to make you even wealthier, whey did he come begging to your door?" (*Homilia in psalmum* 14, 90).

7. Moser, *Die patristische Zinslehre*, 101.

8. Philo, *De virtutibus*, 14.82–83.

9. Maloney, "The Teaching of the Fathers," 243. Maloney notes that Origen's mention of usury in his *Ps.* 36 (PG 12:1347–48) is no more than a mention, for there is no statement for or against the practice.

10. Moser, *Die patristische Zinslehre*, 101. Not to diminish Moser's contribution, however, F.H. Colson, the translator of the text provides a clue in this direction by observing that within this passage there is "obviously an allusion to the original meaning of τόκος" (Philo, *De virtutibus*, 211, n. b.).

11. Philo, *De virtutibus*, 14.87.

12. Gregory of Nyssa, *Contra usurarios*, 299; see also Basil, *Homilia in psalmum* 14, 91–92.

off, he laid down that they too should make a contribution, the
sacrifice of which would not give them pain. He does not allow them to exact money from their fellow-nationals, but does
permit the recovery of dues from the others. He distinguishes
the two by calling the first by the appropriate name of brethren,
suggesting that none should grudge to give of his own to those
whom nature has made his brothers and fellow-heirs. Those
who are not of the same nation he describes as aliens, reasonably enough, and the condition of the alien excludes any idea of
partnership, unless indeed by a transcendency of virtues he con-
verts even it into a tie of kinship, since it is a general truth that
common citizenship rests on virtues and laws which propound
the morally beautiful and the sole good.[13]

In this elegant passage Philo first presents the best of all situations, in
which the lenders would extend liberty to all who find themselves tossed
by that "unsteady wind." But he quickly concedes that one reason or another, the lender does not have it within his capacity to perform this act
of munificence due to heartlessness, greed, or even his own poverty. Lack
of open-handedness of the lender is the reason, Philo claims, for the ordinance against taking interest from one's fellow kinsman because "they are
not capable of showing magnanimity."[14] According to this text, the reason
for the ordinance against usury is not to protect the Hebrews from those
outside the community and keep them in a fair financial state with respect
to neighboring trade communities, but to protect Hebrews from those
within their own society who suffer from the illness of greed; the result is
their willingness to cut down their own people for profit. Philo's distaste
for the lender and his trade is evident in the passage that follows:

Now lending money on interest is a blameworthy action, for
a person who borrows is not living on a superabundance of
means, but is obviously in need, and since he is compelled to
pay the interest as well as the capital, he must necessarily be in
the utmost straits.[15] And while he thinks he is being benefited
by the loan, he is actually like senseless animals suffering further damage from the bait which is set before him. I ask you,
Sir Moneylender, why do you disguise your want of a partner's

13. Philo, *De specialibus legibus*, 2.73–74.

14. Ibid., 2.73.

15. Basil will use this same logic in his *Homilia in psalmum* 14, when he writes:
"Tell me, do you really seek riches and financial gain from the destitute? If this person
had the resources to make you even wealthier, whey did he come begging to your
door?" (*Homilia in psalmum* 14, 90).

feeling by pretending to act as a partner? Why do you assume outwardly a kindly and charitable appearance but display in your actions inhumanity and a savage brutality, exacting more than you lend, sometimes double, reducing the pauper to further depths of poverty?[16]

Philo accompanies this passage with a taunt to "Sir Moneylender," informing him that the public is gleeful at his downfall on the rare occasion that greed has resulted in financial failure, and he concludes the passage with a plea for moneylenders to be content with the return of the loan. In general, Philo's statements on usury speak of little concern for either the salvation or the well being of the lender, and are, overall, primarily concerned with the relief of the individual poor person.[17] While this is hardly a fault, still,

---

16. Philo, *De specialibus legibus*, 2.74–75.

17. Early Christianity owed a debt to Philo for his words against usury, for while he was composing them the behavior of individuals in Christian communities were proof that such condemnations were necessary. An example of treatment doled out to those who engaged in usury is found in the *Constitutions of the Holy Apostles*, in "What are the Characters of Widows Falsely So Called." In this passage the author chastises widows who are supported by the Christian Church, but who—rather than remaining at home and praying—are "not affixed to the altar of Christ." *Constitutions of the Holy Apostles*, Book 3.1.VII, 428. The subsequent passage suggests that usury was not an activity restricted to male members of society: "For when they ought to be content with their subsistence from the Church, as having moderate desires, on the contrary, they run from one of their neighbors' houses to another, and disturb them, heaping up to themselves plenty of money, and lend at bitter usury, and are only solicitous about mammon, whose bag is their god." *Constitutions*, Book 3.1.VII, 428. The woman who participated in such activities was dealt with harshly at the discretion of her bishop: "But if without direction she does any one of these things, let her be punished with fasting, or else let her be separated on account of her rashness." *Constitutions*, Book 3.1.VII, 429. This position against usurious behavior would be supported by a litany of prohibitions in subsequent councils; Canon 17 of the First Ecumenical Council of Nicaea in 325 stated the position clearly: "Forasmuch as many enrolled among the Clergy, following covetousness and lust of gain, have forgotten the divine Scripture, which says, 'Those who do not lend money at interest,' and in lending money ask the hundredth of the sum [as monthly interest], the holy and great Synod thinks it just that if after this decree any one be found to receive usury, whether he accomplish it by secret transaction or otherwise, as by demanding the whole and one half, or by using any other contrivance whatever for filthy lucre's sake, he shall be deposed from the clergy and his name stricken from the list." Ancient Epitome of Canon XVII," I. Nice, 36. The Council of Carthage in 348 reinforced this position, citing the Hebrew and Christian scriptures as authority. Ancient Epitome of Canon V," *African Code, A.D.* 419, 37. Canon 15 of "The Captions of the Arabic Canons Attributed to the Council of Nice" states "that clerics or religious who lend on usury should be cast from their grade," ("Canon XV" of *The Captions of the Arabic Canons Attributed to the Council of Nice*, I. Nice, 46) while Canon 52 states that "usury and the base seeking of worldly

the words of the early Christian authors will demonstrate greater compassion for both parties, balancing worry for the material state of the poor with hope for salvation of the miserly.

In addition to Philo, evidence of an attitude in the east against usury and the usurer can be seen by the end of the second century in the writing of Bishop Apollonius, whose comments on usurious practices in which members of a Christian sect engaged are preserved in the writings of Eusebius and Jerome.[18] Apollonius assembled a disavowal of a Phrygian sect led by Montanus, known as Montanism. In the fragment preserved in Eusebius's *History*, Apollonius first points out the fraudulent character of their leader,[19] next the "alleged" chastity of the group's prophetesses,[20] and finally he addresses the financially unscrupulous behavior of the prophets and prophetesses:

> Don't you agree that all Scripture debars a prophet from accepting gifts and money? When I see that a prophetess has accepted gold and silver and expensive clothing, am I not justified in keeping her at arm's length? . . . Then there is Themiso, who is

---

gain is forbidden to the clergy" ("Canon LII" of *The Arabic Canons*, I. Nice, 49). Conveniently linked to this statement is the additional injunction forbidding "conversation and fellowship with Jews." "Canon LII" of *The Arabic Canons*, I. Nice, 49. Canon 4 of the Synod of Laodicea states that "a priest is not to receive usury nor hemiolioe, ("Ancient Epitome of Canon VI," of *The Canons of the Synod Held in the City of Laodicea, in Phrygia Pacatiana, in which Many Blessed Fathers from Diverse Provinces in Asia where Gathered Together*, 126. *Hemiolioe* is a form of the Latin *hemiolios* [Gk. ἡμιόλιος], which means "consisting of one-and-a-half times as much" (*Oxford Latin Dictionary*, 790). In the absence of any other logical explanation, I can only assume that this measure was meant to keep priests from profiting either intentionally or unintentionally when they lent out money or product to aid those who were in distress) and Canon 5 of the African Code—or Council of Carthage—of 419 states that "as the taking of any kind of usury is condemned in laymen, much more it is condemned in clergymen." "Ancient Epitome of Canon V," of *The Canons of the 217 Blessed Fathers who Assembled At Carthage*," 445. The practice of usury among the clergy continues to be denounced well beyond the era of the early Church: Canon 44 from the synod in Trullo (691–92) reads: "Let a bishop, presbyter, or deacon, who takes usury from those who borrow of him, give up doing so, or be deposed" ("Canon XLIV," *The Apostolical Canons*, 597). For additional information on usury and councils see Maloney, "Early Conciliar Legislation on Usury. A Contribution to the Study of Christian Moral Thought;" see also Moser, *Die patristische Zinslehre*, 189–90, and 204–5.

18. Eusebius, *Historia ecclesiastica* 5.18. See also Jerome, *De viris Illustribus* 40. Tertullian denied this charge in a lost work. Maloney, "The Teaching of the Fathers on Usury," 244.

19. Apollonius, in Eusebius, *Historia ecclesiastica*, 5.18.

20. Eusebius, *Historia ecclesiastica* 5.18.

wrapped up in plausible covetousness, and who failed to raise aloft the standard of confession and bought his release by a heavy bribe . . . The Lord said, "Do not provide yourselves with gold or silver or two coats,"[21] but these people have done the exact opposite—they have transgressed by providing themselves with forbidden things. I can prove that their so-called prophets and martyrs rake in the shekels not only from the rich but from poor people, orphans and widows . . . All the fruits of a prophet must be submitted to examination . . . Tell me, does a prophet dye his hair? Does a prophet paint his eyelids? Does a prophet love ornaments? Does a prophet visit the gaming tables and play dice? Does a prophet do business as a moneylender? Let them say plainly whether these things are permissible or not, and I will prove that they have been going on in their circles.[22]

Apollonius does not censure usury itself, but he does not need to. I quote this passage at length to point out that it is no accident that Apollonius has positioned "money-lending" within a list of other unsuitable behaviors, especially for a prophet or prophetess; together they form a picture of an overall offensive person whose social behaviors are pretentious and rapacious, and who in no way resembles a figure of religious authority: accepting "gifts" and bribes of precious metals, wearing expensive clothing and jewelry, bilking the poor, widowed and orphaned, applying make-up and dyes to face and hair, engaging in gambling sports and other games of chance, and finally, lending money at interest. Apollonius does not cite biblical injunctions against usury, but he applies Jesus's message to his disciples as proof enough that vanities and economic concerns are not to occupy the minds of those who labor for Christianity. Prophet or charlatan, legal or unlawful, Apollonius establishes that engaging in usury or other such behaviors are not consistent with the activity of a Christian, and Christian scripture itself will bear this out. Naturally, it follows that those whose deeds stand in opposition to Christian scripture stand in opposition to the proper authorities of the Christian Church, and further, to Christ himself.

The subapostolic church provides sparse mention to usury, and yet references exist. In the *Didache* one finds strong encouragement for generosity, and a near echo of the words of Christ regarding giving: "Give to everyone that asks thee, and do not refuse, for the Father's will is that we give

---

21. Matthew 10:9–10: "Take no gold, or silver, or copper in your belts, no bag for your journey, or two tunics, or sandals, or a staff; for laborers deserve their food."

22. Apollonius, in Eusebius, *Historia ecclesiastica* 5.18.

to all from the gifts we have received."[23] Reference to lending in *The Epistle to Diognetus* is vague, though the argument could be made—and here I suggest that it should be—that Hesiod and Jesus's counsel to be financially mindful of one's neighbor in times of strife is here upheld: "But whoever takes up the burden of his neighbour, and wishes to help another, who is worse off in that in which he is the stronger, and by ministering to those in need the things which eh has received and holds from God becomes a god to those who receive them,—this man is an imitator of God."[24] Similar counsel is offered as well in the *Epistle of Barnabas*: "You shall not hesitate to give, and when you give you shall not grumble, but you shall know who is the good paymaster of the reward."[25] Not only does one find in these passages the call to common goods, but a reminder of the salvific benefit of engaging in charitable activity, indication that the concern of the author is the salvation of the rich rather than the immediate needs of the poor. Further, one finds the encouragement to give—rather than lend—and the suggestion to *release oneself* from the notion of ownership over what was given (or lent) to another. Most interesting to me, however, is the counsel against grumbling, a fun detail that reveals how people were likely giving: begrudgingly. Of this subapostolic era, the document most devoted to issues of wealth and poverty is second-century *Shepherd of Hermas*. But again, one does not find unambiguous language about lending so much as giving, and giving that is accompanied by a clear motive: "Consider the judgment which is coming. Let therefore they who have over-abundance seek out those who are hungry, so long as the tower is not yet finished; for when the tower is finished you will wish to do good, and will have no opportunity."[26] González rightly notes that this is no "manifesto of social justice,"[27] but it does serves to make the point that the relationship between one's wealth and one's compassion shapes the construction of a religious identity and—ultimately—the case for salvation.

The distinguished Clement of Alexandria (150–215) wrote some of the first censures against usury, in addition to authoring one of the most singularly important methodical inquisitions into matters of wealth and faith: *Who is the Rich Man Who Shall Be Saved?*[28] A convert, Clement

23. *Didache* 1.5.

24. *The Epistle to Diognetus* 10.6.

25. *Epistle of Barnabas* 19.11.

26. *The Shepherd of Hermas* 3.9.5.

27. González, *Faith and Wealth*, 100.

28. Clement of Alexandria, *Liber quis dives salvetur*, PG 9:602–52.

consulted numerous teachers of Christianity before situating himself in Alexandria.[29] He held the position as head of the catechetical school in Alexandria from 180 until 202, when persecution under Emperor Severus forced him to flee the city.[30] Learned like his predecessor Pantaenus and highly inspired by Philo of Alexandria, Clement strove to make Christianity palatable to the educated and intellectual, and believed that Christianity was the fulfillment of both the Hebrew Scriptures and Greek philosophy.[31] To aid in this fulfillment, the missionary-minded Clement wrote *Pædagogus*, or *Instructor*, as an instruction for the convert, a guide to moral life. A brief mention of usury is found in Book 1.10, when at the end of a chapter which expounds upon the way that God—the Instructor—uses different methods to encourage righteousness and discourage sin, Clement quotes Ezekiel 18:4–9. He claims that this passage, in addition to the other passages from Hebrew scriptures and Greek authors quoted within this text,[32] "contain[s] a description of the conduct of Christians, a notable exhortation to the blessed life, which is the reward of a life of goodness— everlasting life."[33] Simply put, salvation for the Christian can be attained by the observance of Jewish proscriptions for righteous living.

Weaving scriptural or classical references into the author's own work was a predictable procedure among the early Christian authors; this method would grant their own texts immediate status and authority by their association with Christian Scripture.[34] In the case of Clement, he saw the Mosaic law as the fountainhead for the moral mandates of the Greeks, and therefore law functioned for the Hebrews as did philosophy for the Greeks. Clement drew from both intellectual methods, and he believed that Christians could learn from both. He placed himself in opposition to Christians who eschewed higher learning or the influence of the law on their Christianity: "Those then," he wrote, "who suppose the law to be

---

29. Clement claims that his work is "truly an image and outline of those vigorous and animated discourses which I was privileged to hear, and of blessed and truly remarkable men." Clement of Alexandria, *The Stromata* 1.1.

30. He never returned to Alexandria after he fled in 202, and he died c. 215.

31. González, *The Story of Christianity*, 71–73.

32. Clement quotes Samian Pythagoras ("When you have done base things, rebuke *yourself*; But when you have done good things, be glad."), an aphorism that is not cited ("For virtue that is praised grows like a Tree."), Isaiah 48:22 and 55:21 and Proverbs 1:10–12 (*Pædagogus*, 1.10).

33. Clement of Alexandria, *Pædagogus* 1.10.

34. Young, *Biblical Exegesis and the Formation of Christian Culture*, 11.

productive of agitating fear, are neither good at understanding the law, nor have they in reality comprehended it."[35]

Additional citations against usury are found in Clement's Stromata, the aim of which was the refutation of Gnosticism and the provision of materials for an alternative philosophy for the intellectual Christian. In Book 2 of the *Stromata*, "The Mosaic Law The Fountain Of All Ethics, And The Source From Which The Greeks Drew Theirs," Clement inserts rather disjointedly the prohibition on usury after his defense of the law and its usefulness:

> Respecting imparting and communicating, though much might be said, let it suffice to remark that the law prohibits a brother from taking usury: designating as a brother not only him who is born of the same parents, but also one of the same race and sentiments, and a participator in the same word; deeming it right not to take usury for money, but with open hands and heart to bestow on those who need. For God, the author and dispenser of such grace, takes as suitable usury the most precious things to be found among men—mildness, gentleness, magnanimity, reputation, renown.[36]

As is pointed out by Maloney in "The Teaching of the Fathers on Usury," a portion of this passage mimics that of Philo, whose fourteenth chapter of his *De virtutibus*[37] is concerned with the problem of usurious activities. In addition to illustrating the influence that writers such as Philo had on early Christianity, the above passage marks the beginning in Clement's text of a section devoted to financial concerns and Israelite provisions for the protection of the poor. Clement's design is to turn from the defense of the morality installed by the Mosaic Code to practical ways in which individuals might use Israelite proscriptions to demonstrate Christian love and charity to one another out of gratitude and devotion to God: "For he shows love to one like himself, because of his love to the Creator

---

35. Clement of Alexandria, *Stromata* 2.18.

36. Ibid.

37. "He forbids anyone to lend money on interest to a brother, meaning by this name not merely a child of the same parents, but anyone of the same citizenship or nation. For he does not think it just to amass money bred from money as their yeanlings are from cattle. And he bids them not to take this as a ground for holding back or showing unwillingness to contribute, but without restriction of hand and heart to give free gifts to those who need, reflecting that a free gift is in a sense a loan that will be repaid, by the recipient, when times are better, without compulsion, and with a willing heart" (Philo, *De virtutibus* 14:82–83).

of the human race."[38] Unlike the passage in *Pædagogus*, Clement provides no explicit passage for this ban against usury. But it is undeniable that he is drawing from the Deuteronomy passages not only because of the mention of "the law" but because of the spin that Clement puts on the injunction. First Clement redefines the Deuteronomic direction not to charge interest "to another Israelite" by first casting the individuals involved as "brother(s)"; he then enlarges the circle by insisting that this definition applies not only to members of the same family or someone who shares the same racial background or even similar beliefs, but to a "participator in the same *word*."[39] This enlarges the possibilities for Christians; those who might have been tempted to disregard business transactions with another simply based on race would be forced to admit that as they share "the same word," which means that they are now expected to treat one another as family in the best sense. The problem created by such an instruction is the enormous loophole that it provides: if one must treat those who participate in "the same word" as family, then the logical conclusion is that those who are not participators in "the same word" can be gouged financially.[40] It is an open invitation to fiscal favoritism.

In an additional chapter of the *Stromata*, in Book 2.22, "Plato's Opinion, That The Chief Good Consists in Assimilation to God, And Its Agreement with Scripture," Clement quotes a second time the complete passage from Ezekiel which includes usury as among vices unknown to the godly individual. In this case, as in the *Pædagogus*, Clement is not writing about usury *per se*, but is using the passage as a list of sins within which the righteous person would not participate. Nestled between passages from Plato's nephew Speusippus—who says that "happiness is a perfect state in those who conduct themselves in accordance with nature, or in the state of good"[41]—passages from Romans[42] and Isaiah,[43] the Ezekiel excerpt is utilized as further evidence to press Clement's final point in this chapter, that by "assimilation to God"—by which he means proper behavior learned through the Mosaic code and wisdom of the philosophers—an individual can become "righteous and holy with wisdom."[44]

38. Clement of Alexandria, *Stromata* 2.18.

39. Ibid., 2.18 (emphasis mine).

40. One wonders to what extent this passage influences Ambrose's *De Tobia*.

41. Speusippus, in Clement of Alexandria, *Stromata* 2.22.

42. Romans 6:22.

43. Isaiah 55:6–9.

44. Clement of Alexandria, *Stromata* 2.22.

In addition to being bishop of Jerusalem as well as a native of the city,[45] Cyril of Jerusalem (c. 315–87) made a career out of being banished from his see a total of three times by zealous Arian bishops.[46] His own orthodoxy was repeatedly under scrutiny, but the question of his right doctrine appears to have been resolved to everyone's satisfaction at the Council of Constantinople in 381.[47] Cyril's see was even visited by Gregory of Nyssa who pronounced it morally corrupt and factious[48] but doctrinally sound.[49] His surviving works provide an illuminating account of Palestinian life in the fourth century.[50] Although Cyril does not make conspicuous use of Scripture in his passage on usury in *Lecture 4; On the Ten Points of Doctrine*[51] to back his claims, still his method can be likened to that of Ezekiel, for Cyril also includes usury within a catalogue of heinous crimes which a Christian should shun. Cyril's list—a register of fiendish and demonic vices—is arguably worse than Ezekiel's:

> But shun every diabolical operation, and do not believe the apostate Serpent, whose transformation from a good nature was of his own free choice: who can over-persuade the willing, but can compel no one. Also give heed neither to observations of the stars nor prophecies, nor omens, nor to the fabulous divinations of the Greeks. Witchcraft, and enchantment, and the wicked practices of necromancy, admit not even to a hearing. From every kind of intemperance stand aloof, giving yourself neither to gluttony nor licentiousness, rising superior to all covetousness and usury. Neither venture to heathen assemblies for public spectacles, nor ever use amulets in sicknesses; shun also all the vulgarity of tavern-haunting. Fall not either into the sect

45. There is a difference of opinion on this point; while Telfer suggests that Cyril was from Caesarea, more recent scholarship suggests that Cyril of Jerusalem was from the very city itself. See Yarnold, *Cyril of Jerusalem*, 3; and Telfer, *Cyril of Jerusalem and Nemesius of Emesa*, 19.

46. Cyril was banished in 357, 360, and finally in 367 (Yarnold, *Cyril of Jerusalem*, 6–7).

47. Yarnold, *Cyril of Jerusalem*, 7.

48. "But as it is, there is no form of uncleanness that is not perpetrated among them; rascality, adultery, theft, idolatry, poisoning, quarrelling, murder, are rife; and the last kind of evil is so excessively prevalent, that nowhere in the world are people so ready to kill each other as there" (Gregory of Nyssa, *On Pilgrimages*, 383).

49. "Cyril, St.," in *The Oxford Dictionary of the Christian Church*, 442–43.

50. Ibid., 442–43.

51. Cyril of Jerusalem, *Lecture 4; On the Ten Points of Doctrine*, Colossians 2.8, 19–28.

of the Samaritans, or into Judaism: for Jesus Christ henceforth has ransomed you.[52]

Cyril's passage contains the most enticing list of depravity encountered yet, ranging from star-gazing to necromancy; usury is simply one among them. But here the practices are not merely activities which one should avoid, for a demonic dimension is added when Satan enters the picture as one who might attempt to persuade an individual to participate in tavern-haunting or charging interest. One can only surmise from this list that Gregory of Nyssa's assertion that Cyril's see was morally corrupt was not too far wrong, and one must pity Cyril for what he was up against. In Cyril's unique list, usury is equated with sins that are in direct opposition to the authority of Christianity: magical practices that stand apart from or in immediate contradiction to the teachings of the Bible and the favor of the early Christian arbitrators.[53] Cyril has demonized the usurer by association in his list with practitioners of the dark arts; naturally, they stand in conflict to Scripture, and therefore Christianity itself.[54] According to this list, usury is not just in violation of the commandment to "love thy neighbor," it is an offence practiced by those who could be classified only as "wicked," under the sway of the "apostate Serpent." Here, the usurer is not just parsimonious, the usurer is evil, wholly inspired by Lucifer.

Gregory Nazianzus, "the Theologian" (c. 329–c. 90) is the third of the three Cappadocian Fathers, and son of the elder Gregory, bishop of Nazianzus, a position which Gregory the younger held later in life. A contemporary of Basil and Gregory of Nyssa, Gregory left school in Athens and adopted the monastic life. He was ordained against his will and appointed to Sasima, but remained residing in Nazianzus where he assisted his father until the elder Gregory's death in 374. During the course of the Council of Constantinople in 381 his elegant preaching resulted in his appointment as bishop of Constantinople, a position which he resigned within the year due to canonical irregularities in his election. He retired to Nazianzus where he spent the remainder of his life writing in monastic solitude.[55] Gregory's mention of usury[56] is contained in his poignant *Introduction to*

---

52. Ibid., 4.37.

53. By comparison, Aristotle's list from the *Nicomachean Ethics*—which focuses on the social rather than moral reprobate—looks pretty tame.

54. See Young, *Biblical Exegesis and the Formation of Christian Culture*, 29–45.

55. Meredith, *The Cappadocians*, 42; see chapters 6 and 7 of McGuckin, *St. Gregory of Nazianzus*, 311–98.

56. In an additional oration, Gregory does not discuss usury, but strongly

Oration 16. On His Father's Silence, Because of the Plague of Hail. Written in 373, one year before his father's death, the text begins by defending his father's silence in the face of a discouraged population who has just suffered through a cattle plague, a drought, and the loss of their crops from rain and hail.[57] Gregory moves the discussion to question the troubles of the natural world: "Tell us whence come such blows and scourges, and what account can we give of them? Is it some disordered and irregular motion…Or are the disturbances and changes of the universe . . . directed by reason and order under the guidance and reins of Providence?"[58] The events are seen as warnings against the society; Gregory implores the community to "worship and fall down, and weep before the Lord our Maker" and "amend our wickedness, lest we be consumed with it,"[59] to abate further divine punishment. Similar to Basil's *Homily in Times of Famine and Drought*, Gregory finds the cause of his community's troubles within the unrighteous actions of its people.

After determining that it is the wickedness of his community that has brought such troubles upon them all, Gregory is resolved to vanquish the evil-doers: "So I will now announce the disobedience of my people."[60] Gregory launches into a list of the potential sins which individuals are committing, sins which set them apart from a godly community, and each of which are accompanied by Scripture to prove their impiety. The first offence he cites is oppression of the poor, under which usury falls, in addition to a variety of other sins connected with financial concerns: acquisition of a neighbor's land and encroaching landmarks,[61] robbing

---

emphasizes lending to the poor in the previously mentioned method of gaining heavenly usury for oneself: "First and before all things, give to him who asks of you, even before he asks: showing mercy all the day, and lending all the day long, carefully seeking back both principal and interest; that is, increase (of God) in him you helped; for he always adds to his store of wisdom who prudently increases in himself the seeds of piety" (Gregory Nazianzen, *Oration 14: On the Love of the Poor and Those Afflicted with Leprosy*, 57). Further, he relies on the gospel to press his point: "And what else does the Scripture say? He that hath mercy on the poor, lends to the Lord. Who would not have such a Debtor, Who in due time will repay both loan and interest?" (*Oration* 14, 62).

57. Gregory Nazianzen, *Ad cives Nazianzenos, Or.* 17 and *Or.* 16; Winslow, "Gregory of Nazianzus and Love for the Poor," 348.

58. Gregory Nazianzen, *Oration* 16, 5.

59. Ibid., 14.

60. Ibid., 17.

61. "One of us has oppressed the poor, and wrested from him his portion of land, and wrongly encroached upon his landmark by fraud or violence, and joined house to

God by denying offerings,[62] oppressing the widows, orphans, the needy and the meek,[63] and generally acting in a rapacious and miserly manner.[64] Then, adding insult to injury, these pikers thank and praise God for what God has "granted" to the rich.[65] Gregory's passage on usury is inspired by the parable of the talents in Matthew 25:26, and while he does not quote the passage, he emulates it in style and content: "Another has defiled the land with usury and interest, both gathering where he had not sowed and reaping where he had not strawed, farming, not the land, but the necessity of the needy."[66] According to Gregory, gathering interest is the work of the morally corrupt; they do nothing yet collect a wage. This reading equates the usurer who has "defiled the land with usury and interest" directly with the wicked master (or harsh man)—who also believed that he was entitled to collect something for nothing.[67] According to Gregory's reading, a proper understanding of the depravity of usury kept the servant from acting wickedly himself on behalf of his master. Like those in the community who are oppressing the widows and children, manipulating

---

house, and field to field, to rob his neighbour of something, and been eager to have not neighbour, so to dwell along on the earth" (Isaiah 5:8, in Gregory Nazianzen, *Oration* 16, 18).

62. "Another has robbed God, the giver of all, of the firstfruits of the barnfloor and winepress, showing himself at once thankless and senseless, in neither giving thanks for what he has had, nor prudently providing, at least, for the future." Malachi 3:8, in Gregory Nazianzen, *Oration* 16, 18.

63. "Another has turned aside the way of the meek, and turned aside the just among the unjust" (Amos 2:7, in Gregory Nazianzen, *Oration* 16, 18).

64. "For this is the most unjust of all, who finds his many barns too narrow for him, filling some and emptying others, to build greater ones for future crops, not knowing that he is being snatched away with hopes unrealised, to give an account of his riches and fancies, and proved to have been a bad steward of another's goods" (Luke 12:18, in Gregory Nazianzen, *Oration* 16, 18).

65. "and keeping the spoil of the poor in his house, has either remembered not God, or remembered him ill—by saying 'Blessed be the Lord, for we are rich,' and wickedly supposed that he received those things from Him by Whom he will be punished" (Zechariah 11:5, in Gregory Nazianzen, *Oration* 16, 18).

66. Gregory Nazienzen, *Oration* 16.18; he quotes Matthew 25:26 as his source. Gregory has here created a new reality based on Scripture; he is giving "other" meaning at the same time that he interprets the passage. See "Allegorical Interpretation as Composition," in Dawson, *Allegorical Readers and Cultural Revision in Ancient Alexandria*, 129–31.

67. Recall that the wicked master/harsh man was told by his servant that the servant did nothing on behalf of his master because "I knew that you were a harsh man, reaping where you did not sow, and gathering where you did not scatter seed; so I was afraid, and I went and hid your talent in the ground" (Matthew 25:24–25).

property lines, robbing God of the first-fruits of the harvest, and building larger barns for their profits rather than distributing the wealth, the
usurer in Gregory's milieu prospers from the hardships of others like a
"wicked master/harsh man." Hence, to align himself with the authority of
Holy Scripture, Gregory rewrites passages[68] using both the Hebrew Bible
and New Testaments to set up perimeters around which Christians must
present themselves: there are those who obey the ordinances (who merit
beneficial spring showers), and then there are those who stand outside the
ordinances (who merit chastising tsunamis).[69]

The final passage to consider in this first section is contained in a
letter of Theodoret, bishop of Cyrrhus (c. 393–c. 460). Theodoret figured
prominently in the Christological controversy of the fifth century, as he
was friends with the infamous Nestorius and a defender of Antiochene
Christology.[70] He also busied himself fighting paganism and heresy, and
those writings that have survived are impressive examples of the Antiochene tradition.[71] Theodoret mentions usury in his letter *To Eusebius,
Bishop of Persian Armenia*,[72] in which he makes use of the parable of
the talents found in Matthew 25:14–30 and Luke 19:11–27, citing, as do
others, what is considered in our day the "traditional" interpretation of
the wicked master as God and the slothful servant who wastes his "talent" as the contemporary individual. The contents of Theodoret's letter
To Eusebius indicates that it was written to encourage Bishop Eusebius to
assume responsibilities which went with his new position, despite the tri-
als implied by Theodoret's words. Strongly cautioning the bishop against
the possibility of shirking his duties, Theodoret uses biblical passages to
remind Eusebius that he will be judged harshly if he fails to shepherd the
Lord's sheep.

> Who does not fear and tremble when he hears the word of God
> spoken through Ezekiel? "I judge between shepherd and sheep
> because you eat the fat and clothe yourselves with the wool and
> you feed not the flocks."[73] And again, "I have made you a watch-

---

68. Concerning this method, Young claims that rewriting the Scriptures within
their texts enabled the Christian authors to offer an alternative to the "stylistic inferior-
ity" of the Bible (Young, *Biblical Exegesis and the Formation of Christian Culture*, 103).

69. Duke et al., "Natural Disasters as Moral Lessons."

70. Theodoret, in *Oxford Dictionary of the Christian Church*, 1600.

71. Ibid., 1600–1601.

72. Theodoret, *Eusebio episcopo Persicæ Armeniæ*, PG 83:1251–56.

73. Ezekiel 24:2, in Theodoret, *Eusebio*, 274.

man unto the house of Israel; when you do not speak to warn the wicked from his wicked way, the same wicked man shall die in his iniquity but his blood shall I require at your hand."[74] With this agree the words spoken in parables by the Lord. "You wicked and slothful servant . . . You ought to have put my money to the exchangers, and then at my coming I should have received the same with usury."[75] Up then, I beseech you, let us fight for the Lord's sheep.[76]

Theodoret uses Ezekiel to connect to Matthew, which functions as a concluding thought. Unlike Gregory of Nazianzus, Theodoret reads the Matthew parable allegorically rather than literally in this particular case; he does not assimilate gaining interest with the sinful master, but instead reads into this passage that the interest gained on one talent is the very least of one's obligations towards the master, who—for Theodoret—is God.

John Chrysostom

No early Christian author addressed affluence as vehemently as John Chrysostom (c. 347–407).[77] Born into a socially well-placed family and educated in the Antiochene tradition, his pull towards the monastic life was thwarted by an inability to prosper under harsh monastic conditions. Made deacon in 381 and ordained in 386, he turned to preaching, his style later earning him the surname "Chrysostom" (golden mouthed). Chrysostom's sermons include not only moral reformation of his community, but expositions of the biblical texts, with emphasis on literal translation and practical application of the Scriptures, consistent with Antiochene exegesis. He was elevated to the position of Patriarch of Constantinople in 398, but lacked the political savvy of the previous Patriarch Nectarius to make the appointment a success. Chrysostom's fracas with Empress Eudoxia led to his exile first in 403 to Armenia and then—after a brief return—again

74. Ezekiel 3:17–18, in ibid.

75. Matthew 25:26–7, in ibid.

76. Theodoret, *Eusebio*, 274.

77. According to Bishop Martyrius of Antioch, Chrysostom's preaching against the sins of the wealthy was so scathing that many of the wealthy did not go to church for fear of being stared at. Some complained that his sermons prevented them from making money in the ways in which they had been accustomed (Liebeschuetz, *Barbarians and Bishops; Army, Church and State in the Age of Arcadius and Chrysostom*, 223). See also, Bishop Martyrius of Antioch, *Ex laudatione in Sanctum Patrem Nostrum Johannem Chrysostomum Archiepiscopum Constantinopoleos*, 1782–1854.

permanently to Pityus in 404. When he did not die quickly enough to suit his enemies, he was forced to travel on foot during harsh weather; his demise came soon after, in 407.[78]

Chrysostom refers to usury in several of his works, many of which stray from the specific scriptural passage under consideration to moral or social concerns that he wished to address, including prayer, virginity, communion, sex, marriage, theatrical shows, work, government, authority and—most of all—wealth.[79] The first three passages that will be considered are *Homilia* 13 and *Homilia* 43 on 1 Corinthians, and *Homilia* 3 on 2 Corinthians.

Chrysostom begins *Homilia* 13 with Paul's sarcastic statements to his shameful and pretentious Corinthians that "we are fools for the sake of Christ, but you are wise in Christ. We are weak, but you are strong. You are held in honour, but we in disrepute."[80] This sets the tone for the homily, as Chrysostom consistently reminds his audience throughout the course of the sermon that although they seek the *honors* of the Apostles, what they should really be seeking is the *condition* of the Apostles, a considerably less attractive offer.[81] After Chrysostom's plea for the nearly impossible imitation of Paul, he eventually brings the homily round to the subject of wealth. It is in the final passage of this homily that Chrysostom mentions debts and usury, and he does so briefly, but without a trace of ambiguity:

> Which, I ask, is more disgraceful? that one clothed with rags should beg, or one who wears silk? Thus when a rich man pays court to old and poor persons, so as to get possession of their property, and this when there are children, what pardon can he deserve? . . . but of what kind are those of the rich? Why, of swine, and dogs, and wolves, and all other wild beasts. For some of them discourse perpetually on banquets, and dishes, and delicacies, and wine of all sorts, and ointments, and clothing, and all the rest of the extravagance. And others about the interest of money and loans. And making out accounts and increasing the mass of debts to an intolerable amount, as if it had begun in the time of men's fathers or grandfathers, one they rob of his house, another of his field, and another of his slave, and all that he has

---

78. González, *Faith and Wealth*, 200–214; Mayer and Allen, *John Chrysostom*, 3–54.

79. Kelly, *The World of the Early Christians*, 95–96; Phan, *Social Thought*, 137.

80. Chrysostom, *Homilia* 13, 1; 1 Corinthians 4:10.

81. Chrysostom, *Homilia* 13, 1.

... Is there any madness and ferocity of wild beasts of any sort
which these things do not throw into the shade?[82]

It is a far less dramatic treatment of the usurer than will be shown below,
but nonetheless some interesting facts come to light in this passage: the
usurer exhibits behaviors not even seen in wild beasts; the usurer seeks
damage on the already disadvantaged members of society; the usurer is
concerned with the trivial and banal things of life; and the usurer is continuing in a tradition which was established before his time, and will no
doubt continue beyond him. Chrysostom is struck by the absolute inhu-
man conduct exhibited by such persons, and his already low opinion of
them flowers in subsequent homilies.

In the second Chrysostom homily to be considered—*Homilia* 43—
a common theme appears that is also in the writings of other early
Christian authors who address questions of wealth: contrary to one's
expectations, it is not always the material poverty of the poor which is
of importance to the author; oftentimes it is the spiritual poverty of the
wealthy individual which the authors are addressing. In this text Chrysostom uses Paul's words to the Corinthians as an excuse to harangue the
wealthy "not so much for the poor, as for your sake who bestow the gift ...
for I vehemently set my heart upon your salvation."[83] Like Plato, Chrysostom is concerned for the spiritual state of the wealthy[84] and he masterfully

82. Ibid., 7.

83. Ibid., 3.

84. As stated in chapter 2, Plato is not concerned solely with the plight of the poor
but also with the "happiness" of the wealthy, which might here be compared with
Chrysostom's desire for the wealthy also to acquire salvation. Chrysostom notes that
it is difficult for the wealthy to attain salvation because they focus their attention on
their worldly wealth rather than on Christian virtue, and that because they do not
understand the transient nature of material goods, their riches become an impediment
for them: "Virtue alone is able to depart with us, and to accompany us to the world
above" (*Epistolam primam ad Timotheum, Homilia* 11, 2.20 [PG 62:501–662]). Similar
to Plato's concern with the mental state of the wealthy is that Chrysostom believed
that all wealth was at some point gained unjustly: "Tell me, then, where do you get
your riches from? From whom did you receive it and from whom did he receive who
transmits it to you? 'From my father and he from my grandfather.' But can you, going back through the generations show that the riches were justly acquired? No, you
cannot. The root and origin of them must have been injustice. Why? Because God in
the beginning made not one man rich and another poor." *Epistolam primam ad Timotheum, Homilia* 12, 4 (PG 62:558–64). Plato too believed that those who were wealthy
only were so because of unjust means; as well, because the wealthy were not able to
be good, therefore they were not able to be happy (Plato, *Laws* 742c–744a). To put
this into Chrysostom's terms, because the wealthy are less likely to practice Christian
charity, they are less likely to attain salvation.

guides his audience through the remaining eight verses, reassuring them in ways which seem always to be intimately connected with the financial, that as Paul struggled with "many adversaries" neither should they be discouraged in their own pursuits when they find their intentions hindered: "Mark, for instance, Paul, not therefore lingering, not therefore shrinking back, because 'there are many adversaries;'[85] but because 'there was a wide door,'[86] pressing on and persevering."[87] He encourages and reminds his audience not to look for their rewards in this time or place,[88] and conversely, not to be too troubled when dealt severe blows to their material situations, such as in the case of the widow or as a victim of disaster.[89] Finally, he encourages the giving process on the simplest level, inviting his audience to offer alms before prayer and bedtime as a "defence against the devil,"[90] and to "give wings to your prayer."[91] It is in the final chapter of the homily that Chrysostom mentions the usurer, as one for whom he has no worry: "For those who demand usury I have no concern, neither with soldiers who do violence to others and turn to their own advantage their neighbours calamities."[92] Why couple the usurer with the corrupt soldier, and why this cavalier attitude towards the usurer? Concerning the former, Chrysostom is equating the two with one another, so consider the interesting parallel: the soldier who does violence to *others*—as opposed to the soldier who fights or abuses only the *enemy*—and who turns his neighbor's woe to his own advantage is a public enemy, a menace, a serpent in the garden, eager for the downfall of the innocent for their own gain.[93] Of Chrysostom's nonchalance, this stems from the conviction that the usurer is so thoroughly in violation of this injunction that they are surely to be rejected

85. 1 Corinthians 16:9b, John Chrysostom, *Homilia* 43.6.

86. 1 Corinthians 16:9a, John Chrysostom, *Homilia* 43.6.

87. John Chrysostom, *Homilia* 43.6.

88. Ibid.

89. Ibid., 43.7.

90. Ibid.

91. Ibid.

92. Ibid.

93. This violates the injunction that the Lord placed before Moses, "You shall not revile the deaf, or place a stumbling block before the blind" (Leviticus 19:11–14). Reiterating what Tamari wrote, one is not to defraud someone who does not understand, or is incapable of understanding, or to take unfair advantage, or do, say or give something to someone that shall bring harm down on them (Tamari, *Jewish Ethics and Economic Life*, 176).

and punished by God, "Since from that quarter God will accept nothing."[94] That such an offence would bring forth so little from the "golden mouthed" indicates that he is solid in this opinion.

Homilia 3 on 2 Corinthians is an exegesis on 2 Corinthians 1:12–23.[95] This passage is less of a financial challenge to Chrysostom, who spends a great deal of time illuminating for his audience Paul's discussion on his travels through Macedonia,[96] the roll of the Spirit in directing Paul's travels,[97] the future royalty of the Christian and the citizenship of heaven,[98] and the extent of God's sacrifice and the righteousness of Abraham.[99] It is within the context of the theme of Abraham and the righteousness of his actions that Chrysostom makes mention of usury: "But here two things were displayed, both the loving kindness of the Master, and the faithfulness of the servant. And before, indeed, he went out from his country: but then he abandoned even nature. For that reason also he received his principal with usury: and very reasonably. For he chose to lose the name of father, to show himself a faithful servant. For that reason he became not a father only, but also a priest; and because for God's sake he gave up his own, therefore also did God give him with these His own besides.[100]" Chrysostom does not use the word "usury" in reference to a financial transaction with moral implications, but with respect to the inheritance which Abraham received as a result of having placed, or "invested" his wealth—faith and family, specifically Isaac—in the proper place, which is with God. Abraham freely and without question invested his son at God's request, and as a result Abraham received from God "with usury" or "with interest" further wealth by way of family, a promise made prior to the sacrificial event, and at a time when Abraham despaired of even having an heir.[101] Previously Chrysostom comments on the potential sacrifice of

94. John Chrysostom, *Homilia* 43.7.

95. Ibid., 3.

96. Ibid., 3.2.

97. Ibid., 3.3.

98. Ibid., 3.5.

99. Ibid., 3.6.

100. Ibid.

101. "He [the Lord] brought him outside and said, 'Look toward heaven and count the stars, if you are able to count them . . . So shall your descendants be.' And he believed the Lord; and the Lord reckoned it to him as righteousness" (Genesis 15:5–6). This promise is reinforced to Abraham after he has passed the Lord's test and made the "investment" in the Lord by way of Isaac: "Because you have done this, and have not withheld your son, your only son, I will indeed bless you, and I will make your

Isaac as one which God would not have accepted, for God "might not accept such bloody offerings; such a table that were of avenging demons."[102] One can identify this passage with the previously quoted *Homilia* 43, in which Chrysostom has almost an indifferent attitude towards the usurer as one whose offering—or in this case "bloody offering"—would not be found acceptable to God.

An additional aspect of Chrysostom's exposition is that here God is the one returning "with usury, and very reasonably"[103] so, rather than the usual connection between the usurer and a corrupt transaction. Chrysostom does not tie in usury here with any biblical injunction against it, as he is using the idea of usury as one which can work for the Christian in proper relationship with God. It reinforces, in fact, the rarely believed plea that "investing" in God brings unheard of reward, while refusing to do so is nothing short of plunder: "Will anyone rob God? Yet you are all robbing me! But you say, 'How are we robbing you?' In your tithes and offerings! You are cursed with a curse, for you are robbing me—the whole nation of you! Bring the full tithe into the storehouse, so that there may be food in my house, and put me to the test, says the Lord of hosts; see if I will not open the windows of heaven for you and pour down for you an overflowing blessing."[104] Chrysostom ends by pleading in the final chapter that all Christians should gain for themselves the interest or "usury" of the kingdom by emulating the investment of the Patriarch: "Do not then only admire this righteous man, but also imitate him."[105] For Chrysostom, the proper investment—and the only one from which we might rightly expect to gain—is with God and the only gain worthwhile is eternal life.

Is this reversal of the common understanding of usury consistent within Chrysostom's examination of Scripture? This can only be answered after an examination of additional uses of the term "usury" within his writings. The subject of usury appears in an additional eight homilies of Chrysostom's, in *Homilia* 5, 18, 28, 37, 45, 56, 64, 78 from his *Homilies on the Gospel of Saint Matthew*.[106] He began writing this group of homilies in

---

offspring as numerous as the stars of heaven and as the sand that is on the seashore . . . because you have obeyed my voice" (Genesis 22:16b–17a).

102. John Chrysostom, *Homilia* 3.6.

103. Ibid.

104. Malachi 3:8–10.

105. John Chrysostom, *Homilia* 3.7.

106. John Chrysostom, *Homiliæ in Matthævm* (PG 57 and 58); John Chrysostom, *Homilia* 5 (PG 57:55–62); *Homilia* 18 (PG 57:265–74); *Homilia* 28 (PG 57:349–58); *Homilia* 37 (PG 57:419–28); *Homilia* 45 (PG 58:471–76); *Homilia* 56 (PG 58:549–58); *Homilia* 64 (PG 58:609–18); *Homilia* 78 (PG 58:711–18).

390, when he had risen to a more powerful position in Antioch. While he was yet not a bishop, scholars of his works have surmised that the tone of these homilies indicates that Chrysostom expected his words would be carefully considered.[107]

The first to be considered is *Homilia V*, which begins with Matthew 1:22–23.[108] After an impassioned plea to allow the entire Sabbath for things pertaining to the Sabbath,[109] Chrysostom engages in a discussion on the importance of righteous living for the sake of salvation, providing through examples how being careless and turning from the way of the Lord can result in damnation.[110] It is within this context that the practice of usury appears. Chrysostom begins the section by referring to the parables of the prodigal son[111] and the ungrateful servant who is forgiven his large debt but is later condemned as he does not forgive a small debt done to him;[112] Chrysostom's point is that if we are careless, no one's help can save us; if we are careful, however, we do not need the guidance of others, only the grace of God.[113] This begins a section of exhortation to give of all that one has, with the controversial "make friends of yourself by means of dishonest wealth"[114] at its core. In passionate prose he implores Christians to unshackle themselves from the burdens of wealth by giving:

> Disperse therefore, that you may not lose; keep not, that you may keep; lay out, that you may save; spend, that you may gain. If your treasures are to be hoarded, do not hoard them, for you will surely cast them away; but entrust them to God, for from there no man makes spoil of them. Do not traffic, for you do not know at all how to gain; but lend to Him who gives an interest greater than the principal. Lend, where is no envy, no accusation, no evil design, no fear. Lend to Him who wants nothing, yet has need for your sake; who feeds all men, yet who hungers, that you may not suffer famine; who is poor, that you may be

---

107. Kelly cites Sir Henry Savile, whom he calls Chrysostom's "greatest editor." Kelly claims that further evidence of this is the contemporary completion of Chrysostom's *Priesthood*, which conveniently ennobles the authority of the priest (Kelly, *The World of the Early Christians*, 100–101).

108. John Chrysostom, *Homilia* 5.1

109. Ibid.

110. Ibid., 5.7–8.

111. Luke 15:13–20.

112. Matthew 18:26–34.

113. John Chrysostom, *Homilia* 5.7.

114. Luke 16:1–9.

rich. Lend there, where your return cannot be death, but life instead of death. For this usury is the herald of a kingdom, that, of hell; the one coming of covetousness, the other of self-denial; the one of cruelty, the other of humanity . . . for nothing, nothing is baser than the usury of this world, nothing more cruel.[115]

Of the many elements worth nothing in this paragraph, two uses of antithesis will be mentioned. First, Chrysostom contrasts the way the world views wealth and the way wealth should be viewed from the Christian perspective: "Give away," he writes, "so that you may gain." This is utterly foolish advice in the mind of an astute business person, who knows full well that it is illogical to expect that if you give something away that it will come back to you in a greater amount, unless there is a contract stipulating its return with appropriate increase. But Chrysostom's advice echoes advice from Jesus to the young man: "If you wish to be perfect, go, sell your possessions, and give the money to the poor, and you will have treasure in heaven."[116] Jesus—and later Chrysostom—consistently turns the world's wisdom against itself, with the result that Christians appear foolish in the eyes of the world when they make civic decisions that go against the flow of public life; it is risky enough to give, but to give in the face of those who scorn such an action is even more difficult.

The discussion then becomes more specific, and the second contrast worth noting is Chrysostom's opposition of the usury of the world with "heavenly usury," in which the individual invests for spiritual profit rather than monetary profit. It is not clear if Chrysostom is encouraging individuals to lend to the poor or to invest in a Church which will then take care of the poor, but regardless, Chrysostom urges repentance on the part of those who have the power to change the lives of those around them simply by dropping some coins. For emphasis, he differentiates between the results of the two types of usury: heavenly usury is the harbinger—or herald—of the kingdom of God, of life, of self-denial, and of humanity, while the usury of the world is the herald of cruelty, covetousness, death and hell.[117]

Chrysostom advances from a discussion on moral choices which can aid in one's salvation, to a social discourse on the wretched nature of usury and the usurer: "Why, other person's calamities are such a man's traffic; he makes himself gain from the distress of another, and demands wages for

115. John Chrysostom, *Homilia* 5.9.

116. Matthew 19:21.

117. John Chrysostom, *Homilia* 5.9.

kindness, as though he were afraid to seem merciful, and under the cloak of kindness he digs the pitfall deeper, by the act of help burdening a man's poverty, and in the act of stretching out the hand thrusting him down, and when receiving him as in harbor, involving him in shipwreck, as on a rock, or shoal, or reef.[118]" Having cast the usurer implicitly in the role of murderer, Chrysostom proceeds into a fictitious discussion between a lender and himself, the lender wanting to know why he should be expected to entrust to another that which he could use for himself, and yet receive nothing in return. Chrysostom assures the lender that in fact his intention is not for the lender to go without: "I say not this: yea, I earnestly desire that you should have a recompense; not however a mean nor small one, but a greater; for in return for gold, I would that you should receive Heaven for usury."[119] You are poor, Chrysostom writes, if you concern yourself only with the wealth of this world, no matter what your bankbook reads.[120] Here is a second text in which Chrysostom reverses the direction of usury, enlarging the scope of the discussion to include that which God gives in return for financial trust invested in the poor among mortals—God's people: "my people, the poor among you"[121]—and spiritual trust invested by the giver in God; God will not abandon the cause of the lender.[122]

Chrysostom's *Homilia* 18[123] focuses on Matthew 5:38–40 and differs from previous sermons, as he does not depart from the text or provide extensive introductory statements, but launches into a concise and tight examination of the Scripture, encouraging his audience to turn their actions heavenward and consider ceaselessly the benefit of both neighbors and enemies.[124] This comprises not just behavior, but possessions as well.

---

118. Ibid.

119. Ibid.

120. Ibid.

121. Exodus 22:25.

122. This is seen in both Basil's text ("When you are about to give to a poor person on the Lord's account, that same gift is also a loan: it is a gift because you do not hope to receive it back again, but a loan because the Master in his great beneficence undertakes to make repayment for the poor person. He receives a little in the guise of the poor, but gives back much on their behalf. 'The one who has mercy on the poor lends to God.' Would you like to have the Master of all as your guarantor for full repayment?" (*Homilia in psalmum* 14, 97–98) and Gregory's as well ("Make a pledge to him who is immortal and believe in his reliable bond which can never be sundered. Do not demand gain but give bountifully and without corruption (Proverbs 19:17)." (Gregory of Nyssa, *Contra usurarios*, in McCambley, 297).

123. John Chrysostom, *Homilia* 18.

124. Ibid., 18.1–3.

Enclosing his passage on usury and unrighteous uses of money within Jesus's explicit statements on lending, Chrysostom's explanation follows:

> "Give to everyone who begs from you, and do not refuse any-one who wants to borrow from you."[125] These last are less than what went before; but marvel not, for this He is ever accustomed to do, mingling the small with the great. And if these be little in comparison with those, let them give heed, who take the goods of others, who distribute their own among the harlots, and kindle to themselves a double fire, both by the unrighteous income, and by the pernicious outlay. But by "borrowing," here, He means not the compact with usury, but the use merely. And elsewhere He even amplifies it, saying that we should give to them, from whom we do not expect to receive.[126]

Chrysostom clarifies that Jesus is not referring to a contractual loan but a simple loan, perhaps even interest-free, between family members or friends.

Homilia 28 begins with Matthew 8:23–24. Chrysostom moves the examination of the passage into an eerily interesting portion on specters and departed souls, as he comments on the casting of the demons into the swine.[127] From this Chrysostom provides a comparison between the demoniac and the sinful person, who "goes naked like him, clad indeed in garments, but deprived of the true covering, and stripped of his proper glory; cutting himself not with stones, but with sins more hurtful than many stones."[128] It is a sympathetic vision of sin, and a contrast from ti-rades against the rich sinner clad in luxurious garments, gorging on costly foods and ignoring the plights of the poor. That, however, is to come, for Chrysostom changes his tone when he confronts the problems of the cov-etous, and the remainder of the discourse is dedicated to this concern: "I for my part would sooner consent to dwell with ten thousand demons, than with one diseased in this way."[129] After launching into a fanciful de-scription of a demonic,[130] Chrysostom claims that the money-orientated

125. Matthew 5:42 in John Chysostom, *Homilia* 18.3.

126. John Chrysostom, *Homilia* 18.3. Luke 6:34–35: "If you lend to those from whom you hope to receive, what credit is that to you? Even sinners lend to sinners, to receive as much again. But love your enemies, do good, and lend, expecting nothing in return" (NRSV). See chapter 3 for discussion on this text.

127. Matthew 8:28–34, in John Chrysostom, *Homilia* 18.3–4.

128. John Chrysostom, *Homilia* 18.4.

129. Ibid.

130. Ibid., 18.5.

man is faraway more frightening, fearsome and dangerous than such a creature could be: "Yet is the covetous man much more fierce even than this, assailing all like hell, swallowing all up, going about a common enemy to the race of men . . . you will see him snatching up a sword, laying violent hands on all, and sparing none; neither friend, nor kinsman, nor brother, nor even his very parent."[131] Chrysostom cites usury as one of the ways by which covetous persons lose their fortunes when they wager that they will gain from one who has nothing to begin with: "Many, for instance, on many occasions, wishing to lend at large usury, and through the expectation of gain not having inquired about them who receive their money, have together with the interest lost also their capital."[132] Here there is neither a scriptural nor social condemnation of the practice of usury, merely the message that gluttonous desire for profit can result in bad business, foolish decisions made while blinded by the prospect of unjust gain, or the previously mentioned "unrighteous income."[133] This passage is Chrysostom's fiscal version of Jesus's caution to the crowd: "If any want to become my followers, let them deny themselves and take up their cross and follow me. For those who want to save their lives will lose it, and those who lose their life for my sake, and for the sake of the gospel, will save it."[134] If pressed, Chrysostom might have said that the covetous person deserved to lose their wealth if they were so blinded by their greed that they could not even conduct business transactions with proficiency, but "by some trifling meanness they have lost all."[135] He comes close to these very words with his pronouncement that "because they know not how to sow, but have ever practised reaping, they of course continually fail of their harvest."[136] The theme of sowing and reaping and its connection to both spiritual and material benefits is ever-present in the Hebrew Bible and New Testament; and though the Christian scriptures are filled with numerous examples that support Chrysostom's allusion, perhaps the best is found in Galatians: "Do not be deceived; God is not mocked, for you reap whatever you sow.

---

131. Ibid.

132. Ibid., 18.6.

133. Ibid., 18.3.

134. Mark 8:34; Jesus follows this counsel with a question very pertinent to the discussion at hand: "For what will it profit them to gain the whole world and forfeit their life?" (Mark 8:36).

135. John Chrysostom, *Homilia* 28.6.

136. Ibid.

If you sow to your own flesh, you will reap corruption from the flesh; but if you sow to the Spirit, you will reap eternal life from the Spirit."[137]

Homilia 37 analyses Matthew 11:7–25, the passage in which Jesus sends out his disciples with instructions for their well-being. After preaching on this passage Chrysostom launches into a tirade against biblical examples of disobedience contrasted with John the Baptist's obedience.[138] In this passage the subject of usury arises: "In order then that both our houses may be continually open to the one, and our ears to the others, let us purge away the filth from the ears of our soul. For as filth and mud close the ears of our flesh, so do the harlot's songs, and worldly news, and debts, and the business of usury and loans, close up the ear of the mind, worse than any filth; moreover, they do not close it up only, but also make it unclean."[139] Chrysostom notes a difference between "usury" and "loans," but both are equated as dung in the ears of the unfaithful.[140] It is not just the usurer who is condemned in this passage but also the one who disobeys Jesus's injunction to "love your enemies, do good, and lend, expecting nothing in return."[141] The one who lends without any usury is equally as damnable as the one who attempts to profit off another's need, for both are eager for revenue: the one in principal, the other in principal and additional returns. Chrysostom does not let the borrower off the hook, for here the one with "debts" also is indicted. I think it is reasonable to conclude that in this particular passage Chrysostom was not condemning the needy person who borrowed for consumption, but probably the individual who borrowed to maintain a certain lifestyle, as we have noted was common practice. As evidence, Chrysostom ends this homily with a passionate plea against the corruptness of theatrical pleasures and other such scandalous activities which cost money, and holds up the chaste and simple life of marriage, children and friends as a life which is not harmful to one's soul: "And in chastity too you would profit more, should you refrain from going there."[142]

Homilia 45 concerns Matthew 13:10–11, and while Chrysostom begins with a speech on the wisdom of the disciples, he soon forms an

---

137. Galatians 6:7–8.

138. John Chrysostom, *Homilia* 37.1–6.

139. Ibid., 37.7.

140. Ibid., 37.7.

141. Luke 6:34–35.

142. John Chrysostom, *Homilia* 37.9. The phrase "should you refrain from going there" refers to the wicked theatre.

argument on material wealth out of what he refers to as the "unspeakable justice" behind Jesus's injunction that "for those who have, more will be given, and they will have an abundance; but from those who having nothing, even what they have will be taken away."[143] Chrysostom carries this theme for the remainder of the first chapter, covers the parable of the sower in the second, and in the third he reflects upon all the gifts of the spirit granted to the Christian. Finally, Chrysostom concludes that the Christian—who actually deserves the very "deep of hell"[144]—should feel obligated out of both a sense of gratitude and fear of damnation to depart from being "slaves of money."[145] He shames his audience with reminders that others have shed both blood and life for Heaven, and yet they cannot even sacrifice "superfluities":

> And of what favour can you be worthy? of what justification? who in his sowing of the earth, gladly pours forth all, and in lending to men at usury spares nothing; but in feeding his Lord through His poor is cruel and inhuman? Having then considered all these things, and calculated what we have received, what we are to receive, what is required of us, let us show forth all our diligence on the things spiritual. Let us become at length mild and humane, that we may not draw down on ourselves the intolerable punishment. For what is there that does not have the power to condemn us? Our having enjoyed so many and such great benefits; our having no great thing required of us; our having such things required, as we shall leave here even against our will; our exhibiting so much liberality in our worldly matters. Why each one of these, even by itself, would be enough to condemn us; but when they all meet together, what hope will there be of salvation? In order that we may escape all this condemnation, let us show forth some bounty towards those who are in need.[146]

In this long passage quoted from a short homily, Chrysostom's use of usury is not extraordinary; here the practice stands as it does in previous homilies, a base custom whose practitioners should expect only "the fire that is being prepared for the devil and his angels"[147] as eternal reward.

---

143. Matthew 13:12.
144. John Chrysostom, *Homilia* 45.3.
145. Ibid.
146. Ibid.
147. Ibid.

Homilia 56, which examines Matthew 16:28—17:10, contains Chrysostom's longest tirade against usury. The first six chapters of the account cover the transfiguration and the reaction of the disciples to the event.[148] Chrysostom's application of the text to his audience begins in the seventh chapter with the following statement: "But if we will, we also shall behold Christ, not as they then on the mount, but in far greater brightness."[149] Familiar now with Chrysostom's style and method, we know that he is going to state how it is that an average Christian would be able to surpass in sight that of the beloved disciples, "even the three, who even in the cloud were counted worthy to be under the same roof with the Lord."[150] Consistently, Chrysostom connects the possibility of eternal damnation with participation in usurious pursuits, and it is his longest diatribe yet against the practice in his homilies: "Tear in sunder every unjust compact"; thus calling men's bills about the interest due to them, and the sums they have lent. "Set at liberty them that are bruised"; them that are afflicted. For such a being is the debtor; when he sees his creditor, his mind is broken, and he fears him more than a wild beast . . . For what is more vexatious than to be lending, and taking thought about usuries and bargains, and demanding collateral, and fearing and trembling about securities, about the principal, about the writings, about the interest, about the bondsman?"[151] This passage functions for us as a window to Chrysostom's world, and provides a modern reader with some understanding of his audience: a church filled with sinners simultaneously loved and chided by their priest. He acknowledges that while many do not like to hear what he has to say, their punishment would be the same whether he spoke or not; in fact, he would be included in their punishment for not having attempted to deter them from their wicked deeds.[152] Like a parent forced to discipline a wayward child, Chrysostom informs them that "I must make you sorry here, that we may not suffer punishment there."[153] Note that he is included in the latter half of the sentence; they are his flock and he will not abandon them, even in their punishment.

Surely Chrysostom's audience is in heaven now, for no one could sit through this peppery priest's sermons and be unmoved. Utterly

148. Ibid., 56.1–6.
149. Ibid., 56.7.
150. Ibid.
151. Ibid., 56.8.
152. Ibid.
153. Ibid.

disregarding "laws that are without,"[154] Chrysostom brandishes usury as a "dreadful disease"[155] that has gripped them. In the remainder of his sermon he says nothing about usury that others before him have not said, but it is the intensity poured into his work that gives the text its wondrous quality. Unlike the normal brief asides granted to this problem, here Chrysostom attacks both usury and the usurer with vengeance that makes even the modern reader feel uneasy as he likens turning an honest wage into unjust increase through usury as obliging "a fair womb to give birth to scorpions."[156]

It is not simply that Chrysostom condemns usury from a social perspective, here he addresses it from the previously mentioned alternative reading as well: he chides the usurer not only for the futility of making an investment in one who can in no way repay, but also for failing to invest in the spiritually responsible or proper manner. Claiming that one percent per month legal allotment that the lender receives is but a "small price for so good a deed,"[157] Chrysostom urges the lender to give money to the needy rather than lend it, for then God would return that investment with "a hundredfold and eternal life."[158] It is no accident that Chrysostom alludes here to the response Jesus gave to the disciples when they asked, "Look, we have left everything and followed you. What then will we have?"[159] As well, this passage immediately follows the conversation between Jesus and the man who is told that in order to have eternal life he must—in addition to obeying an edited version of the ten commandments—sell all his possessions and give the money to the poor.[160]

Chrysostom criticizes the usurer for being so foolish as to entertain such misplaced greed, and notes that usurious loans do not guarantee a high return: "How many have lost their very principal for the interest's sake? How many have fallen into perils for usurious gains?"[161] Reminiscent

---

154. Ibid., 56.9. His statement is a reminder that although the conciliar laws were against clergy participating in usurious pursuits, still it was legal for the secular public. For laws contemporary to Chrysostom, see chapter 2.

155. Ibid.

156. Ibid.

157. Ibid.

158. Matthew 19:29, in John Chrysostom, *Homilia* 56.9.

159. Matthew 19:27.

160. Matthew 19:16–22.

161. John Chrysostom, *Homilia* 56.9.

of 1 Timothy 6:9–10,[162] Chrysostom implores the proper use of one's funds, for to lose one's money by donating all to the poor is noble; to lose one's money while waiting on a "hoped for" return of "unrighteous income" is the apex of covetousness, for not only is the lender taken to the nadir of poverty but the debtor remains there as well. Pushing this interpretation to its farthest degree, one senses that the usurer could be held indirectly responsible if sin led to the death of another due to a deprivation of basic life needs.[163]

Insisting that the "old law" is still active, Chrysostom cites Exodus 22:25; Leviticus 25:35–36; and Deuteronomy 22:19 as his foundation;[164] he rejects the complaint of the usurer who wishes to receive praise for turning the interest over to the church and insists that God wants no such offerings;[165] finally, he refers to the Law of Honorius of 397 CE as his defense that even the honorable lawgivers find the practice contemptible.[166] It could be suggested that Chrysostom is acknowledging that reasonable usury might be acceptable as it is legal. However, his next paragraph would negate that interpretation: "Is it not a horrible thing, if you ascribe

162. "But those who want to be rich fall into temptation and are trapped by many senseless and harmful desires that plunge people into ruin and destruction. For the love of money is a root of all kinds of evil, and in their eagerness to be rich some have wandered away from the faith and pierced themselves with many pains" (1 Timothy 6:9–10).

163. Although not writing directly about usury but about the sins of the wealthy in general, in *Homilia* 11 from his *Homilies on the Epistle of St. Paul the Apostle to the Romans*, Chrysostom writes that the one who inflicts financial oppression—in whatever form that might take—is indirectly a murderer: "Is it not murder, pray, and worse than murder, to hand the poor man over to famine, and to cast him into prison, and to expose him not to famine only, but to tortures too, and countless acts of insolence? For even if you do not do these things yourself to him, yet you are the occasion of their being done, and do them more than the ministers who execute them." John Chrysostom, *Homilia* 11, *Epistolam ad Romanos* (PG 60:583–682), 414. Basil demonstrates agreement with this assessment: "Starvation, the distress of the famished, is the supreme human calamity, a more miserable end than all other deaths . . . But famine is a slow evil, always approaching, always holding off like a beast in its den . . . Whoever had it in his power to alleviate this evil but deliberately opts instead for profit, should be condemned as a murderer" (Basil, *Homilia dicta tempore famis et siccitatis*, in Holman, *The Hungry Are Dying*, 190). See chapter 2 for comments by Cicero on the murder of a man through debt, for the link between financial sins and murder. See chapter 5 for Gregory of Nyssa's comparison of the two.

164. John Chrysostom, *Homilia* 56.9.

165. Ibid.

166. Ibid.

not even so much honour to the polity of Heaven, as the legislators to the council of the Romans."[167]

Chrysostom's next barb is another reference to the etymology of τόκος.[168] Alluding either to Basil's *Homilia in psalmum* 14,[169] or Plutarch's *Moralia*,[170]—or perhaps to both—Chrysostom writes that the moneylender is never even able to enjoy what is gained, for "before this evil offspring is brought forth complete, he compels it also to bring forth, making the interest principal, and forcing it to bring forth its untimely and abortive brood of vipers."[171] Naturally Chrysostom's evocative vocabulary would immediately connect the listener with Jesus's famous tirade against the scribes and Pharisees, in which Jesus refers to them as snakes and as "a brood of vipers."[172] Here, Chrysostom has cast himself as the critic of the current social order, as Jesus in his day. Further, his choice of the phrase "brood of vipers" in connection with usury brings to mind the ancient myth of the Medusa, whose hair of snakes—a brood of vipers—rendered her so unsightly that to look upon her brought about instant death; truly, what better mascot for the usurer than the Medusa?

In a passage that would make any feminist eager to condemn this feisty preacher—and most queasy—Chrysostom counsels that one should "cut out the evil womb of usurious gains, let us deaden these lawless labours, let us dry up this place of pernicious teeming, and let us pursue the

---

167. Ibid.

168. As a reminder, τόκος can be defined as birth, offspring, interest or oppression.

169. "It is said that rabbits give birth and breed again while still nursing their young. And for those who set rates of interest, their money is loaned out and bears interest and produces even more. You did not even have the money in your hands, and already the lender was demanding the interest payment for the current month" (Basil, *Homilia in psalmum* 14 [PG 29:273], in Schroeder, *On Social Justice*, 95).

170. "They say that hares at one and the same time give birth to one litter, suckle another, and conceive again; but the loans of these barbarous rascals give birth to interest before conception; for while they are giving they immediately demand payment, while they lay money down they take it up, and they lend what they receive for money lent . . . And then they make a laughing stock forsooth of the scientists, who say that nothing arises out of nothing; for with these men interest arises out of that which has as yet no being or existence" (Plutarch, "On Borrowing," in *De vitando aere alieno*, 325).

171. John Chrysostom, *Homilia* 56.9. Chrysostom is here speaking about one of the abuses of usury, that of *anatocism*, wherein the accumulation of interest is capitalized on the original interest. See chapter 2 for Solon's reform of this practice.

172 "You snakes, you brood of vipers? How can you escape being sentenced to hell?" (Matthew 23:33).

true and great gains only."[173] There is no inventive use of the word usury by Chrysostom in this homily, only a scalding invective with Christian scripture, philosophy, and Roman law as his defense against a practice that he fears has afflicted Christians as a disease.

Further comments against usury are fairly anti-climactic, but they are present nonetheless and always accompanied by biblical passages. *Homilia* 64 begins with Matthew 19:27, and addresses the parable of the landowner who hires throughout the day yet pays the same wage for those who worked many hours or a few. Chrysostom moves from this discussion to that of the biblical code, "for even a part of it overlooked brings upon one great evils."[174] His concern here is almsgiving; though he admits that almsgiving is only part of the whole, still it is a large enough part that to neglect to participate in almsgiving "casts into hell them that have come short in it."[175] Chrysostom insists that his audience is to emulate and override the giving that was expected of Pharisees and Scribes, who gave almost a full one-third of their income.[176] It is within this section that almsgiving is connected with usury, for it is not that the Pharisees and Scribes simply gave one-third of their income, but additional "untainted" gifts as well: "And together with these, first fruits, and first born, and other things besides, as, for instance, the offerings for sins, those for purification, those at feasts, those in the jubilee, those by the canceling of debts, and the dismissals of servants, and the lendings that were clear of usury." In addition to such obligations as those listed, the offerings themselves could not be befouled by base transactions. Chrysostom's lack of condemnation on usury is interesting; it is possible that this passage could be considered a tacit acknowledgement of usury as an accepted part of secular society, but his refusal to consider as favorable a gift which came from such a transaction indicates that money gained under such a transaction—the "unrighteous income"—is indicative of the spiritual life of the lender/giver.

Homilia 78 includes a unique treatment of usury; Chrysostom's text begins with the parable of the ten virgins, and concludes with the parable of the ten talents. To my surprise, just as Theodoret of Cyrrhus does only a few years later, the Antiochene-educated Chrysostom reads the parable allegorically rather than literally and equates the Lord in the account—

---

173. John Chrysostom, *Homilia* 41.9.

174. Ibid., 64.4.

175. Ibid.

176. Ibid.

a "hard man"—with God,[177] and reads the talents as allegorical as well: "For the talents here are each person's ability, whether in the way of protection, or in money, or in teaching, or in any way of the kind."[178] Chrysostom's response to the passage on usury is puzzling as well: "What could be more gentle than this? For men indeed do not [do this], but him that has put out the money at usury, truly do they make him responsible to demand it again. But He not so; but, you ought, He says, to have put it out, and to have committed the demanding of it again to me. And I should have demanded it with increase; by increase upon the hearing, meaning the showing forth of the works. You ought to have done that which is easier, and to have left to me what is more difficult.[179]" This is an intriguing response. Undeniably Chrysostom is not speaking of usury as the financial practice of gaining interest on a loan or increasing one's wealth at another's expense, but here "usury" is the investment of one's "talent," the development or increase of that talent by God, and the subsequent restoration of that talent with interest to the investor as a gift. In addition, Chrysostom is saying that the collection of not only the investment but the interest as well is the job of the master—in his view, God—not the responsibility of the one who makes the investment. Therefore the servant is chastised not just for failing to increase the investment, but because the servant failed to trust in the Master to aid in the endeavor in the first place; Chrysostom's point is that the Master would never have abandoned the servant even in any attempt: "Let no man say, 'I have but one talent, and can do nothing'; for you are not poorer than that widow; you are not more uninstructed than Peter and John, who were both 'unlearned and ignorant men'; but nevertheless, since they showed forth a zeal, and did all things for the common good, they attained to Heaven."[180]

Chrysostom also attends to the parable of the ten talents within a lengthy introduction to *Homilia* 41 from his series on Genesis,[181] the final passage of Chrysostom's to be considered.[182] Overcome with unhappiness

177. Ibid., 78.2.

178. Ibid.

179. Ibid., 78.2.

180. Ibid.

181. John Chrysostom, *Homiliæ in Genesin* (PG 53 and 54). *Homiliæ* 41 (PG 53:375–86).

182. There is an additional Homily of Chrysostom's which deals with "covetous gain" (*Homilia* 10 *in Thess.* 10.4 [PG 62. 455–62]). However, as the homily does not *explicitly* discuss usury but only alludes to it under the expansive subject of greed, its existence will here be noted, but not scrutinized. Seipel is the only author who includes this homily among his primary sources; see chapter 1.

over those who choose instead to go to the races rather than to church, Chrysostom ignores the day's Scripture until he has first delivered a reprimand for the sins of those who are absent. He uses as his text the parable of the ten talents, with a conclusion similar to that previously stated. In the case of material wealth, Chrysostom claims, God forbids the taking of interest because it is detrimental to both parties; however, in the case of spiritual matters, the more "interest" the debtor pays, the more generous reward from above the debtor will receive. In Chrysostom's case, he urges Christians to look out for one another, to "snatch them from the jaws of the devil,"[183] and urge their neighbors to go to church; by doing so, he assures them, their spiritual rewards will be great, and they will hear at the time of reckoning: "You have been faithful in a few things, I will put you in possession of many."[184]

Conclusion

Before addressing the questions posed in the statement at the beginning of this chapter, I would like to summarize the scripture passages that these authors employed to support their condemnation of the practice of usury, and comment briefly on the ways that they made use of the term "usury" within their writings. First, Clement of Alexandria twice quotes in total the passage from Ezekiel, and mentions "the law" in a direct reference to Deuteronomy 23:19–20e; his position is biblically based, and focused on right behavior. Cyril of Jerusalem cites nothing biblical, but in a style reminiscent of Ezekiel he includes usury within a list of devilish crimes all loosely connected with enchantment and wizardry, activities which would be utterly condemned by the authorities, much less scripture; Cyril's text precisely places the usurer outside the walls. Usurious activity is cited by Gregory of Nazianzus as one of the reasons why his irreverent community has been struck by various natural disasters. Although there is no mention of biblical ordinances, Gregory bases his understanding of usury on what some would consider a proper reading of the parable of the talents in Matthew 25:26: he equates the usurer—one who is "gathering where he had not sowed and reaping where he had not strawed"[185]—with the wicked master, eager for gain earned by the sweat of another's brow. Making use of the parable of the talents found in Matthew 25:14–30 and Luke 19:11–27,

183. John Chrysostom, *Homilia* 41.6.

184. Ibid.

185. Gregory Nazienzen, *Homilia* 16.18.

Theodoret of Cyrrhus mentions usury in his letter to Eusebius as a method of fearful encouragement to the new bishop. Contrary to Gregory of Nazianzus, but like Chrysostom, Theodoret equates the master with God, and the "talents" with the obligations that the Christians have before God. Although Casimir McCambley's statement that the authors used "forgive us our debts" as justification for their position[186] is correct in the case of Gregory of Nyssa, not one of the authors considered in this chapter uses this phrase in his text as justification for a position against usury.

While one could look—as González has—at the hundreds of passages written by John Chrysostom on wealth and draw significant conclusions about Chrysostom's opinions on the connections between wealth, communal property and injustice,[187] with regard to usury it is not possible to wrap it in so tidy a package. Chrysostom, who at times simply echoes what has been said before on the subject, condemns both the practice of usury and the usurer. But unique to his sermons is that he uses the idea of usury to his own advantage to compound a point that is either worldly or celestial. By affixing the subject of usury to his sermons as chastisement, he presents usury as an example of worldly behavior in which he does not want to see Christians engaging, such as in *Homilia* 43 on 1 Corinthians, and *Homilies* 5, 18, 28, 37, 45, 56, and 64 on Matthew. Chrysostom's "spiritual" use of usury works allegorically; he reverses the concept from earthly interest to eternal salvation in *Homilia* 3 on 2 Corinthians and in *Homilia* 56 and 78 on Matthew, obliging God to provide the interest for what has been invested in by the believer. Despite his allegorical renderings, one could never conclude that Chrysostom approves of the legal practice of usury; his unambiguous condemnation of usury and usurers within his writings perfectly balances any attempt to finger him for inconsistency.

In addition to noting the use of Scripture, this chapter has considered the ways in which references to "usury" and "usurers" have been included in various writings of a selection of Greek early Christian authors for the purpose of addressing two questions: first, to whom does the term "usurer" refer within these writings? Does the term "usurer" refer only to a monetary "usurer," or does the term "usurer" come in time to refer to simply one among many wicked characteristics in a corrupt and sinful individual? To generalize, by using the term "usurer" the Greek early Christian writers intend an individual who is extracting interest—perhaps a life-threatening degree of interest—from another. While the usurer might very well be an

---

186. McCambley, "Against Those Who Practice Usury by Gregory of Nyssa," 288.

187. González, *Faith and Wealth*, 200–213.

unknown business person, one is left with the impression that it is more likely an opportunistic "neighbor," someone within the Christian community. Regardless of relationship, this person is lending when they should give, and lending to a degree that is causing grave harm to the individual to whom the money is being lent. This surely includes situations in which the borrower is merely borrowing so to continue to live in the style to which they have grown accustomed, but it is unlikely that they would speak out against the practice of usury so strongly if irreparable damage was not being brought upon individuals and households as a result of what were probably consumptive loans. This definition of a "usurer" includes one who fails to follow either biblical prohibitions which state that usury is forbidden among members of a community or the injunction of Jesus to "lend, expecting nothing in return."[188] Contrary to what I had at first suspected, after a closer reading it does not appear that the early Greek authors reduced the practice of "usury" or the term "usurer" to a simple insult, or indication of a sinful individual; it appears that for the most part the writers are addressing the problem of usury *specifically* as the practice plagues their individual communities, and that by the term "usurer" they mean expressly and quite simply "one who engages in usury."

This leads to the second question: is the Deuteronomic injunction against usury within the society—while allowing for the practice outside the community (Deuteronomy 23:19–20)—found within the works of the early Greek authors, or is the practice prohibited to all, regardless of relationship? If so, what was the scriptural or legal defense for any such condemnation? The author who most directly refers to the Deuteronomy passage is Clement of Alexandria, who writes quite specifically that an individual must consider as a brother "designating as a brother not only him who is born of the same parents, but also one of the same race and sentiments, and a participator in the same word."[189] In fourth-century eastern Christianity the "community" of the chosen now appears to be applicable to anyone regardless of their racial makeup and/or previous religious affiliation as long as they now embrace Christianity. As a result—according to the above texts—the biblical proscriptions against usury are applied but without racial/ethnic distinctions previously held. In none of the above texts did there appear to be any distinction made between the religion or racial composition of the usurer and lender; Paul would delight that in these writings there are no distinctions, no "Jew" or "Christian," only a

188. Luke 6:34–35.
189. Clement of Alexandria, *Stromata* 2.18.

blanket condemnation against the practice of usury and the usurer, whose character—rather than whose race—is being slandered.[190] Although there is a heavy presence of biblical condemnation against the practice of usury, the scriptural and/or legal defense for the condemnation of usury among the above authors seems to rest heavily on the New Testament. The economic philosophy of the New Testament was not unnoticed by these thoughtful bishops, most especially John Chrysostom.

Appeals to righteous behavior are characteristic of a problem such as usury or other social diseases associated with poverty. But unlike other stumbling blocks that the early Christian bishops and theologians faced such as Montanism or Arianism, usury is a different kind of dilemma for two reasons: first, it is not an act of heresy to engage in usury and so it is not as straightforward a problem as the theological battle between blasphemy and sanctity. To be a usurer does not preclude that the usurer is not a Christian; that is, one can be both a Christian and a usurer at the same time, just as one can be an adulterer or some type of addict and a Christian at the same time—a fact which must have been as galling for the early Christian bishops as it is to modern day pastors and priests. Second, usury was legal, so any one who engaged in usury was not breaking the civil law. Consequently, early Christian leaders were faced with a difficult situation: how to make people engage in righteous behavior without resorting to threatening them with an expired religious code. In short, how do you force someone to "be good?" They attempted to answer this question by continuing to uphold Christian scriptures as binding in an allegorical or spiritual way, without being forced to admit that any of the other injunctions in the Hebrew Bible were literally required as well, such as circumcision or other such unpleasantness. The best possible way to do this with respect to usury was to connect the ordinance of the Israelite code against usury with the sayings of Jesus, thereby demonstrating continuity and progression of the Law and applicability for the Christian in their day. In a sense, they had to extract the "Hebrew" from the Hebrew Bible; by this I mean they had to keep the moral centre of the Hebrew Bible while at the same time discarding a constricting Law which did not apply to a way of life that was neither nomadic nor anxious to remain distinct from

190. The majority of the texts examined above are slanderous to the usurer, with authors portraying the usurer as an individual who practices the sinister art of entrapment. But a sympathetic element is added as well; in addition to being evil they are also portrayed as misguided, for while they are not ignorant of the extent of damage that their actions are causing to others, they are ignorant to the damage being done to their own souls.

other societies.[191] The allowance that Jews may lend with usury outside of their community does not rise as a point of debate within these texts. Usury allowed outside the community but not within is a rather uncomfortable distinction which does not appear among authors in the eastern provinces of the Empire, who seek a blanket moral condemnation of what is a legally valid practice. Because usury appeared to be prohibited to all regardless of relationship, happily, the deliberation over usury in the life of early Christianity in the east appears to be relatively free of racial biases which fetter the debates in the early west, in the Carolingian age, and in the Middle Ages.[192]

191. Rosemary Radford Reuther writes that by the end of the first century, Christianity had moved from the Jewish to the Hellenistic milieu, and had detached itself from its Jewish identity, with the exception of the Scriptures, which were interpreted through the gospels (Reuther, *Gregory Nazianzus, Rhetor and Philosopher*, 157).

192. Recall Bishop Ambrose of Milan's harsh words concerning usury and the "other": "Upon him whom you rightly desire to harm, against whom weapons are lawfully carried, upon him usury is legally imposed. On him whom you cannot easily conquer in war, you can quickly take vengeance with the hundredth. From him extract usury whom it would not be a crime to kill. He fights without a weapon who demands usury; without a sword he revenges himself upon an enemy, who is an interest collector from his foe. Therefore, where there is the right of war, there is also the right of usury" (Ambrose, *De Tobia* 15.51 [PL 14:779]). For the Christian, however, there is to be another way: "The more blameworthy is usury, the more admirable is the one who abstains from it. If you have money, give it away. The money that you keep idle, make it useful for others. Give it with the intention of not recovering it; and if it is returned to you, do not receive profit from it. If the borrower cannot pay your money back to you, let him repay you his gratitude; if you are cheated of your money, you will acquire justice, because he is just who has compassion and lends. If you lose your money, you will gain mercy, as it is written: 'He is merciful who lends to his neighbor'(Sirach 29.1)" (Ambrose, *De Tobia* 32.2.521, in *Corpus scriptorum ecclesiasticorum latinorum (Vienna)*. The ninth-century scholar Rabanus Maurus wrote that the injunction of Deuteronomy 23:19–20e is a demonstration of charity to the "other" rather than fraud. To all "catholic" Christians one should lend freely, but to the "alien" (criminals and infidels) one lends with usury as compensation for the good work of the Christian. In the twelfth century, Christians began to apply this to Moslems, and it was praised as a useful economic weapon for recovery of Christian heritage. Jews in Europe saw it as an opportunity to extract usury from the Christians, who did not much like this. Joseph the Zealot wrote concerning this: "They [the Gentiles] reproach us for doing usury and quote what David says (Ps 15): '. . . who do not lend money at interest . . . shall never be moved.' Answer: David was Moses' disciple, he could not, therefore, place himself in contradiction to his master by making additions or omissions in the Law: now Moses has said: 'On loans to a foreigner you may charge interest, but on loans to another Israelite you may not charge interest.' Our persecutors will perhaps pretend that they are our brothers in virtue of the verse 'You shall not abhor any of the Edomites, for they are your kin' (Deut 23:8[7]) but to that R. Moses of Paris has

replied: 'The prophet Obadiah has established that this brotherhood no longer exists, for he has said: "foreigners entered his gates and cast lots for Jerusalem, you too were like one of them." (Obad. 11)'" (Nelson, *The Idea of Usury*, 5–6). For further discussion of usury and the Jewish relationship, see Grayzel, *The Church and the Jews in the 13th Century.*

5

Basil and Gregory

Credit Where Credit is Due[1]

THE TEXTS UNDER CONSIDERATION in this chapter—Basil's *Homilia in psalmum 14*[2] and Gregory of Nyssa's *Contra usurarios*[3]—are the two most fully developed sermons against usury from early Greek Christianity. Rather than treating usury as a secondary subject that emerges during the course of a scriptural exegesis on greed, wealth or poverty, the two bishops take usury as their primary subject and compose sermons around it.[4] As was noted in the introduction, Patrick Cleary championed

1. The central argument for this chapter was crafted into an article that was published in the *Journal of Early Christian Studies* titled "Basil and Gregory's Sermons on Usury: Credit Where Credit is Due," 16 (2008) 403–30.

2. Basil, *Homilia in psalmum 14* (PG 29:263–80). In his chronology of Basil's works, Paul Fedwick places *Homilia in psalmum 14, prima* and *secunda* between the years 363 and 378 (Fedwick, *Basil of Caesarea*, 9–10). Two fine translations of this sermon exist in English, in Way (trans.), *Exegetical Homilies*, 181–91; Schroeder, *On Social Justice*, 89–99.

3. Gregory of Nyssa, *Contra usurarios* (PG 46:433–52), in McCambley, "Against Those Who Practice Usury, by Gregory of Nyssa." Jean Daniélou ("Chronologie des Sermons de Saint Grégoire de Nysse," 348) dates this homily to 379. Bernardi does not support Daniélou's date unequivocally, but in light of a more convincing alternative, agrees. "S'il est vrai que les voyages de Grégoire en 380 ne lui permirent guère de prêcher, comme l'avait établi Diekamp, il ne s'ensuit pas nécessairement que l'année 379 puisse seule être retenue, bien qu'elle soit assez probable en définitive" (Bernardi, *La prédication des pères cappadociens*, 264–65).

4. Neither sermon stands independently; Basil's *Homilia in psalmum 14 secunda* is Part 2 of his *Homilia in psalmum 14 prima* (PG 30:352–57), which addresses justice, moral thought, philanthropy, and the distribution of goods, rather than poverty. See

Basil's sermon as a foundational document on this topic, claiming: "St. Basil's magnificent effort is the source of inspiration. His homily on the fourteenth psalm is professedly used by St. Gregory of Nyssa and by St. Ambrose, and both borrow freely from it."[5] Though Stanislas Giet more accurately notes that Gregory offered his homily as a "supplement" to his brother's[6]—referring to Gregory's deferential citation of Basil's earlier work[7]—this minor concession does not account for the many differences within these two very distinct sermons. Though Gregory's sermon is more original and less dependent upon Basil than was Basil's upon an earlier treatise on usury, when historians ponder early Christian authors who address usury,[8] Basil's text customarily garners more attention. While there is no dispute that the texts have elements in common, even those elements are used differently; therefore, the goal of this chapter is an analysis of Basil of Caesarea's *Homilia in psalmum* 14 and Gregory

---

Holman, *The Hungry Are Dying,* 111–12. Gregory's *Contra usurarios* is one of three sermons delivered during the same period, all of which address the problems of poverty. It is only these two sermons of the total five, however, that address specifically the issue of usury. Translations for the two additional sermons by Gregory—*On the Love of the Poor:* 1: "On Good Works" (PG 46:543–64) and *O the Love of the Poor:* 2: "On the Saying 'Whoever Has Done it to One of These Has Done It to Me'"* (PG 46:472–89)— are provided in translation in Holman's *The Hungry Are Dying,* 193–99 and 199–206, respectively. While the former of the two homilies addresses the attitude of the Cappadocian population toward those who are twice poor (in poverty and illness; the disease described by Gregory refers most likely to leprosy), the latter sermon, while entirely devoted to the plight of the poor, does not specifically address the subject of usury, and therefore will be considered only as it harmonizes with the scope of this volume.

5. Cleary, *The Church and Usury,* 49.

6. "Grégoire de Nysse, en condamnant le prêt a intérêt, s'attaque aux mêmes désordres que son frére; il présente même son homélie comme complétant, à l'usage des usuriers, celle que Basile avait spécialement adressée aux emprunteurs" (Gregory of Nyssa, in condemning the loan at interest, opposes the same licentiousness as his brother; he even presents his homily as a supplement, for the use of the usurers, [to] that which Basil had especially addressed to the borrowers.) (Giet, "De Saint Basile à Saint Ambroise," 105).

7. "Our words pertaining to usury should suffice because the example of persons condemned in court is adequate for me. May God bestow repentance upon them. But those who are quick to loan and pierce themselves with hooks of moneylending, recklessly harm their own lives. I remain silent in this matter because our holy father Basil's advice is sufficient. He has wisely and abundantly furnished it in his homily to persons who are foolish enough to make loans out of greed." Gregory of Nyssa, *Contra usurarios* (PG 46:452), in McCambley, "Against Those Who Practice Usury, by Gregory of Nyssa," 301–2.

8. See chapter 1.

of Nyssa's *Contra usurarios*. Such a study will reveal noteworthy mutual qualities and differences and will provide an answer to the following question: to what extent does Gregory's homily depend on Basil's? Is it accurate to refer to Gregory's offering as "supplemental" to Basil's? To this end, and to place the homilies in proper context, this chapter will first offer a synopsis of their life in Cappadocia, considering the opinions of Gregory and Basil regarding poverty, debt and usury as they are distinguished in selections of their ascetic writings, including one of Gregory's aforementioned two sermons against the poor, and Basil's *Homilia dicta tempore famis et siccitatis*.[9] Finally, this chapter will examine each of the brother's texts on usury in turn. Use of the word τόχος will be noted as it pertains to interest. As well, I will consider the attitudes of the brothers regarding the financial responsibilities of the poor or the debtor, and the degree to which they admonish the wealthy.

Finally, it is worth noting that I recognize that the era in which the brothers lived is not comparable to ours; I make no attempt to justify their understanding of how economics operate, why scarcity exists or why people suffer in light of our own understanding of—or wrestling with—these concepts. In short, their cultural framework is completely different from ours with respect to economics, politics and status. Basil owned slaves, and both brothers operated under a patronage model and within a honor/shame system; further, they differed radically from us culturally and geographically. Most especially, in light of patristic eschatological vision—a vision that placed an emphasis *not* on this world and the ways in which we might make it better, but, rather looked towards a finality to the injustices of the world in the restoration of the created order within Christ[10]—we cannot expect them to care about the things that we care about, or even to care about "human rights" as we understand them.[11]

9. Basil, *Homilia dicta tempore famis et siccitatis* (PG 31:303–28).

10. Daley, The *Hope of the Early Church*.

11. Allen, "Challenges in Approaching Patristic Texts," 33–35; see also Holman, "The Entitled Poor," 476–89; see also Grieg, "Throwing Parties for the Poor," 145–61.

The Cappadocian Brothers

Saint Basil the Great

Brothers Basil and Gregory were two of nine children born to Basil the Elder and Emmelia, a land-owning couple of Cappadocia.[12] An affluent province of the Empire since 191 BCE, the alpine Cappadocia was bordered on the west by the Alys River, and on the north by the Black Sea; land neighbors included Pontus to the north, Cilicia to the south, Armenia to the east, and Galatia to the west. A desolate country positioned in the far eastern part of the Empire, its major exports were horses and grain,[13] as well as olives and grapes.[14] According to sources in antiquity[15] the populations of Cappadocia were comprised of thick, grasping inhabitants—who, having been previously controlled by the Hittites and Persians,[16] largely resisted Hellenization[17]—and land-hungry magnates.[18] Largely the peasants worked the lands as serfs to emperors, aristocrats or Anatolian gods and goddesses, who were land owners of vast territories in their own right;[19] we can conclude that they likely understood themselves as living a life of grueling work that served the needs of others. Those who lived in the mountains were semi-nomadic, and fully hostile to those unlucky enough to be charged with the task of collecting local or national tribute.[20]

12. Meredith, *The Cappadocians*, 20. It has generally been assumed that Basil and Gregory came from a wealthy family; for the discussion concerning whether or not the family was wealthy, aristocratic, noble, or even senatorial, see Karayannopoulos, "St. Basil's Social Activity," 375–91. Whatever their status in life, Basil the Elder and Emmelia seem to have been good parents, and Gregory of Nazianzus, in his *Panegyric on St. Basil*, speaks highly of them (Gregory Nazianzen, *Oration* 43 [PG 36:504–5]).

13. Meredith, *The Cappadocians*, 2.

14. Holman, *The Hungry Are Dying*, 70.

15. According to Meredith, sources include the sixth-century poet Pseudo-Demodocus, in *Anthologia Lyrica Graeca* I, and Pseudo-Lucian, in *Epigram* 43. Meredith, *Cappadocians*, 8 notes 3–4.

16. Rostovtzeff, *The Social & Economic History of the Hellenistic World*, 1:573.

17. Meredith, *The Cappadocians*, 2; Holman, *The Hungry are Dying*, 27.

18. Meredith, *The Cappadocians*, 2. Land magnates of Cappadocia were particularly rapacious, to the extent that Emperor Justinian I (527–65) complained that daily he was besieged with requests from clergy and women who lost their land, and lamented that "almost all the Imperial Estate has become private property." Bury, *History of the Later Roman Empire: From the Death of Theodosius I to the Death of Justinian*, vol. 2, 341. Bury does not provide a citation for his Justinian quote.

19. Rostovtzeff, *Social and Economic History*, 1:258.

20. Ibid., 258.

While there is scholarly consensus that the peasant population was most likely illiterate, there is dispute over what would have meant with respect to reception of the orations of Cappadocia's famous bishops. Though he does not condemn them, Anthony Meridith writes that the level of illiteracy suggests that inhabitants of Cappadocia were very likely unmoved by the eloquent sermons of their high-brow bishops; on the other hand, Susan Holman, also notes that Cappadocia was "a region characterized by widespread illiteracy," but claims that the verbally gifted bishops would have been especially effective amongst such people. Either way, success in such an environment often depends on the attitude of the educated toward the uneducated; despite a lack of "book learning," the uneducated can smell contempt, and while contempt existed for the people of Cappadocia, it did not come in the orations of fourth-century Cappadocian bishops. One of the more contemptuous statements made about native Cappadocians comes from Lucian, who writes that "it would be easier to find white crows and flying tortoises than a Cappadocian who was a reputable orator."[21] Even the pronunciation of the Cappadocians came under attack when Philostratus writes that Pausanius, a sophist, "used to deliver his declamations with a coarse and heavy accent, as is the way with the Cappadocians . . . Hence he was commonly spoken of as a cook who spoiled expensive delicacies in the preparation."[22] And while such sources evoke a population of coarse agriculturalists, they also imply an elitist denigration of those peasants, which suggests to us the low value in which the inhabitants were held.

Although biblical evidence suggests that there were Christians in Cappadocia by the end of the first century,[23] Christianity in Cappadocia

---

21. Lucian, *Epigram* 43, in Philostratus, *Philostratus and Eunapius: Lives of the Sophists* (trans. Wright), 240–41, n. 2.

22. Philostratus, in *Philostratus and Eunapius*, 241–43.

23. "Peter, and apostle of Jesus Christ, to the exiles of the Dispersion in Pontus, Galatia, Cappadocia, Asia, and Bithynia . . ." (1 Peter 1:1). Eusebius also mentions Bishop Alexander of the Cappadocian see, which indicates the presence of an organized Christian community prior to the arrival of Gregory Thaumaturgus in the mid-third century (Eusebius, *The History of the Church from Christ to Constantine* (Williamson, trans.), 6:11. Meredith, *Gregory of Nyssa*, 1–2.

is credited to Gregory Thaumaturgos,[24] whose teacher was Origen.[25] Basil credits his mother and grandmother with the "conception of God" which he and his "most divinely-favoured brother Gregory"[26] received in childhood.[27] In addition to their religious tutelage, Basil (c. 330–77 or 79) was educated initially by his father Basil the Elder and later by Libanius, the famous pagan rhetorician.[28] Basil's decision to leave secular life and adopt a life of asceticism was dual in nature, for though it was accompanied by a clear understanding of his social failings, it was at the same time marked by a profound and hopeful vision:

> When I finally woke up as from a deep sleep, I saw the wonderful
> light of the Gospel's truth, and I realized how useless the wisdom
> of the transitory archons of this world is. Then I cried bitterly
> for my pitiful way of life and prayed to find my way toward an
> understanding of the pious doctrines. Before everything else I
> longed to change my ways that had been perverted on account
> of my long association with the wicked. Reading the Gospel and
> realizing that the basic prerequisites for human completion are
> the renunciation of one's fortune, the giving to the poor, and

24. Meredith, *Gregory of Nyssa*, 3. The *Life* of Gregory Thaumaturgus (c. 217–70), a native of Pontus and student of law and rhetoric, was written by Gregory of Nyssa: *In Praise of Gregory Thaumaturgus* (PG 46:893–958). In *Letter* 204, Basil refers gratefully to Gregory Thaumaturgus, former bishop of Neocaesarea (233–70) as the reason for the bond between Basil and the Neocaesareans: "And, secondly, if sharing the same teachers contributes at all greatly to union, both you and we have not only the same teachers of God's mysteries, but also the same spiritual fathers who from the beginning have laid the foundations of your church. I mean the famous Gregory" (Basil, *Letter* 204 *To the Neocaesareans*, in Deferrari [trans.], *Saint Basil, The Letters*, 3:157.

25. Meredith, *Gregory of Nyssa*, 10.

26. Basil, *Letter* 223 *Against Eustathius of Sebaste*, in Deferrari, *Saint Basil, The Letters* 3:303.

27. In *Letter* 204, Basil writes to the Neocaesareans that "what indeed could be clearly proof of our faith than that we were brought up by our grandmother, a blessed woman who came from among you? I mean the illustrious Macrina, by whom we were taught the sayings of the most blessed Gregory (as many as she herself retained, preserved to her time in unbroken memory), and who moulded and formed us while still young in the doctrines of piety," in Deferrari (trans.), *Saint Basil, The Letters*, 3:169. Further, in *Against Eustathius of Sebaste*, Basil writes that the theological training he received from his mother and grandmother was a sound foundation for later learning: "Nay, the conception of God which I received in childhood from my blessed mother and my grandmother Macrina, this, developed, have I held within me; for I did not change from one opinion to another with the maturity of reason, but I perfected the principles handed down to me by them." Basil, *Against Eustathius*, in Deferrari, 299.

28. Meredith, *Gregory of Nyssa*, 20–21; Gregory of Nazianzus provides a detailed description of Basil's education (Gregory Nazianzen, *Oration* 43 [PG 36:510–16]).

also the retiring from all worldly cares and affections, I searched to find someone else who felt the way I did, so that together we could overcome the adversities of human life. And I found many in Alexandria and the rest in Egypt . . . Palestine and Coele-Syria, and Mesopotamia.[29]

Basil's goal was not the abandonment of wealth for the purpose of entering into a life of ascesis and solitary contemplation, but a life that reflected philanthropy and spiritual *evergetism*. Like Plato's ideal upper class, Basil, freed from material distractions, would be free to devote himself to the needs of his community.[30] Basil's own testimony was enhanced by Gregory's comments about his brother's conversion in Gregory's *Life of St. Macrina*, which largely credits Macrina with Basil's spiritual transformation:

> The great Basil returned home. He was the brother of the afore-mentioned Macrina, and during all this long period, he had been receiving training in rhetoric in the schools. Macrina found that he had become excessively exalted by the idea of his own gift of oratory. He despised all those who held public office and was puffed up with pride, regarding himself as a man above the notabilities of the province. She therefore drew him too towards the ideal of philosophy, so rapidly that he renounced worldly fame. He despised the admiration which he had won through his eloquence and became, as it were, a deserter to a hard life of manual labor. Through his complete detachment from material possessions he prepared for himself a way of life in which he would be unhindered in his pursuit of virtue.[31]

Basil embraced the monastic life, became ordained, and by 370 was bishop of Caesarea,[32] an important city situated at the convergence of approximately all the major roads through Asia Minor. Despite this benefit, Cappadocia was not immune to the difficulties of the era and a famine due to poor harvests in 369 provided Basil with the opportunity to activate and cultivate a sense of social responsibility in his congregations. A man of action, he appealed to the individual sense of divine justice, and

29. Basil, *Adversus Eustathium Sebastenum* 2, in Karayannopoulos, 383.

30. Plato, *Republic* 7.521b.

31. Gregory of Nyssa, *Vita S. Macrinæ Virginis* (PG 46:959–1000); *The Life of Macrina* in *Handmaids of the Lord* (trans. Peterson), 56.

32. Rousseau, *Basil of Caesarea*, 2. While his life from boy to bishop was not nearly so tidy as these two sentences suggest, it is not for this project to question the progression of events.

never hesitated to shame the wealthy into aiding the poor.[33] In a passage from his famous *Panegyric*, Gregory of Nazianzus reports that in addition to writing sermons, Basil used word and conduct to influence the wealthier members of the community[34] to open their warehouses—if not their hearts—for the benefit of the poor:

> For by his word and advice he opened the stores of those who possessed them, and so, according to the Scripture dealt food to the hungry, and satisfied the poor with bread, and fed them in the time of dearth, and filled the hungry souls with good things. He gathered together[35] the victims of the famine with some who were but slightly recovering from it, men and women, infants, old men, every age which was in distress, and obtaining contributions of all sorts of food which can relieve famine, set before them basins of soup and such meat as was found preserved among us, on which the poor live . . . his succour of the famine gained no profit, having only one object, to win kindly feelings by kindly treatment, and to gain by his rations of corn the heavenly blessings.[36]

33. "What will you tell the Judge? You who dress up your walls and leave humans naked? You who groom and adorn your horses and will not look at your naked brother? You whose wheat rots, and yet do not feed the hungry?" Basil, *Homilia in divites* 4 (CPG 2581); González, *Faith and Wealth*, 178.

34. Karayannopoulos, after listing the variety of military and civil authorities to whom Basil addressed his letters, notes that not only is it puzzling that Basil threw his net so widely towards individuals whom he did not even know, but that Basil was—in the process—engaging in duties not previously engaged in by a bishop. Karayannopoulos claims that as Basil had abandoned wealth and status, the only thing that could have possibly influenced the elite recipients of his letters was the respect they were forced to admit for a man who so freely offered his life as a witness of the Christian ascetic ideal (Karayannopoulos, "St. Basil's Social Activity," 378–84).

35. Karayannopoulos notes that it was probably during this time that the Basiliad—Basil's "city of the poor"—originated. Rousseau writes that the system was likely already in place, but that Basil took advantage of the opportunity to make more permanent arrangements for the poor (Rousseau, *Basil of Caesarea*, 139–40, 375). See also Holman, *The Hungry Are Dying*, 74–75, for a more recent discussion of the Basiliad. The historian Sozomen writes about the "Basileias," in his *Ecclesiastical History*: "It was established by Basil, bishop of Caesarea, from whom it received its name in the beginning, and retains it until today" (Sozomen, *The Ecclesiastical History of Sozomen* [NPNF 2]), 6.34. For additional information the Basiliad and on additional Early Byzantine philanthropic institutions, see Constantelos, *Byzantine Philanthropy and Social Welfare*, 152–84. For the influence of the eccentric Eustathius of Sebaste on Basil's ascetic method and philosophy, see Rousseau, *Basil of Caesarea*, 74–76.

36. Gregory of Nazianzus, *Oratio* 43 (PG 36:541–48). Gregory of Nyssa also defends Basil's generosity (against Eunomius), writing that Basil "ungrudgingly spent

Unlike wealthy donations of aristocracy anxious for earthly praise, Basil's actions promote not a mortal but a spiritual distinction; his renunciation of wealth and distribution to the needy take to a logical conclusion Plato's aspiration for the individual to seek the welfare of the community against one's individual desires. As stated in Chapter Two, in an environment of philanthropy the leaders are from among those "who are really rich, not in gold, but in the wealth that makes happiness—a good and wise life."[37] True wealth is visible in the actions of a righteous person.

During the period of famine Basil wrote three sermons emphasizing that surplus wealth is to be shared with others.[38] Rousseau, who dates these sermons to 369, writes that they were weak and abstract, with Basil pointing to the famine as punishment for the collective sins of the community.[39] F. X. Murphy, on the other hand, claims that within these sermons "Basil's moral teaching on social and economic justice is most effectively expressed."[40] In these and other sermons, Basil offers more than chastisement or moral instruction, he offers a concrete conclusion: famine is not the problem, the problem is greed.[41] With this came a stunningly simple piece of advice: if the rich—whose wealth alone cannot even produce a drop of rain[42]—would share with the poor such misery could be avoided.[43]

---

upon the poor his patrimony even before he was a priest, and most of all in the time of the famine, during which he was a ruler of the Church, though still a priest in the rank of presbyters; and afterwards did not hoard even what remained to him." Gregory of Nyssa, *Against Eunomius*, book I.10, in *Against Eunomius*, 45. See also Gregory of Nyssa *In laudem Basillii* 17, in *Encomium of Saint Gregory, Bishop of Nyssa, on His Brother Saint Basil, Archbishop of Caesarea*.

37. Plato, *Republic* 7.521b, 145.

38. Basil, *Homilies 322, In illud dictum evangelii secundum Lucam: "Destruam horrea mea, et maiora aedificabo"; itemque de avaritia* (PG 31:261–78); 325, *Homilia dicta tempore famis et siccitatis* (PG 31:303–28); and 336, *Homilia quod Deus non est auctor malorum* (PG 31:329–54); in Rousseau, *Basil of Caesarea* 137–38.

39. Rousseau, *Basil of Caesarea*, 137–38.

40. Murphy, "Moral and Ascetical Doctrine in St. Basil," 320–26.

41. Holman also disagrees with Rousseau, claiming that Basil's sermon encouraged a "ceremonial economic exchange" (Holman, *The Hungry Are Dying*, 96). By this Holman means Basil encouraged the wealthy to shift their sights from the profits gained in the market to the starving bodies of those who are neither profiting nor shopping, but dying in the market.

42. Basil, *Homilia dicta tempore famis et siccitatis*, in Holman, *The Hungry Are Dying*, 187. In another portion of the homily he says, with respect to gold, that "you gathered it and still you lack one thing: the power to feed yourself."

43. "The superfluous must be distributed among the needy" (Basil, *Homily 322, In illud dictum evangelii secundum Lucam: "Destruam horrea mea, et maiora aedificabo"; itemque de avaritia*, in González, *Faith and Wealth*, 177).

Even worse than their stingy behavior, the rich seek to profit from the destitute nature of the poor by hoarding their supplies[44] and engaging in unjust lending practices, and what more than this could be cause for God's wrath? Basil's solution consists of a process of repentance on the part of the citizen, a process which begins with recognition of sin, continues with heartfelt and tearful repentance, and, finally, a conscious effort to relieve the poor in their misery:

> This is the right response for those who serve. This is repentance for those alienated by sin. Yet we sin much and repent carelessly and slothfully. Who in his prayer is pouring out tears to grasp a thunderstorm and seasonable rains? Who, to wipe out sin, imitates the blessed David who waters his bed with lamentations? ... Who nourishes the fatherless child so that God might nurture for us the orphaned grain that is oppressed by the impotence of the wind? Who provides for a widow who is distressed by life's difficulties, so that the necessary food might be distributed?[45]

The final step, Basil insists, is to turn away from the market and separate oneself from the seduction of greed and the distraction that it causes in one's heart.[46] The ability to separate oneself from sterile coin will release God's fertile favor, which up until now has been prevented from natural augmentation by the prosperity of unnatural products: "Destroy the unjust account books, that sin might be dissolved. Without the oppressive contract of usury that earth might bear appropriately. For when copper, gold, and inert substances multiply contrary to nature, then that which is naturally fecund becomes barren, condemned to fruitlessness, as vengeance on the established practices. God is right to be angry."[47] Basil has not asked the Christian community to do anything that he has not

---

44. "Our sheep multiply, yet the naked outnumber them. The storehouses are crowded with narrow corridors with abundant reserves, yet we have no mercy on those who mourn" (Basil, *Homilia dicta tempore famis et siccitatis*, in Holman, *The Hungry Are Dying*, 185).

45. Basil, *Homilia dicta tempore famis et siccitatis*, in Holman, *The Hungry Are Dying*, 187.

46. "O men, except for a few, you devote yourselves to market profit; you women collude with them in their materialism. Few remain at prayer with me, and these are distracted, yawning, constantly looking around and waiting for the cantor to finish the psalms, so they will be dismissed, as if from prison, from the church, and the required prayer" (Basil, *Homilia dicta tempore famis et siccitatis* in Holman, *The Hungry Are Dying*, 185–86).

47. Basil, *Homilia dicta tempore famis et siccitatis* in Holman, *The Hungry Are Dying*, 185–86.

already demanded of the monastic; in *Discourse on Ascetical Discipline: How the Monk Should Be Equipped*[48] he reminds monks to be preoccupied with good works and deeds: "Swear not at all, nor lend money for interest, nor sell grain and wine and oil for profit."[49] In this way, by refusing to entangle themselves in obligations of the secular world they will "heap up treasure in heaven."[50] Selling and lending are not problematic, but doing so for profit destroys the community. Greedy Christians with misplaced devotion fail to aid the needy while they build up an earthly account for fear of someday being in want; they have chosen what is fleeting over that which is permanent. Though Basil condemns those who prey on the poor, he also implores them to turn their misplaced lust from the material to the spiritual. How much better, Basil would claim, to be seen in heaven as one who has functioned as a physician of society rather than a disease: "Then the whole people, standing about our common judge, will call you nourisher, benefactor, and all those other titles that attach to philanthropy."[51] Though harsh on the wealthy and wicked, neither does he neglect to gently chastise the poor, and he cautions them to consider that their status does not exempt them from charitable actions, even though one may be down to the last loaf.[52]

---

48. Basil, *Discourse on Ascetical Discipline: How the Monk Should be Equipped*, in *Saint Basil: Ascetical Works* (PG 31:647–52), in Wagner, *Saint Basil: Ascetical Works* 9:33–66.

49. Basil, *Discourse on Ascetical Discipline: How the Monk Should Be Equipped*, in Wagner, *Saint Basil: Ascetical Works* 9:34.

50. Ibid.

51. Basil, *Homily on Wealth* (PG 31:265), in Rousseau, *Basil of Caesarea*, 139; see also, Siepierski, "Poverty and Spirituality," 322–24. In *Homilia dicta tempore famis et siccitatis* Basil writes that at the Final Judgment those who have fed the poor will hold primacy of honor: "The supplier of bread will be called before everyone else; the kind and bountiful will be escorted to life before all the other righteous." On the other hand, the miserly "will be handed over to the fire before all other sinner" (Basil, *Homilia dicta tempore famis et siccitatis*, in Holman, *The Hungry Are Dying*, 191).

52. "Are you poor? There is someone much poorer than you . . . Do not shrink from giving of the little you have; do not treat your calamity as if it is worse than the common suffering. Even if you possess only one loaf of bread, and the beggar stands at the door, bring the one loaf out of the storeroom" (Basil, *Homilia dicta tempore famis et siccitatis*, in Holman, *The Hungry Are Dying*, 189–90).

Basil is equally severe and hopeful in two homilies written on the subjects of detachment[53] and envy,[54] two phenomena which, like usury, do not discriminate between the monastic and the lay, but plague all alike. In *On Detachment From Worldly Goods* Basil addresses the transitory nature of the wealth of the rich,[55] for such pleasures are "absolutely foreign to our nature, superfluous, and not capable of being really possessed by anyone."[56] The only possession worth acquiring is one's own soul, housed in one's own body, and Basil equates "wicked and avaricious men" who seek to gain more at another's expense to the "Enemy [who] lurks in secret and spreads his nets for our destruction."[57]

Destruction is easily wrought by the progenitor of greed—the envious one—who is more to be pitied than feared as he grieves over his "brother's joy and . . . cannot endure the sight of other's blessings."[58] Equivalent to usurers, the envious seek the downfall of society by infecting their neighbors with a poison until their plumpness "wastes away under the gaze of the envious, as if washed away by a destructive flood."[59] The envious are

53. Basil, *Homily* 21, *On Detachment From Worldly Goods and Concerning the Conflagration Which Occurred in the Environs of the Church* (PG 31:539–64), in Wagner (trans.), *Saint Basil: Ascetical Works* 9:487–505.

54. Basil, *Homily* 11, *Concerning Envy* (PG 31:371–86), in Wagner, *Saint Basil: Ascetical Works* 9:463–74.

55. "Even if certain individuals should gather together an immense store of gold in this life, it would not remain permanently in their possession . . . it would either escape them while they were yet alive, passing into the hands of persons stronger than they, or it would presently be lost to them at their death, its nature not being such that it could accompany them at their departure hence" (Basil, *On Detachment from Worldly Goods*, in Wagner, *St. Basil: Ascetical Works* 9:492.

56. Ibid., 494.

57. Ibid., 488. In Basil's *Homily* 7, *Creation of Crawling Creatures* from the *Hexaemeron*, Basil compares the aquatic food chain to the divine retribution visited upon the rapacious: "The majority of fish eat one another, and the smaller among them are food for the larger. If it ever happens that the victor over a smaller becomes the prey of another, they are both carried into the stomach of the last. Now, what else do we men do in the oppression of our inferiors? How does he differ from the last fish, who with a greedy love of riches swallows up the weak in the folds of his insatiable avarice? . . . Beware, lest the same end as that of the fish awaits you—somewhere a fishhook, or a snare, or a net. Surely, if we have committed many unjust deeds, we shall not escape the final retribution" (Basil, *Homily* 7 [PG 30:937–48], Way (trans.), *Saint Basil: Exegetical Homilies*, 109. Basil considers the hierarchy of the animal world as both a superior paradigm and a warning for the human world; what is natural in their world is immoral in ours.

58. Basil, *Concerning Envy*, in Wagner (trans.), *St. Basil: Ascetical Works*, 464.

59. Ibid., 469–70.

recognized by their features, Basil writes, with their "eyes [which are] dry and lustreless; their cheeks, sunken, their brow, contracted; their mind, distorted and confused by their passion and incapable of making valid judgments and in handling their affairs."[60] Much like Plutarch's vultures,[61] the envious consume what is already rotten. Basil's advice is profoundly practical: recognizing that compulsive factors are at work, he urges the greedy to turn their preoccupation for gain towards that which might lead to salvation rather than destruction. He urges that one combat envy by turning the mind towards the acquisition of virtue rather than material goods: "At all events, if you are desirous of glory and wish to outshine the crowd and if, for this reason, you cannot bear to hold second place, turn your aspirations, as one would change the course of a stream, toward the acquisition of virtue."[62]

A radical change in behavior is customarily the result of a radical change in attitude, but sometimes the reverse is true as well. Basil, who experienced his own revolutionary conversion and who recognized the need to rid himself of the wealth which stood as a barrier to his relationship with God, must have been optimistic about the possibility of change in the hearts of the greedy. Surely such change could be brought about by the adoption of virtuous habits[63] to replace nefarious practices, such as lending with interest, or other sinful behavior.

The adoption of virtuous habits requires that the sinner participate actively in their rehabilitation. The first of Basil's "Canonical Letters"[64] to his former disciple and bishop of Iconium Amphilochius addresses necessary penitence for an assortment of sins, including those who extract usury, those who murder, those who engage in serial marriages, and adulterers. Echoing the seventeenth canon of Nicaea,[65] Basil makes the condition that

---

60. Ibid., 470.

61. Plutarch, in Fowler (trans.), *Love Stories*, 335.

62. Basil, *Concerning Envy*, in Wagner, *St. Basil: Ascetical Works*, 9:473.

63. Holman writes extensively about "Redemptive Almsgiving" in *The Hungry Are Dying* and in "The Entitled Poor" While almsgiving forms a portion of both Basil and Gregory's sermons, it shall not be considered as extensively as it is in Holman's text because this project is concerned primarily with usury; therefore I will only address almsgiving as Basil and Gregory connect it with usury.

64. Basil, *Homily 188, To Amphilochius, on the Canons*; *199, To Amphilochius, on the Canons*; *217, To Amphilochius, on the Canons*, in Deferrari, *Saint Basil, the Letters* 5–48; 103–34; 241–66. These letters were written in 374.

65. *Canon* 17: "If anyone shall receive usury or one hundred fifty percent, he shall be cast forth and deposed, according to this decree of the Church." "The First Ecumenical Council: The First Council of Nice," NPNF 14.36.

"he who takes usury, if he consents to spend his unjust gain upon poor, and thereafter to be freed of the disease of avarice, shall be received into holy orders."[66] Unlike the canon, Basil's statement is considerably more severe and humane at the same time: the individual may gain the favor of the Church and receive holy orders despite the fact that he has sinned against the community; yet, the individual must first demonstrate that he is freed from the sin of avarice by parting with his "unjust gain." This is not a question of turning the money over to the Church for the Church to determine its rightful use, but the usurer himself must aid in his personal rehabilitation by dismantling his golden shackles.

Gregory of Nyssa

Possibly due to financial strains placed on the family by the death of Basil the Elder, the younger Gregory (c. 335–95) was not endowed with the privileged education of his elder brother. Therefore the education of Gregory, according to his own letters, fell to Basil.[67] In addition, Gregory was highly influenced by both the intellectual culture and ascetic lifestyle of his elder sister Macrina the Younger, whose *Life*[68] he composed, and whose deathbed conversation provided the *mise en scène* for his momentous *On the Soul and the Resurrection*.[69] Also unlike brother Basil, Gregory differed in that he was not a monk, he married,[70] and he was not the most successful bishop of his see.[71]

---

66. Basil, *Homily* 188, *To Amphilochius, on the Canons*, 14, in Deferrari, *Saint Basil, the Letters*, 199.

67. Gregory of Nyssa, *Letter* 13.5 (MG 46:1049A); Meredith expresses doubt that Gregory could have received such vast knowledge in philosophy and theology solely from Basil, and adds that if such a statement were true, that it "says much for the teaching abilities of the one and the docility of the other" (Meredith, *The Cappadocians*, 52).

68. See note 29.

69. Gregory of Nyssa, *De Anima et Resurrectione Dialogus* (PG 46:11–160).

70. A woman believed to have been Gregory's wife is mentioned in Gregory of Nazianzus's *Letter* 197.6; Gregory of Nazianzus writes that he had heard of "the passing of our saintly and blessed 'sister,'" and referred to Theosebeia as "a saint and the wife of a priest" (Gregory of Nazianzus, *Letter* 197, in Barrois, *The Fathers Speak*, 216).

71. See Basil, *Letter* 58, *To Gregory, His Brother*, in Deferrari, vol. 1, 357–61, and *Letter C, To Eusebius, Bishop of Samosata*, in Deferrari, *Saint Basil, the Letters* 2:183–87, for conflict between the brothers. See also Meredith, *Gregory of Nyssa*, 4.

Although in his youth Gregory had desired to be a priest,[72] sometime after the year 362 he chose to follow in his father's footsteps and adopt the life of a teacher of rhetoric, for which he was later criticized by family friend Gregory of Nazianzus.[73] He was eventually persuaded the leave his secular job and retire to a monastic foundation in Pontus,[74] though there is no evidence that he led a traditionally "ascetic" lifestyle.[75] When Basil was elevated to Bishop of Caesarea in 370, he successfully persuaded his brother to accept the bishopric of Nyssa in 372, which Gregory accepted reluctantly.[76] In retrospect this might have been considered a mistake by Basil, who was attempting to increase his influence and surround himself with trustworthy allies by appointing his brother to Nyssa. Further, Gregory's problems with management, leadership, heretics and finances may have led Basil later to regret his choice.

While Gregory might have floundered as an ecclesiastical authority in the early years of his career, he flourished as a theologian and philosopher[77] in the later half, emerging as one of the dominant personalities of the early Christian era. His contributions to the world of Christian thought include the refutation of heresy,[78] dogmatic theology,[79] and spirituality.[80] And though additional works stand in the shadows of these theological pillars, they are in no way *over*shadowed by them, for his sermons and homilies have something different but no less important to offer: they are

72. Graef (trans.), *The Lord's Prayer; The Beatitudes*, 3.

73. "You had rather be thought of as a rhetor than as a Christian" (Gregory of Nazianzus, *Letter 2*, in Meredith, *Gregory of Nyssa*, 3–4). Meredith does not give any citation information about this well-known quote.

74. Ibid., 4.

75. Daniélou, *From Glory to Glory*, 3.

76. Roth, *On the Soul and Resurrection*, 9; See also, Gregory of Nyssa, *De Vita Moysis* (PG 44:298–430). Two years earlier, against another Gregory's wishes, Basil had placed Gregory of Nazianzus as bishop of Sasima. (Daniélou, *From Glory to Glory*, 3).

77. Meredith puts the situation quite succinctly: "Gregory's importance for posterity, however, is not to be sought in his ecclesiastico-political addresses and activities. It is as a writer, and above all as one whose views change importantly under certain external influences, that he claims our attention" (Meredith, *The Cappadocians*, 53).

78. Gregory of Nyssa, *Contra Eunomium* (PG 45:243–1122).

79. Gregory of Nyssa, *Oratio catechetica* (PG 45:11–106).

80. Gregory of Nyssa, *De Vita Moysis, De virginitate,* or *On Virginity* (PG 46:317–416); *De Anima et Resurrectione Dialogus,* or *On the Soul and Resurrection* (PG 46:11–160).

soundly practical, and reflect a thorough understanding of the difficulties of ordinary human life.[81]

One would be hard-pressed to find a more ordinary human difficulty than poverty, and surely Nyssa—just to the west of Caesarea—experienced similar economic conditions. As has become evident, debt is the ugly stepsister of poverty, and Gregory addresses debt of a material and a spiritual nature in his sermons on the Lord's Prayer. In the fifth sermon of this collection, *Forgive us our debts, as we also forgive our debtors,*[82] Gregory asserts that an individual who is capable of forgiving the debts of others is no longer reflecting human nature in his actions, but godly ones, for in the forgiveness of debts the lender has performed a task which is the prerogative of God alone to do: "If a man imitates in his own life the characteristics of the Divine Nature, he becomes somehow that which he visibly imitates."[83] For Gregory, the forgiveness offered from one person to another returns the forgiver to the state of original creation when there was no petty bickering over ownership. Hence this portion of the prayer functions as a reminder to those praying that actions *previous to praying* dictate how God should look upon this petition for their own mercy.[84]

The greater portion of the sermon is concerned with debt that the individual sinner owes to God as a result of having turned from the beauty of the Divine to gaze instead on shameful sin.[85] Gregory cautions those who might boldly claim that as they had not offended against the Com-

81. Hilda Graef writes that the intensely practical nature of Gregory's homilies are one of their most striking characteristics: "In fact, his mystical theology rests on a solid basis not only of sound dogmatic theology, but also of a wide acquaintance with ordinary human life and non-theological scholarship, which is as characteristic of him as it is of his brother Basil" (Graef [trans.], *The Lord's Prayer. The Beatitudes,* 7).

82. Gregory of Nyssa, *Sermon 5, Forgive us our debts, as we forgive our debtors. And lead us not into temptation. But deliver us from evil,* in Graef (trans.), *The Lord's Prayer. The Beatitudes,* 71–85; Gregory of Nyssa, *Oratio* 5 (PG 44:1178–94).

83. Gregory of Nyssa, *Sermon 5,* in Graef (trans.), *The Lord's Prayer. The Beatitudes,* 71. The doctrine of deification manifests itself briefly in this passage, in which the emphasis is placed on the personal and organic union which occurs between God and an individual when one engages in actions of a benevolent nature. For scriptural references to deification, see John 17:22: "The glory that you have given me I have given them, so that they may be one, as we are one." See also 2 Peter 1:4: "Thus he has given us, through these things, his precious and very great promises, so that through them you may escape from the corruption that is in the world because of lust, and may become participants in the divine nature."

84. Gregory of Nyssa, *Sermon 5,* in Graef (trans.), *The Lord's Prayer. The Beatitudes,* 71.

85. Ibid., 74–75.

mandments, the phrase in question might not apply: all who are dressed
as Adam in the garments of skin, all who put hope in transitory fig leaves
sewn together have rejected Divine garments for apparel of ephemeral luxuries, honors, and reputation: "Having been wrapped up in these things,
let us imitate the Prodigal Son after he had endured the long affliction of
feeding the swine. When, like him, we return to ourselves and remember the Heavenly Father, we may rightly use these words: 'Forgive us our
debts.'"[86] Though praying for forgiveness for debts, the words of such an
individual, though they are a "Moses" or a "Samuel," are ineffectual unless
they themselves have already demonstrated the very mercy for which they
plead.[87] Gregory writes that the unforgiving sinner who pleads for mercy
might receive from the Judge the following chilly response:

> You ask me to love men, and yourself do not give love to your
> neighbour? You ask to have debts forgiven, how can you strangle
> your debtor? You pray that I may blot out what is written against
> you, and you preserve carefully the acknowledgements of those
> who owe you something? You ask to have your debts cancelled,
> but you increase what you have lent by taking interest? Your
> debtor is in prison while you are in church? He is in distress
> on account of his debts, but you think it is right that your debt
> should be forgiven? Your prayer cannot be heard because the
> voice of him who suffers is drowning it.[88]

If God forgives, we should also forgive; what audacity to accept
benefits of grace without bestowing the same. Gregory points to a vivid
example of this in the previously discussed Matthew 18:23–35, in which a
miserly servant is forgiven great debt, but, in turn, refuses to remit a minor
debt owed to him.[89] The actions of a servant or slave against the "superior"
mirror those of the human before God; therefore, Gregory writes, look
beyond social status imposed by irrational forces and recognize that all
humans are equal in nature. It is not just poverty, but the response of the
wealthy to poverty that distorts the creation. Therefore, proper understanding of shared humanity results in a goodness which moves both individuals involved towards the original state of purity; acts of benevolence
towards the needy clarify the divine image: "For as you practice goodness

86. Ibid., 77.
87. Ibid.
88. Ibid., 80.
89. Ibid., 80–81.

you are clothed in Christ and as you become like Christ you become like God."[90]

Becoming like God is difficult for persons who set pleasure as a goal, and poverty sermons of both Basil and Gregory indicate that they were determined to strike a blow against the imbalance of gluttony and starvation in their Cappadocian communities. In his sermon titled *Concerning Beneficence* Gregory reminds his audience that for the past two days he has spoken to them against the "pleasures of the mouth and the belly."[91] But rather than continue in that vein, that as their behavior has indicated to Gregory that his "council was not in vain,"[92] and therefore he shall proceed with greater, more mature teachings, as is appropriate to their spiritual bearing. While he is pleased with their change in behavior, at the same time he expresses concern with what lies behind the façade of their ascesis; in addition to self-control over food, he wants them to advance righteous behavior beyond the dinner plates and apply it to how they view their neighbor's possessions and profit:

> Practice self-control in your appetite for other people's belongings! Renounce dishonest profits! Starve to death your greed for Mammon! Let there be nothing in your house that has been acquired by violence or theft. What good is it to keep meat out of your mouth if you bite your brother with wickedness? What good does it serve you to observe a strict frugality at home if you unjustly steal from the poor? What kind of piety teaches you to drink water while you hatch plots and drink the blood of a man you have shamefully cheated? Judas, after all, fasted along with the eleven, but failed to master his greed; his salvation gained nothing by fasting.[93]

Though the concept of "usury" is not explicit in this brief passage, what is evident is that Gregory draws a parallel between unjust business practices and grave sin. "Dishonest profits" is a clear indicator of usury, and can refer either to excessive interest or to other forms of theft, such as overcharging on products or services. Taking a "bite" out of one's brother is reminiscent of one of the aforementioned Hebrew words for usury, *nèsèk*,

90. Gregory of Nyssa, *In verba "faciamus hom."* 1, in González, *Faith and Wealth*, 180.

91. Gregory of Nyssa, *Concerning Beneficence*, in Holman, *The Hungry Are Dying*, 193.

92. Ibid.

93. Ibid.

meaning a literal "bite," as in the debtor being "bitten" by the lender.[94] To end this censure of the incongruity of outward ascesis but inward greed, Gregory reminds the audience that the infamous Judas was once held in the inner circle of Christ's ministry, and yet all the good works of Judas—service, fasting and careful administration over the common purse—all were useless, for the end result was that eventually greed overwhelmed his soul and captured Judas's salvation.

In a more pointed text against those who gouge the poor, Gregory's *Fourth Homily* in his *Commentary on Ecclesiastes*[95] takes its cue from the second chapter, in which Ecclesiastes[96] attempts to create happiness for himself by refusing nothing for his pleasure. Gregory sadly concludes that abundance of wealth does not guarantee that one "will thereby become wise, sagacious, reflective, learned, a friend of God, prudent, pure, passion-free, detached and aloof from all that draws him towards evil;"[97] neither does it make a man "physically strong, pleasant to look at, extending life for many centuries, free from ageing, disease and pain, and all the things sought for in the life of the flesh."[98] Rather, he claims, he sees "many endowed with such wealth living in a pitiful state of health."[99] Gold, Gregory notes, might transfer its luster to our bodies, but it cannot cover a deformity or heal an ailment.[100] His text initially reflects pity for people

94. Neufeld, "Prohibitions against Loans," 355.

95. Gregory of Nyssa, *Fourth Homily, In Ecclesiasten* (PG 44:615–754), in Hall and Moriarty.

96. Gregory refers to the author as "Ecclesiastes," therefore this text will as well.

97. Gregory of Nyssa, *Homily 4*, in Hall and Moriarty (trans.), *Gregory of Nyssa, Homilies on Ecclesiastes*, 76–77. Aristotle claimed that the abundance of wealth did not guarantee that one would not die of hunger. In his *Politics* he writes that when barter ceased to be an effective means of exchange, individuals constructed a mechanism which would enable them to acquire what they needed: small metals, first measured by weight and size, and later imprinted with an image. Wealth came to be assumed by some to be the accumulation of these coins, but others, including Aristotle, shunned the notion that an abundance of such coins could mean one is wealthy (Aristotle. *Politics* 1257).

98. Gregory of Nyssa, *Homily 4*, in Hall and Moriarty (trans.), *Homilies on Ecclesiastes*, 77.

99. Ibid.

100. "Even if the gold is well-made and shaped, and even if you set in it stones which are green or fiery-bright, the person does not any more for that assume the appearance of what is attached to him, but if there is some blemish on his face or if he is without some feature—an eye lost, or a check gouged out in an ugly scar—the deformity remains in his appearance, not at all concealed by the gleam of gold; and if someone happens to be in some bodily pain, the stuff brings him no comfort in

who put their faith in material possessions, asserting that they must surely not be of sound mind; if they were, they would not place such importance on an object which—in the dark—is indistinguishable from lead.[101] Further proof that the avaricious are not of sound mind is their inability to distinguish wrong from right behavior when it comes to the possession of such objects: "If, therefore, for right-thinking people it would be a kind of curse to acquire the properties of this inanimate stuff, what is the mindless frenzy over the acquisition of things whose goal is futility, so that for this reason those who are driven mad with the desire for riches even commit murders and robbery?"[102] In sum, in the dark, the avaricious person can no more distinguish sin from virtue as they can gold from lead, and therefore their greed has resulted in the birth [τόκος] of evil thoughts, the agent of subsequent sins: envy, robbery, murder, usury.[103] This is not the first time that the usurer has been lumped into the same category as the murderer,[104] and Gregory's tone becomes less sympathetic as he describes the role of the usurer in the downfall of the poor: "What a misuse of words! 'Child' (τόκος <= interest>) becomes a name for robbery. What a sour marriage! What an evil union, which nature knows not, but which the vice of the covetous invented between inanimate parties! What intolerable pregnancies, from which such a 'child' is produced!"[105]

In an interesting play on the word τόκος, Gregory explores the perversity surrounding the fertility of an infertile object. For Gregory, there is only one way to properly reproduce, and that is if the parents of what is begotten are properly ordered; only animate creatures can reproduce as only animate beings have male and female, and God has fairly demanded

---

his distress" (Gregory of Nyssa, *Homily* 4, in Hall and Moriarty [trans.], *Homilies on Ecclesiastes* 78).

101. "'But fire goes out,' he says, 'and the sun sets, and the beauty of the bright display is not displayed.' Tell me, what is the difference in the dark between gold and lead?" (Gregory of Nyssa, *Homily* 4, in Hall and Moriarty [trans.], *Homilies on Ecclesiastes*, 77–78).

102. Ibid., 79.

103. "What is the difference between getting someone else's property by seizing it through covert housebreaking or taking possession of the goods of a passer-by by murdering him, and acquiring what is not one's own by extracting interest?" (ibid., 79).

104. For previous connections between usury and other nefarious practices, see chapter 2.

105. Gregory of Nyssa, *Homily* 4, in Hall and Moriarty (trans.), *Gregory of Nyssa, Homilies on Ecclesiastes*, 79.

their reproductive activity with an order to "increase and multiply."[106] It follows that the reproduction of inanimate objects—objects which cannot be defined as either male or female—cannot produce acceptable offspring, as they cannot be properly ordered.[107] Because reproduction is attempted where no true reproduction is possible, τόκος, or interest, is therefore conceived by corruption and delivered in hate: "This is the 'child' with which greed was in labour, and to which wickedness gave birth, and whose midwife is miserliness."[108] Further, the usurer denies being "pregnant in the wallet,"[109] sufficient proof that he is swollen in sin.

Gregory's final thoughts on usury and the usurer are more vitriolic than what came before, and he does not end on a hopeful note, unlike Basil's texts above. Gregory compares the "benefits" of usury to the extinguishing of a flame with oil, to a hook concealed by attractive bait, and the usurer to a fish flayed by misfortune.[110] Finally, he identifies the irony that those who cloak theft in contracts are praised for their so-called humanitarian actions: "If someone takes someone else's money by force, or steals it secretly, he is called a violent criminal or a burglar or something like that; but the one who advertises his felony in financial agreements, and who provides evidence of his own cruelty, and who enforces his crimes by contracts, is called a philanthropist and a benefactor and a saviour and all the worthiest of names."[111] Gregory ends this section with a return to Scripture, quoting from Ecclesiastes that "I gathered for me both silver and gold."[112] In doing so he reminds his audience that statements such as these are not included in Scripture as affirmation of greed, but as dem-

106. Genesis 1:22, 28; Gregory of Nyssa, *Homily 4*, in Hall and Moriarty (trans.), *Gregory of Nyssa, Homilies on Ecclesiastes*, 79.

107. Aristotle disagreed with the ancient belief that dead matter could contain within itself some degree of fertility. See chapter 2.

108. Gregory of Nyssa, *Homily 4*, in Hall and Moriarty (trans.), *Gregory of Nyssa, Homilies on Ecclesiastes*, 79.

109. Ibid. This is also known in Basil's *Homilia in psalmum* 14: "He swears up and down, even calling down curses on himself, that he is at a complete loss for funds, and that he too is searching for someone from whom to procure a loan . . . He confirms the falsehood with an oath, thus acquiring perjury as an evil fringe benefit of misanthropy" (PG 29:265–68), in Schroeder, *On Social Justice*, 90.

110. "It is then he reaches out his hand full of money, as the line reaches out the hook concealed in the bait, and the victim, snapping at his momentary prosperity, disgorges all his hidden inner parts with the hook when it is pulled." Gregory of Nyssa, *Homily 4*, in Hall and Moriarty (trans.), *Gregory of Nyssa, Homilies on Ecclesiastes*, 80.

111. Gregory of Nyssa, *Homily 4*, in ibid.

112. Ecclesiastes 2:8.

onstration that such behavior came to nothing for those who engage in single-minded acquisition of wealth. Through such passages many might learn to guard themselves against such evil, and "pass unscathed by places infested with robbers and wild animals through the previous knowledge of others previously imperiled there."[113] Perhaps, knowing the experience of Ecclesiastes, even the usurer can turn his former shame to glory.

Far too briefly, I have traced some of the themes found in Gregory and Basil's writings regarding poverty, debt and usury as they are distinguished in a few selections outside of their sermons specific to usury. To a certain extent these fragments are able to reflect the Cappadocian writers' ascetic ideas and ideals. First, both Gregory and Basil understand wealth to be ultimately transitory and useless; ultimately, the object of money itself cannot produce what is truly needed, such as healing, relief, rain, or salvation.[114] Second, the brothers both urge the wealthy to turn a zeal for consumption of earthly treasure to heavenly virtues: Basil outwardly by adoption of virtuous actions and Gregory inwardly by recognition of Christ in both lender and debtor, self and other. Third, they both insist on public restitution for the sinner: Basil through virtuous actions, and Gregory through verbal disavowal. Finally, while they are intensely harsh on the usurer, they never condemn the usurer entirely, but always leave room in any reproof for the possibility of rehabilitation of the sake of salvation of the sinful soul. The following section charts whether similarities continue—and whether condemnation is coupled with hopefulness—in the two sermons that deal exclusively with usury.

Homily 12: A Psalm of David against Usurers

Basil Repays His Debt

Basil's *Homilia in psalmum* 14 begins with acknowledgement of his own debt, in which he describes himself as a "good-natured debtor"[115] to his audience, a shrewd portend of his theme. The previous day he had spoken on Psalm 14, but due to time constraints he had neglected to finish his sermon. But because he understands the "this brief verse concerns matters

113. Gregory of Nyssa, *Homily* 4, in Hall and Moriarty (trans.), *Gregory of Nyssa, Homilies on Ecclesiastes*, 80.

114. And neither—according to Gregory—can the outward renunciation of wealth bring these about.

115. Basil, *Homilia in psalmum* 14 (PG 29:265) in Schroeder, *On Social Justice*, 89.

of great interest to us"[116] with which his members struggle and which this small passage addresses, omitting even the smallest portion of the Psalm would diminish its importance. The actual degree of significance is indicated by the layering of biblical passages which uphold a position he has not yet even established: in addition to quoting twice the portion of the Psalm which concerns usury, Basil identifies five additional passages against usury: Ezekiel 22:12; Deuteronomy 23:19; Jeremiah 9:6; Psalm 54:12; and Matthew 5:42. A glut of biblical quotations at the beginning of his work implies a strong scriptural foundation; surprisingly, this is not the case, nor does it appear that Scripture is even the sole foundation for Basil's homily, though he uses it liberally throughout his text, as will be later noted. But while Maloney remarks that Basil's text is marked by influences of Aristotle[117] and Philo of Alexandria,[118] a close reading suggests that it was Plutarch who made the greatest impression on the Cappadocian bishop. In the nineteenth century, Eugene Fialon noted the similarities, providing a side-by-side examination of seven passages from Basil's *Homily* and Plutarch's "That We Ought Not To Borrow" from *Moralia* in his *Étude historique et littéraire sur Saint Basile suivie de l'hexameron*.[119] Fialon's conclusion—which was summarily dismissed by Giet[120]—is that prior to delivering his homily Basil read and removed portions of Plutarch's treatise against debtors.[121] But, Fialon asserts, the bishop does not reproduce Plutarch verbatim, but introduces some significant differences to the text: primarily, Basil removed the mythology and secular history inserted by Plutarch and replaced it with biblical truth.[122] Despite this structural change, and though Basil's homily is more lively, animated and sympathetic to the misfortunate person,[123] it is in the end, Fialon claims, Plutarch who speaks from the Christian pulpit through the mouth of Ba-

---

116. Ibid.

117. Maloney, "The Teaching of the Fathers on Usury," 248.

118. Ibid., 249.

119. Fialon, *Étude historique et littéraire sur Saint Basile suivie de l'hexameron*, 191–95. Portions of the text in which Basil mirrors Plutarch will be noted as they are met.

120. Giet, *Les idées et l'action sociales de saint Basile*, 121–22. See also Giet, "De Saint Basile à Saint Ambroise," 120.

121. Fialon, *Étude historique et littéraire sur Saint Basile suivie de l'hexameron*, 191.

122. "La mythologie et l'histoire profane ont disparu dans l'homélie pour faire place à la Bible" (Fialon, *Étude historique et littéraire sur Saint Basile suivie de l'hexameron*, 195).

123. Fialon, *Étude historique et littéraire sur Saint Basile suivie de l'hexameron*, 195.

sil.[124] As Basil's audience has received a properly Christian ethical position concerning wealth and specifically usury, one wonders why such a notion as Plutarch's influence should be problematic to Giet, who works hard to demonstrate Basil's scriptural basis for his position. As stated above, Giet dismisses Fialon's claim as "not without obvious exaggeration,"[125] and eventually settles with Basil's main scriptural passage—from Psalm 14—and legislation of the Council of Nicaea. Two paragraphs after the discharge of Fialon and a list of Christian authors who echo the scriptural condemnations in their works,[126] Giet admits: "It is difficult to know if Basil knew some of these texts since he does not quote any; but he was not unaware of—and perhaps we have here the reason for which, among all the texts of the Old Testament, he was attached to the commentary of Psalm 14—the seventeenth canon of Nicaea against clerics who took to usury . . ."[127] Therefore, this chapter will proceed from the understanding that the spirit of Plutarch sat to the right of Basil as he composed his sermon, and that Plutarch's "That We Ought Not to Borrow" functioned as the intellectual—if not spiritual—inspiration for Basil's *Homily*. While Hans Urs von Balthasar was writing about Gregory of Nyssa, he might as well have been writing about the influence and connection between Plutarch and Basil: "Never will looking backward towards the sources and the basic elements replace a looking forward that endeavors to grasp the synthesis that has been effected, the irreducible novelty that has been attained. The fruit of these labors, even though it is contained in the roots, is always something new and unexpected."[128] Writing a sermon or public address against lending is neither new nor unexpected, and many of the passages which Basil employs are also neither new nor unexpected. What then, does Basil contribute to the reasoned doctrine against lending? After having dissected Basil's text, addressed his method to attempt to solve

124. "Toutefois, il faut le reconnaître: à part ces differences, c'est Plutarque qui parle dans la chaire chretiénne par la bouche de Basile" (Fialon, *Étude historique et littéraire sur Saint Basile suivie de l'hexameron*, 196).

125. "non sans une exagération évidente" (Giet, "De Saint Basile à Saint Ambroise," 120).

126. Giet, "De Saint Basile à Saint Ambroise," 120–21.

127. "Il est difficile de savoir si Basile a connu quelques-uns de ces textes puisqu'il n'en cite aucun; mais il ne pouvait ignorer—et peut-être avons-nous ici la raison pour laquelle, entre tous les textes de l'Ancien Testament, il s'est attaché au commentaire du psaume 14—le dix-septième canon de Nicée contre les clercs adonnés a l'usure" (Giet, "De Saint Basile à Saint Ambroise," 121).

128. Balthasar, *Presence and Thought*, 17.

the problem of usury in his congregation and demonstrated the similarity in style to that of Plutarch, I will conclude this section by addressing the element or elements of Basil's *Homilia in psalmum* 14 that are "new and unexpected."

Basil does not expound upon the five biblical passages previously mentioned, but after quoting them launches straight away against the practice of usury. According to Basil, the act of usury begins with deceit, proof alone that the usurer knows that such actions are foul, and therefore must formulate a ruse in order to bring about the desired result:

> He swears up and down, even calling down curses on himself, that he is at a complete loss for funds, and that he too is search-ing for someone from whom to procure a loan. He confirms the falsehood with an oath, thus acquiring perjury as an evil fringe benefit of misanthropy. When, however, the one seeking the loan mentions rates of interest and names collateral, then he winks and smiles, suddenly recalling come old family ac-quaintance, and calls him "friend" and "neighbor." He says "Let me see if I can find some money set aside somewhere. I have a deposit entrusted to me by a friend for trading, but he set heavy terms of interest on it. For you, however, I will reduce the rate somewhat and lend it to you at a lower interest."[129]

Basil has presented his audience with a miscellany of falsehood in his description of the initial transaction: first, the usurer claims that he has no money; second, the usurer has taken oaths to this end; third, the usurer claims that his own money is the possession of a friend or relative to whom the funds have been entrusted, in order to remove himself from the act of usury itself; finally, the amount of interest is "lowered" for the debtor, as the usurer feigns that he is taking a loss—no doubt on account of his great humanitarianism, for which the debtor should be appropri-ately grateful. Wondering how someone might consider this façade to be indicative of any good business sense, Basil first questions the logic of these actions—"Tell me, do you really seek riches and financial gain from the destitute? If this person had the resources to make you even wealthier, why did he come begging to your door?"[130]—then attempts to shame the usurer: "He came seeking an ally, but found an enemy. He came seeking medicine, and stumbled onto poison. Though you have an obligation to

---

129. Basil, *Homilia in psalmum* 14 (PG 29:265–68), in Schroeder, *On Social Justice*, 90.

130. Ibid., 90. See chapter 3 for Philo's similar argument in *De specialibus legibus* 2.74.

remedy the poverty of someone like this, instead you increase the need, seeking a harvest from the desert. It is as if a doctor were to go to the diseased, and instead of restoring them to health, were rather to rob them of the last remnant of their strength. Thus you make the hardships of the miserable an occasion for profit."[131] Basil contrasts this offensive prayer of the usurer for community poverty to increase his gain with the inoffensive prayer of the farmer for rain to increase his crops, and ends this portion of the *Homily* with a clever word problem for the usurer: the interest claimed by a loan made to a poor person is a lesser sum than the accumulation to the usurer's personal multitude of sins.[132] In other words, what the usurer stands to gain financially, he loses spiritually; he has not considered the big picture, or life beyond what is to be gained in the present. Like the hypocrites praying in the synagogues and on street corners, the usurer receives his reward in this lifetime, but fails to gather reserve for the next.[133]

Basil moves next from transaction to effect, and presents a different image of the debtor. Previously he has described the debtor bereft of dignity or self-respect, "one who acts in such an undignified manner."[134] But the debtor is even more pitiable than one who is simply in need of the basic necessities of life—including pride—for this one type of debtor has borrowed and adopted a lavish lifestyle which he could not otherwise afford, and the money—his or not—has attracted the usual bottom-feeders of society: "After receiving the money, on the first day he is joyful and festive, decked out in borrowed splendor, the change in his circumstances in clear evidence. There is a richly laden table and lavish clothing. Even the servants have brightened in their appearance. He is surrounded by the multitude of flatterers and drinking companions, hovering around the house like drones."[135] The situation grows desperate, however, as the time for payment approaches, until "in his sleep he sees the lender as a nightmare floating over his head. If he wakes up, the interest consumes his thoughts and is a constant source of worry."[136] The usurer and the debtor

131. Ibid., 90–91.

132. Ibid.

133. Matthew 6:5–8.

134. Basil, *Homilia in psalmum* 14 (PG 29:265), in Schroeder, *On Social Justice*, 90.

135. Ibid., 91.

136. Ibid. The opening scene of an early fifth-century-BCE Hellenic comedy by Aristophanes, *The Clouds*, deftly depicts a man torn by just such fears; having enjoyed a classical education Basil might possibly have been familiar with and influenced by this powerful opening scene: "Damn! I'm so bitten up by all these blasted bedbuggering debts and bills and stable-fees, I can't catch a wink. And all because of YOU! Yes,

have this in common: they are both consumed day and night with concern over the interest; their only other common ground, Basil claims, is that their anxiety is not unnoticed: "When lender and debtor meet one another, the Lord visits them both."[137] Though he might suffer materially, and worry internally, the debtor is not without divine protection.

Enlisting a passage from Proverbs 5—a proverb which cautions against adultery—and drawing directly from Plutarch, Basil encourages the poor to tap into all available resources before dipping into another's well: "'Drink water at your own cistern;'[138] that is, look to your own means. Do not turn to other springs, but draw forth from your own springs the comforts of life. Do you have utensils of bronze, clothing, a beast of burden, vessels for all your needs? Sell them all; choose to give up everything rather than your freedom."[139] Plutarch's advice is stunningly similar, having offered much the same advice earlier: "Ought there not, then, to be a law about money also, that people shall not borrow from others or resort to other people's springs who have not first examined their own resources at home…Why do you pay court to the banker or broker? Borrow of your own table; you have drinking-cups, silver dishes, *bonbonnières*. Pawn these for your needs."[140] Cautioning the poor against bad spending habits, Basil urges them to consider debt as a loss of autonomy, despite any momentary respite which the money might bring: "By borrowing, however, you will not become rich, and you will surrender your freedom."[141] Plutarch too, considers debt as enslavement: "No, let us preserve our liberty by taking off what is useless from our table, our bed, our vehicles, and our daily expenses, intending to pay it back if we are fortunate."[142] As well, borrowing places the poor in the position of having to engage in lies of their own, specifically those of supplication and fawning when in need, and curses and charges of counterfeit money when the time of payment arrives.[143]

---

you and your damned horses! Gigs, rigs, nags, ponytails . . . Hell, horses everywhere! Horses in your dreams! But *me*? *I'm* bankrupt, broke, ruined, waiting for the end of the month when all these debts come due" (Aristophanes, *The Clouds*, in Arrowsmith, et al., *Three Plays by Aristophanes*, 23.

137. Proverbs 29:13 LXX, in Basil, *Homilia in psalmum* 14 (PG 29:268–69), in Schroeder, *On Social Justice*, 91.

138. Proverbs 5:15.

139. Basil, *Homilia in psalmum* 14 (PG 29:269), in Schroeder, *On Social Justice*, 92.

140. Plutarch, *De vitando aere alieno* 318–19.

141. Basil, *Homilia in psalmum* 14 (PG 29:269), in Schroeder, *On Social Justice*, 93.

142. Plutarch, *De vitando aere alieno*, 319.

143. Basil, *Homilia in psalmum* 14, PG 29:269, in Schroeder, *On Social Justice*, 92.

Further, the process instigated by the debtor only serves to increase the possibility of sin in the lender as well as the debtor, for far from being pacified by having gained any money at all and unlike a cur who has captured his prey, once having profited, the lender wants more. To detail the extent of the lender's inhumane treatment, Basil presents a list of activities in which the lender will engage, all of which effectively limit the freedom of the debtor:

> Dogs become tame if you feed them, but when the creditor receives back what was borrowed, he becomes even more enraged. He does not stop his howling, but on the contrary, demands even more. Although you swear you will pay, he does not believe you. He pries into your private affairs, and inquires about your transactions. If you emerge from your home, he seizes you and drags you away; if you hide yourself within, he stands outside and pounds at the door. He shames you before your spouse, treats you disgracefully in front of your friends, seizes you by the throat in public places. Even a chance meeting at a festival is a disaster; he makes life unbearable.[144]

After questioning the wisdom of deferring the day of poverty by adding the shame of debt to destitution, Basil informs his audience that it is not a crime to be poor: "Now no one blames you for being poor, since this misfortune came upon you involuntarily. But if you make yourself liable for loans at interest, then everyone will fault you for your lack of good judgment."[145]

Referring to borrowing as an "evil freely chosen"[146] Basil shames childish individuals unable to reconcile themselves to their present circumstances; rather than working themselves up from poverty bit by bit, such persons, he claims, instead gamble on an uncertain future, putting their faith in false hopes and swimming "like fish to the bait."[147] He points

144. Ibid., 92–93.

145. Ibid., 93.

146. Ibid.

147. Ibid., 94. It is surprising that Basil does not chide the debtor here for putting his faith and hope in another person rather than in God, as he does in Question 42 of his *Long Rules*: "A man who relies upon himself, however, or even upon the person whose duty it is to provide for his needs, and thinks that his own activity or that of his associate is a sufficient resource for his livelihood, runs the risk, as he places his hope in man, of falling under the curse which reads: 'Cursed be the man that trusteth in man and maketh flesh his arm and whose soul departeth from the Lord.' Now, by the words 'that trusteth in man,' the Scripture forbids a man to place his hope in another, and by the words, 'and maketh flesh his arm,' it forbids him to trust in himself. Either

to the near impossibility of gaining money for repayment *in addition* to the interest, when the individual has not the initial sum to begin with. Comparing both poverty and debt to illness or disease, the spiritual doctor offers the following prescription to his audience: "No one can heal wounds with more wounds, nor remedy evil with more evil, nor alleviate poverty with loans at interest."[148]

Basil turns from this remedy to bombard his audience with a series of short exclamatory and repetitive questions, again an echo of Plutarch, who wrote: "Have you money? Do not borrow, for you are not in need. Have you no money? Do not borrow, for you will not be able to pay...Being unable to carry the burden of poverty you put the money-lender on your back, a burden difficult for even the rich to bear."[149] Basil too, questions his audience: "Are you rich? Do not borrow. Are you poor? Do not borrow. If you are well off, you have no need of the loan; if you have nothing, you will not be able to repay it. Do not give your life over to bitter regret, lest you count the days before you took the loan as the happiest of your life."[150] The unhappiness of the debtor is subsequently charted in detail, as Basil describes the descent of disquiet into which the debtor sinks as the time of payment draws near. As the debtor is no richer than he was prior to the loan, sleepless, anxious, covetous, and heavy-hearted, the debtor fears each knock on the door, each barking dog, and desperately begins to formulate lies to defer the usurer.[151]

Basil employs metaphors from the natural world to describe the foul human whose envy has made them venomous:[152] the usurer is lower than a dog, unable to be satisfied once he receives what he wants;[153] the usurer is a "quickly reproducing beast"[154] to which the debtor has yoked himself; and the rapid growth of interest is compared to the fecundity of rabbits:

---

course is termed a defection from the Lord . . . the Scripture declares that anyone for anyone to place his trust in himself or in anyone else is to alienate himself from the Lord." Basil, *Question 42*, in *The Long Rules* (PG 31:890–1052), in Wagner (trans.), *Saint Basil: Ascetical Works* 9:318. See chapter 4 for Philo of Alexandria's imagery of an individual who has been "baited" by a lender.

148. Basil, *Homilia in psalmum* 14 (PG 29:268), in Schroeder, *On Social Justice*, 94.

149. Plutarch, *De vitando aere alieno*, 327–39.

150. Basil, *Homilia in psalmum* 14 (PG 29:272–73), in Schroeder, *On Social Justice*, 94.

151. Ibid., 94.

152. See also Basil, *Homilia de invidia* (PG 31:371–86).

153. Basil, *Homilia in psalmum* 14 (PG 29:273), in Schroeder, *On Social Justice*, 93.

154. Ibid., 95.

"It is said that rabbits give birth and breed again while still nursing their young. And for those who set rates of interest, their money is loaned out and bears interest and produces even more. You did not even have the money in your hands, and already the lender was demanding the interest payment for the current month. And when this was loaned to you as well, it brought forth more evil, and still more, evil without end."[155] Although the notes in the Basil text direct the reader to Aristotle's *History of Animals*, it seems clear that Basil's text still mirrors Plutarch's *Moralia* in both text and tone: "They say that hares at one and the same time give birth to one litter, suckle another, and conceive again; but the loans of these barbarous rascals give birth to interest before conception; for while they are giving they immediately demand payment, while they lay money down they take it up, and they lend what they receive for money lent."[156] Because of interest which gives birth to interest, Basil follows the fertility of the hares with a brief consideration of the fertility of money. Authors Maloney and González suggest that Basil's use of the word τόκος is reminiscent of Aristotle,[157] but Basil does not give the question of the fertility of money as much reflection as did the philosopher. Aristotle considered the breeding of interest to be unnatural because money was to be used in exchange, not to breed from itself; the reproduction of self from self would be considered a perversion of the natural order.[158] Basil, on the other hand, does not address whether or not money might rightly be considered fertile, but considers the reproduction of evil born of greed to be a far greater problem than the reproduction of interest; wicked offspring are borne of wicked parents, and such offspring never cease their expansion.[159] Unlike the natural world, in which animals and plants bring forth their offspring in due time, τόκος is unnatural because the offspring is born immediately, immediately begins to consume, and never grows to maturity: "Seeds take time to grow, and animals take time to fully mature, but interest is born today, and today begins to bear. Those animals that begin bearing at an

---

155. Ibid.

156. Plutarch, *De vitando aere alieno*, 325.

157. Maloney, "The Teaching of the Fathers on Usury," 248; González, *Faith and Wealth*, 176.

158. Aristotle, *Politics* 1258b.

159. "For it seems to me that loans are said to 'bear' (τόκος) interest on account of the great fecundity of evil. How else? Or perhaps interest is said to 'bear' (τόκος) on account of the pains and travails which it naturally produces on the souls of those who borrow" (Basil, *Homilia in psalmum* 14 [PG 29:273], in Schroeder, *On Social Justice*, 95.

early age also cease bearing early. But money immediately begins to multiply, and possesses limitless ability to reproduce. And every animal, once it reaches its proper size, stops growing. But the silver of the greedy never stops growing as time passes. And animals, once they have raised their young to maturity, cease bearing. But when it comes to borrowed silver, the newborn gives birth, and the elderly continues to bear. You should have nothing to do with this monstrous creature."[160]

The influence of Plutarch continues along themes of health and gender, as Basil chastises those who borrow merely to "devote themselves to unconstrained expenditures and useless luxuries, those who serve the passionate desires of women,"[161] much as Plutarch did when he complained about debtors who "because of their luxury and effeminacy or their extravagance, they make no use of what is their own, though they possess it, but take form others at a high rate of interest, though they have no need of doing so."[162] Later in his text Plutarch writes more graphically that such persons are "much like persons ill with cholera, who do not accept treatment, but vomit up the prescribed medicine and then continue constantly to collect more disease."[163] In like fashion, Basil complains that those with loans who take on more loans before another is paid off are as "[t]hose who suffer from cholera," who "constantly disgorge what they have eaten, and before their system is properly cleansed, they fill themselves up with a second portion, vomiting this up too with terrible, racking pains . . ."[164]

An oft repeated theme throughout Basil's *Homilia in psalmum* 14 is the loss of personal freedom, an understated facet of the lending process. Here Basil departs from the influence of Plutarch[165] and stresses emphatically that as an individual contracts a monetary debt, simultaneously they have placed themselves into both a physical and a spiritual bondage, and that this is not an individual's natural state before God: "You behold the sun as a free person. Why do you begrudge the liberty you now enjoy?"[166]

160. Ibid.

161. Ibid.

162. Plutarch, *De vitando aere alieno* 317.

163. Ibid., 335.

164. Basil, *Homilia in psalmum* 14 (PG 29:277), in Schroeder, *On Social Justice*, 96–97.

165. Plutarch highlights loss of personal freedom as a problem of debt (*De vitando aere alieno* 323, 333–35), but he does not emphasize repeatedly this to the extent that Basil does in his homily, so I would not say that Plutarch was so great an influence on Basil with respect to this particular theme.

166. Basil, *Homilia in psalmum* 14 (PG 29:277), in Schroeder, *On Social Justice*, 95.

No matter that Solon eliminated the practice of "loans on the person"[167] in 594 BCE, nearly one thousand years later the practice of usury still carries the taint of enslavement, and the usurer the stench of Master. Basil states the conditions of usury from the outset as a binding contract of slavery of which the debtor is completely ignorant, "depriving him of freedom even more than the poverty that already oppressed him. The one who has made himself liable for rates of interest he cannot pay has incurred self-inflicted slavery for life."[168] Here Basil stresses to his audience that they have not understood borrowing and lending with interest from the proper perspective; previously, lending had seemed to them to be a series of physical maneuvers that simply dealt with money, maneuvers that carried no particular ulterior motives other than being an uncomplicated business deal, a transaction to "tide one over," or perhaps even an "arrangement" that emerged between friends. Basil pleads with the poverty-stricken individual not to allow themselves or their families to be destroyed for want of possessions, by being led astray by being "rich in a dream,"[169] a dream which comes to ruin in reality. Basil's "poor man" protests that "many have become rich by taking out loans;"[170] to this the bishop wisely points out that more have fallen to the gutter by this process than have landed upright, and appeals to fathers to deprive their sons of neither the dignity of their own freedom nor of having had a free father, no matter how poor: "Children are not brought to court for the penury of their parents, but the debt of a parent leads straight to prison. Do not leave behind a ledger that will go down as a parental curse upon your children and grandchildren."[171] Basil wants his listeners to see beyond these simple actions to the tangled net and piercing hook which lie behind them; this is not a fair exchange between equals, it is not an act of *leitourgia* in the most positive sense but an act of *leitourgia* which equals enslavement. In the case of usury, the loan is a prison in which one is entrapped not only by the loss of money, but by harassment encountered at the hands of the creditor, by shame incurred that one could not provide for self or family, by anxiety as days of payment due draw near with no means of acquiring the money in sight, by heavy-heartedness as

167. See chapter 2.

168. Ibid., 90. Holman points out that Basil's use of the term "servitude" here carries a derogatory message to serve as a slave, rather than the more positive form of *leitourgia*, which is "to serve public offices at one's own cost" Liddell and Scott, *A Greek-English Lexicon*, 1036; Holman, *The Hungry Are Dying*, 25.

169. Basil, *Homilia in psalmum* 14 (PG 29:277), in Schroeder, *Basil the Great*, 97.

170. Ibid.

171. Ibid.

the luxuries of those around the debtor fill him with envy, and ultimately by prison for the debtor if the debt remains in arrears.[172]

Having said his piece to the poor and to those who borrow unnecessarily, Basil ends his homily with an invective against the rich. He questions if the rich among his listeners have noted that he has encouraged the poor and destitute that it is better to remain in such a condition rather than to put themselves at the mercy of such afflictions as are accompanied by interest. Sadly, Basil notes that had his listeners been heeding scripture[173] that this sermon would be completely superfluous,[174] and he encourages the richer members of his flock to place themselves in a more favorable position before God by lending to the poor without hope for repayment. Maloney, in "The Teaching of the Fathers on Usury," writes that Basil's closing resembles Philo's *On the Virtues*,[175] but it is difficult to find such visible influence as is found in the Plutarch text. Perhaps the best example is Philo's statement that "this is the best course, but, if they are unwilling to give, they should at least lend with all readiness and alacrity, not with the prospect of receiving anything back except the principal."[176] It appears that the two are in agreement of spirit, and one could make the claim that Basil's allegation that "if you must seek a return on your investment, be satisfied with what comes from the Lord; he himself will pay the additional amount on behalf of the poor"[177] resembles Philo's statement.[178] This follows from Basil's exhortation for the miserly to consider that their free gift to the poor is yet a loan, and here he quotes Proverbs 19:17 as assurance: "Whoever is kind to the poor lends to the Lord, and will be repaid in full."[179] He states this more explicitly in his *Homilia dicta tempore famis et siccitatis*, where he boldly asserts: "O poor one, lend to the rich God. Believe in the one who is at all times taking up the cause of the afflicted in his own person and supplying grace from his own stores. Trustworthy guarantor, he has vast treasuries all over the earth and sea. In fact, even if

172. Basil, *Homilia in psalmum* 14 (PG 29:268–69), in ibid.

173. Here Basil quotes Luke 6.35 (ibid., 97).

174. Basil, *Homilia in psalmum* 14 (PG 29:277), in ibid.

175. Maloney, "Teaching of the Fathers on Usury," 249.

176. Philo, *On the Virtues* 14.83.

177. Basil, *Homilia in psalmum* 14 (PG 29:280), in Schroeder, *On Social Justice*, 98.

178. For the influence of Philo of Alexandria on the writings of the early Christian authors, see Moser, *Die patristische Zinslehre*, 96–105.

179. Proverbs 19:17.

you were to demand back the loan in the middle of the ocean, you would be guaranteed to receive the capital with interest."[180]

Consummate misanthropy influenced Plutarch's opinion on lending, for he concludes "That we Ought Not to Borrow" on a purely fatalistic note; without a drop of sympathy, he resolves that "people in debt are content to be dunned, mulcted of tribute, enslaved, and cheated."[181] The benefit of hope-filled Christianity, in this case, is evident: Basil winds up his homily with sure-fire proof of the wickedness of the usurer and his interest,[182] and points out that the merciless usurer reaps without sowing, claims the seed along with the produce, and harvests the fruits along with demands for the principal.[183] Despite such sins, the bishop nevertheless ends his homily with an appeal for the wicked to do good, to not turn away from those in need in order that when it might be their time to pass on the advantaged wealthy might also "depart to the Lord with a good hope, receiving there the interest upon your good works."[184]

Against Those Who Practice Usury

Gregory Accepts the Challenge

For one text allegedly based on another, Gregory of Nyssa's *Contra usurarios* could not begin more differently than Basil's. While Basil begins the first sentence of *Homilia in psalmum* 14 with reference to the Psalm,[185] Gregory begins his sermon with an introduction brimming with a proper Platonic definition of those who love virtue as ones who "live in accord with reason by following beneficial laws and ordinances."[186] He further

---

180. Basil, *Homilia dicta tempore famis et siccitatis*, in Holman, *The Hungry Are Dying*, 190. Through such a statement Basil works to change the perception that money that is not working for the wealthy is unfaithful, and as such will lead the wealthy to their ruin. But God, assures Basil, is not inhumane, and will no more let the poor go to ruin than the rich. Loans, Basil would claim, are not the enemy; it is interest that crushes the poor, for "this interest, which you take, is full of extreme inhumanity" (Basil, *Homilia dicta tempore famis et siccitatis*, in Holman, *The Hungry Are Dying*, 190).

181. Plutarch, *De vitando aere alieno*, 339.

182. "Woe to those who call the bitter sweet and the sweet bitter." From Isaiah 5.20, in Basil, *Homilia in psalmum* 14 (PG 29:280), in Schroeder, *On Social Justice*, 98.

183. Ibid. 99.

184. Ibid.

185. Ibid., 89.

186. Gregory of Nyssa, *Contra usurarios* (PG 46:433), in McCambley, "Against

claims that virtuous persons are noted by two common characteristics: the first distinction is that of being "inimical to wickedness,"[187] and the second is that they "favour good deeds."[188] Without these qualities, Gregory claims, an individual is unable "to live well,"[189] excepting he "has virtue for a mother and puts evil to flight."[190] Further, while Basil's homily was based on Psalm 14 (and a single line, at that), Gregory's sermon is thematic; although he quotes Ezekiel 22:12 in the first paragraph, he never returns to it, but instead uses a variety of scriptural defenses for his position, all of which will be considered below.

Jean Daniélou, in "Chronologie des sermons de Saint Grégoire de Nysse," writes that this sermon was probably delivered during the month of March, in the season of Lent in 379, and possibly in Caesarea.[191] If Basil died January 1 of 379, and if Gregory was delivering this sermon in Caesarea only a few months later, perhaps Gregory's audience might have been familiar with the Basil's previous sermon on usury. This could explain why Gregory initially adopts a tone of reluctance, loath to compete with his brother's memory, Basil having so recently departed.[192] He states

Those Who Practice Usury, by Gregory of Nyssa." 294. This passage is reminiscent of Plato's *Republic*, in which Socrates queries, "And is it not likewise the production of justice in the soul to establish its principles in the natural relation of controlling and being controlled by one another, while injustice is to cause the one to rule or to be ruled by the other contrary to nature? 'Exactly so,' he said. Virtue, then, as it seems, would be a kind of health, and beauty and good condition of the soul, and vice would be disease, ugliness, and weakness? 'It is so.' Then is it not also true that beautiful and honorable pursuits tend to the winning of virtue and the ugly to vice? 'Of necessity'" (Plato, *Republic* 4.444d–e).

187. Gregory of Nyssa, *Contra usurarios* (PG 46:433), in McCambley, "Against Those Who Practice Usury, by Gregory of Nyssa," 294.

188. Ibid.

189. Ibid.

190. Ibid.

191. "Nous pensons donc que ce sermon a été prononcé au début de Carême de 379." (Daniélou, "Chronologie des Sermons de Saint Gregoire de Nysse," 348). Jean Bernardi, in his brief section on Gregory of Nyssa's *Contra usurarios* in *The Preaching of the Cappadocian Fathers: The Preacher and His Audience*, does not support Daniélou's date unequivocally, but in light of a more convincing alternative, agrees: "S'il est vrai que les voyages de Grégoire en 380 ne lui permirent guère de prêcher, comme l'avait établi Diekamp, il ne s'ensuit pas nécessairement que l'année 379 puisse seule être retenue, bien qu'elle soit assez probable en définitive" (Bernardi, *La prédication des pères cappadociens*, 264–65).

192. Bernardi suggests that this sermon was delivered during the Feast of the Forty Martyrs, when the Cappadocian bishops gathered together in Caesarea to assist the Metropolitan, and, in this case, to elect a successor to Basil (Bernardi, *La prédication*

that his treatment of the subject matter is that of being "yoked to an ass or ox,"[193] and asks his audience not to reproach him—one who is "skilled in speaking and philosophy and trained in every type of learning"[194]— for having thus far not spoken on the subject of usury,[195] but promises that now he shall "descend to the contest at hand."[196] However, a fuller definition of καθήκα is "come, or go down, (esp.) to fight,"[197] while a more comprehensive definition for ἡ ἄμιλλα includes "contest for superiority, conflict,"[198] and "rivalry, generally a struggle."[199]

Of course Gregory did not use the opportunity of his Lenten sermon to "one-up" his recently deceased brother, but it is noted by more than one scholar that Gregory often worked as a spiritual complement to Basil. Anthony Meredith notes that Gregory made a career of composing mystical versions of works already accomplished by Basil: *On Virginity*, which he claims is a "philosophical underpinning" to Basil's own *Rules*, and Gregory's *On the Six Days of Creation* and *On the Making of Man*, which Meredith labels as "critical continuations of Basil's own works in the same areas."[200] Daniélou makes a similar claim about Gregory's relationship with Basil's scholarship, that Gregory's obligation was "not merely to carry on the work of Basil; he has also to bring it to completion."[201] Virginia Woods Callahan also states that Gregory's theological output consistently reflects a passionate commitment to Basil's interests.

---

des pères cappadociens, 265). It would not have been uncommon for Gregory and the others to deliver several sermons at this time: "Il est normal que Grégoire ait eu, au cours de ce séjour, comme ses collègues, et peut-être plus qu'eux en sa qualité de frère et d'héritier spirituel du défunt, l'occasion de prêcher devant les fidèles de Césarée" (Bernardi, *La prédication des pères cappadociens*, 265).

193. Gregory of Nyssa, *Contra usurarios* (PG 46:436), in McCambley, "Against Those Who Practice Usury, by Gregory of Nyssa." 294–95.

194. Ibid., 294.

195. Gregory mentions in a letter that "Divine Scripture forbids accumulation and usury as well as the appropriation of another person's possessions, even though it is done under the pretext of a contract." Gregory of Nyssa, *Epistola Canonica AS S. Letoium Melitines Episcopum* (PG 45:233B), in McCambley, "Against Those Who Practice Usury by Gregory of Nyssa," 291.

196. Gregory of Nyssa, *Contra usurarios* (PG 46:433), in McCambley, 294.

197. καθήκα, in Liddell and Scott, *A Greek-English Lexicon*, 852.

198. ἡ ἄμιλλα, in ibid., 83.

199. Liddell, *A Lexicon*, 40.

200. Meredith, *The Cappadocians*, 53.

201. Daniélou, *Glory to Glory*, 5.

She notes that four of Gregory's treatises are against Eunomius,[202] and claims that his *Life of Moses, On the Psalms*,[203] and *On the Canticle of Canticles*[204] reflect Gregory's desire to provide philosophical, theological and mystical interpretation of Basil's *Rules*.[205] With this in mind, Gregory's *Contra usurarios* surely functions in a similar way to many of the works mentioned above: as a *complement* to Basil's earlier homily, as an attempt to *complete* the homiletic exploration of the topic, and as further evidence of a theological rivalry, which may or may not have existed at least in the mind of Gregory, if not his brother's as well.[206] But in addition to the conception of competition lies that of responsibility, and Daniélou acknowledges the tension that surely existed between the two and—at the same time—claims that Gregory was fully aware of the responsibilities that fell to him at his brother's death; Gregory rose to the occasion: "It may well have been that Basil's dominant personality had, up till then, prevented Gregory from expressing himself. For despite Basil's affection for his brother, he had no true notion of Gregory's worth. Their characters were essentially too opposed for that. But now, with Basil's death, Gregory was forced to stand on his own, and thus in the years that followed he was able to reveal himself as he really was.[207]

Regardless of motive, Gregory wholeheartedly tackles the subject with vigor. Urging the poor to take the example of John the Baptist and scorn usurers as a "brood of vipers,"[208] Gregory stretches the comparison to further warn the poor against a "poisonous serpent"[209] which preys on

202. Gregory of Nyssa, *Contra Eunomium*, in Callahan, *Gregory of Nyssa: Ascetical Works*, xii.

203. Ibid., xiii.

204. Ibid.

205. Gregory of Nyssa, *In Canticum Canticorum*, in ibid., xiii.

206. It is not likely that Werner Jaeger would tolerate my suggestion of competition, for he claims that it is not by chance that Gregory's texts often complement Basil's, for Basil "must have impressed him from the beginning with the idea that they could prevail only if they combined their forces, and Gregory clung to this ideal even after Basil's death" Jaeger, *Two Rediscovered Works of Ancient Christian Literature*, 19.

207. Daniélou, *From Glory to Glory*, 5.

208. Gregory of Nyssa, *Contra usurarios* (PG 46:436), in McCambley, 295; reference to Matthew 3:7: "You brood of vipers! Who warned you to flee from the wrath to come?"

209. Gregory of Nyssa, *Contra usurarios* (PG 46:436), in McCambley, 295; Referencing the appearance of the serpent in Genesis 3:1, Gregory uses this metaphor for greed in his *Commentary on Ecclesiastes* as well: "Perhaps that is why the sense of pleasure is called in scripture a *serpent* (Genesis 3:1), which has the natural ability, if its

the soul of the needy. Interestingly, his statement that "although you allow a trifling [pleasure] to delight you now, a poisonous serpent later brings harm upon your soul"[210] could apply to the usurer as well as the debtor. In fact, a great deal of this initial portion of the text is hampered—or perhaps enlivened—by ambiguity, as a few of the phrases can be construed to apply to either the debtor or the usurer. Either way, by the time Gregory is quoting Matthew 5:42—"Do not refuse him who would borrow from you"—it is apparent that he is addressing the usurer, whose action he immediately condemns as a "superficial good deed."[211] Gregory's text does not quote, but yet provides allusion to the parable of the rich man and Lazarus found in Luke 16:19–31, a parable which emphasizes the hard-heartedness of the wealthy even against the wisdom of Moses and the prophets. Gregory reminds his congregation that they are blind to the needs of those seated at their gates: "The destitute person is making supplication and is seated outside your door."[212] Hearing this, the audience might remember that while starving and covered with sores licked by dogs, destitute Lazarus sits at the gates of an unnamed rich man, who dresses in finery and feasts daily on fine linens.[213] As Gregory exclaims that "in his need he seeks your wealth to bring relief,"[214] those listening might recall that while both men died, only one received comfort in the afterlife, while the other—the selfish and unnamed rich man—received the torment of Hades for his outrageous comportment.[215] Gregory warns his audience that their refusal to aid the poor will do more than provide stability for the bankbook of the wealthy, but will, in fact, "turn him [the poor] into an adversary." This is exactly how the rich man now views Lazarus, who resides under the protection of

---

head slips into a chink in the wall, to pull all the rest of its coils in behind it. What do I mean? Nature makes housing necessary for humans, but pleasure, slipping by means of this need into the clink in the soul, turns the need into an immoderate extravagance in beautification and transfers the urge to that . . . After this she comes to a peak of arrogance and winds pride around her, fastening under her the dominion of over her own kindred. She drags her coil of desire for money over these, and with that necessarily goes license, the hindmost part and tail of the bestiality of pleasure." Gregory of Nyssa, *Fourth Homily*, in Hall and Moriarty, 82.

210. Gregory of Nyssa, *Contra usurarios* (PG 46:436), in McCambley, "Against Those Who Practice Usury by Gregory of Nyssa," 295.

211. Ibid.

212. Ibid.

213. Luke 16:19–21.

214. Gregory of Nyssa, *Contra usurarios* (PG 46:436), in McCambley, "Against Those Who Practice Usury by Gregory of Nyssa," 295.

215. Luke 16:22–26.

Abraham and enjoys the comforts which the rich man denied during their time on earth. Gregory's metaphors in this passage are similar to Basil's, for Gregory too uses Hippocratic imagery to skewer hypocrites: he here refers to the usurer as a "murderous physician"[216] who kills the patient for profit under the pretext of healing. After these accusations, Gregory digresses from the usurer, focusing attention on money-lending itself. Gregory personifies money-lending as an evil, beast-like spirit, describing it as rapacious and valueless, delighting in banquets and producing that which it has not tilled.[217] Cleverly, Gregory writes that "money-lending" has alternative, if not unnatural, tools: "A reed for a plough, papyrus for a field, and black ink for seed."[218] His description grows disturbingly vivid:

> Usury's home is a threshing-floor upon which the fortunes of the oppressed are winnowed and where it considers everything its own. It prays for affliction and misfortune in order to destroy such persons. Moneylending despises people contented with their possessions and treats them as enemies because they do not provide money. It watches courts of law to find distress in persons who demand payment and follows tax collectors who are a nest of vultures in battle array prepared for war. Money-lending carries a purse and dangles bait as a wild beast to those in distress in order to ensnare them in their need. Daily it counts its gain and cannot be satisfied. It is vexed by gold hidden in a person's home because it remains idle and unprofitable.[219]

Vaguely reminiscent of God's warning to Cain: "If you do not do well, sin is lurking at the door; its desire is for you, but you must master it,"[220] Gregory's device demonstrates the all-consuming nature of an evil which so penetrates the soul of the money-lender that the person no longer exists as a "being," but as a personification of evil. But as quickly as he begins this theme, Gregory drops it, and addresses briefly the incongruity that exists for money-lenders: they often have not two coins to rub together, yet have tremendous wealth on paper.[221] Referring to this as a "convenient form of

---

216. McCambley, "Against Those Who Practice Usury by Gregory of Nyssa," 295.

217. Ibid.

218. Ibid.

219. Ibid., 295–96.

220. Genesis 4:7b.

221. Gregory of Nyssa, *Contra usurarios* (PG 46:436), in McCambley, "Against Those Who Practice Usury by Gregory of Nyssa," 296.

destitution," Gregory ridicules those whose misplaced and greedy hope in an uncertain future empties their present life of basic necessities.[222]

Gregory works diligently to unlock active fear in the lender, fear which makes the lender think that he can gain a paradise by placing a corruptible bond on a poor person; instead, he writes to the lender, construct a pledge with God, the caretaker of an incorruptible bond.[223] Gregory urges his listeners to put away the need for written contracts and bonds, for one must "give and make restitution with regard to any recorded public debt."[224] The only written contract with which one need be concerned is the Gospels, and those—Gregory claims—were written and authorized by four persons, not one; in addition, the oath of the Gospels is not limited to one transaction, but is relevant beginning from the time of the salvation of Christians.[225] Through the contract of the Gospels the Christian has the assurance of a "pledge of paradise and a worthy token."[226] Although Basil and other authors refer to such "heavenly usury," God's stated role is never more explicit than in Gregory's sermon. Using a bold twist of terminology that seems almost profane, Gregory refers to God as the "Debtor."[227] But this is not a "debtor" as either we or Gregory's audience understands the term, but one who has control over the "entire world and its possessions,"[228] and one who will wisely attend to all the lender's needs if the lender will only give abundantly rather than demand what is not theirs to secure.[229] Like Basil, who reminds the debtor that they "behold the sun as a free person,"[230] Gregory beseeches the lender to consider as their pledge the present bounty of the earth, and all which is inheritable from God: "Consider the sky's expanse, examine the boundless sea, learn from the earth's magnitude and count the living beings which it nourishes . . . Do not demand gain but give bountifully and without corruption (Prov 19:17).

---

222. Ibid.

223. Ibid., 296–97.

224. Ibid., 296.

225. Ibid.

226. Ibid.

227. Ibid.

228. Ibid.

229. Ibid.Gregory also uses this language in *Sermon 5* on the Lord's Prayer: "For the forgiving of debts is the special prerogative of God, since it is said, *No man can forgive sins but God alone*," in Graef (trans.), *Gregory of Nyssa: The Lord's Prayer. The Beatitudes* 71.

230. Basil, *Homilia in psalmum* 14 (PG 29.276), in Schroeder, *On Social Justice*, 95.

Then you will see God who abundantly dispenses his grace."[231] Gregory offers as insurance the promise Christ makes to Peter, who wonders for what benefit have they left their homes and families behind: "Truly I say to you that everyone who has left houses or brothers or sisters or father or mother or wife or children or lands will receive a hundred-fold and will inherit eternal life."[232] Gregory's rhetorical question to the lender—"Are you aware of his generosity and goodness?"[233]—leads to his statements on the generosity of God who freely gives to those who are charitable, which he contrasts with the miserable condition of the money-lender who gives and spends his days and nights agonizing over the return: "Why do you harm yourself with anxiety by calculating days, months, the sum of money, dreaming of profit, and fearing the appointed day whose fruitful harvest brings hail?…Such an impatient disposition results in obsession. If the usurer has loaned to a sailor, he would sit on the shore, worry about the wind's movement, constantly examine their diminishment and await the report of a wreck or some other misfortune. His soul is disquieted whenever he sees the sea angered; he examines dreams and reveals his disposition through the events which had transpired during the day."[234] This passage is similar to one within Basil's text,[235] in which Basil describes the anxiety which accompanies the debtor throughout the month; here, however, Gregory once again complements his brother's work by presenting the money-lender rather than the debtor as the one who suffers undue anxiety over the loan. Gregory's suggestion that the usurer loses his own personal freedom through his occupation echoes that of Seneca, who wrote: "He who craves riches feels fear on their account. No man,

231. Gregory of Nyssa, *Contra usurarios* (PG 46:440), in McCambley, "Against Those Who Practice Usury by Gregory of Nyssa," 296.

232. Matthew 19:27, in Gregory of Nyssa, *Contra usurarios* (PG 46:440), in McCambley, "Against Those Who Practice Usury by Gregory of Nyssa," 297. Gregory's quotation leaves out an interesting phrase, which is the implication that individuals will receive their "hundredfold" at the consummation of God's purpose, rather than during the individual's earthly lifetime.

233. Gregory of Nyssa, *Contra usurarios* (PG 46:440), in McCambley, "Against Those Who Practice Usury by Gregory of Nyssa," 297.

234. Ibid., 297.

235. "But as the money begins to dwindle, the interest ever increasing as time passes, the nights do not bring rest to him, nor does the coming of the day bring joy, nor does the sunrise seem beautiful. Rather, he despises his own life and loathes the days as they hasten onwards towards the appointed day of repayment, and hates the months as producers of interest" (Basil, *Homilia in psalmum* 14 [PG 29:268], in Schroeder, *On Social Justice*, 91).

however, enjoys a blessing that brings anxiety; he is always trying to add a little more. While he puzzles over increasing his wealth, he forgets how to use it. He collects his accounts, he wears out the pavement in the forum, he turns over his ledger,—in short, he ceases to be a master and becomes a steward."[236]

Those whose hearts are not stewards to the earth and its cares and anxieties, but who look heavenward instead are rewarded, Gregory assures, by a benevolent and charitable God who sees to the needs of those who are virtuous, such as Moses, Elizabeth, Hannah and Mary.[237] Virtuous individuals honor God by petitioning God directly for their needs instead of looking for grain in a barren field, while the usurer humiliates their own nature by deigning to this action. If one considers Gregory's understanding of the purification of the soul from *On the Soul and Resurrection* as it might apply to this text, then the aforementioned humiliations of the usurer will not condemn him merely to the misery of the present time; the "scent" of the material world will cling to the body and soul of an individual through death into the afterlife, and contaminate their post-death life either with further pains or with diminished pleasure:

> The rich man still sticks to the fleshly life as if with bird-lime which he has not thoroughly cleaned off even when he has ceased from life. He is still concerned with flesh and blood . . . Those who spend most of their time in evil-smelling places, even if they go out into the fresh air, are not cleansed from the unpleasantness which has adhered to them from prolonged contact. In the same way, even when the transition has been made to the invisible and rarified life, the lovers of the flesh would doubtless be unable to avoid bringing with them some of the fleshly odor. This makes their pangs more grievous, as their soul has become partly materialized from such an environment.[238]

Gregory's concern with the nature of the body results in the application of metaphors of metal, seen not only within this text but also

---

236. Seneca, *Ad Lucilium Epistulae Morales* 110. See chapter 2.

237. Gregory of Nyssa, *Contra usurarios* (PG 46.441), in McCambley, "Against Those Who Practice Usury by Gregory of Nyssa," 298; see Exodus 16:15b, Luke 1:3, 1 Sam 1:20, and Luke 2:7.

238. Gregory of Nyssa, *On the Soul and the Resurrection* (Roth, trans.), 75–76. Both Meredith and Roth note the influence which Plato's *Phaedo* had on Gregory's *On the Soul*, not only in Gregory's staging of the text, but in the relationship between the Platonic immortality of the soul and the Christian resurrection of the body. See Roth, *On the Soul and Resurrection*, 75; Meredith, *Gregory of Nyssa*, 2, 5, 85.

in his *Homilia IV* from *In Ecclesiasten*.[239] In *Contra usurarios* he makes reference to the usurer's body as already being "composed of copper and gold,"[240] implying that seeking more of the same is equivalent to consummation of the flesh of the poor, who still share in nature if not in wealth. The rich creation of the human body means that an individual is already in possession of great fortune, but despite this, some still fall into need; those who are petitioned for more are asked to recall that "the need for a loan is a request for mercy cheerfully bestowed,"[241] not an opportunity to "force poverty on those who are rich."[242] He reminds his audience of scriptural injunctions against usury in the Hebrew Bible,[243] Luke 6:32 and the parable of the unjust servant,[244] and asks the same question to which he addresses the usurer in *Sermon 5, Forgive us our debts, as we forgive our debtors*: "How can you pray like this, oh usurer? How can you make a request from God in good conscience since he has everything and you do not know how to give?"[245] One must consider that the inability of the lender to give is the least of his sins, as the prayers of the lender consist of "contemptuous words," paid for by the "misfortunes, tears and lamentations of others."[246] Gregory offers a suggestion that the debtor—as in Basil's text—is not fully aware of the implications of his loan or of the source from which it comes, for had he, "he would not have taken it as tasting his brother's flesh and the blood of his relatives,"[247] and writes in the voice of the needy begging mercy from the consumer: "Do not, oh man, sustain

---

239. Gregory questions the contribution of metals for happiness, as they cannot make a fool wise, a body strong, or the ill well: "Even now one may see many of those already better endowed with such wealth living in a pitiful state of health, so that if their servants were not at hand they would not be able to go on living" (*Homilia 4*, in Hall and Moriarty, *Gregory of Nyssa: Homilies on Ecclesiastes*, 77). As Pontus (north of Nyssa) was known for its extensive mineral wealth (notably copper, iron and silver), perhaps Gregory used metals metaphorically because it was a wealth that people in his area readily understood (Rostovtzeff, *Social & Economic History of the Hellenistic World* 1:572).

240. Gregory of Nyssa, *Contra usurarios* (PG 46:441), in McCambley, "Against Those Who Practice Usury by Gregory of Nyssa," 298.

241. Ibid.

242. Ibid.

243. Exodus 22:25.

244. Matthew 18:28–34.

245. Gregory of Nyssa, *Contra usurarios* (PG 46:444), in McCambley, "Against Those Who Practice Usury by Gregory of Nyssa," 298.

246. Ibid.

247. Ibid.

yourself on your brother's tears and do not give as food to the hungry the groans of those who have suffered calamity."[248]

Like Basil, Gregory draws from nature to describe the usurer, whom he likens to birds soon to be caught after greedily feasting on seed, or hunters who deplete each populated valley of wildlife, then move on with their nets to the next fertile valley.[249] The imbalance in the human world contrasted with the natural balance in the wild kingdom is a theme adopted from the Greek philosophers, who would hold the two domains up against one another for unfavorable comparisons.[250]

Gregory prefaces his conclusive tirade against the usurer with a parable about a miserly moneylender who hoarded wealth but provided not even the necessities of life for his family. At his death, his children razed his house and questioned all who knew him, but the man died so suddenly and concealed his riches so cleverly that his sudden death meant that the fortune remained permanently undetected.[251] Redolent of Ecclesiastes,

248. Ibid.

249. Ibid. Gregory does not dwell on this as much in *Contra usurarios* as he does in *Concerning Beneficence*, where he writes movingly about the rape of the natural world to gorge the maw of the self-indulgent: "Our gourmands do not, in fact, even spare the bottom of the sea, nor do they limit themselves to the fish that swim in the water, but they also bring up the crawling marine beasts from the ocean bed and drag them to shore. One pillages the oyster banks, one pursues the sea urchin, one captures the creeping cuttle fish, one plucks the octopus from the rock it grips, one eradicates the mollusks from their pedestal. All animal species, those that swim in the surface waters or live in the depths of the sea, all are brought up into the atmosphere. The artful skills of the hedonist cleverly devise traps appropriate to each" (Gregory of Nyssa, *Concerning Beneficence*, in Holman, *The Hungry Are Dying*, 198).

250. One example can be found in Plutarch, who writes: "Swallows do not borrow, ants do not borrow, creatures upon which natures has bestowed neither hands, reason, nor art; but men, with their superior intellect, support through their ingenuity horses, dogs, partridges, hares and jackdaws in addition to themselves . . . Do you not see how many opportunities are offered on land and in the sea?" (Plutarch, *De vitando aere alieno*, 329–31). Philo also employed this technique; see chapter 3.

251. Gregory of Nyssa, *Contra usurarios* (PG 46:449), in McCambley, "Against Those Who Practice Usury by Gregory of Nyssa," 300–301. Bernardi dislikes this passage, and claims that Gregory does not even make his point with this story. "A dire vrai, Grégoire ne semble pas s'être rendu compte que son exemple ne prouvait pas grand chose. Celui qu'il présente expressément comme un usurier avait caché sa fortune, il n'avait pas laissé derrière lui de reconnaissances de dette susceptibles s'être recouvrées par ses héritiers" (Bernardi, *La predication des peres cappadociens*, 267). I would maintain that Gregory makes his point, as the man gained interest he lost his soul; usury consumed him, to the degree that he failed to provide for the needs of his heirs. This man's love for money radically outweighed his love for his own children. Thus, he hid their inheritance and left them penniless, vagrant and shamed in an age when people

Gregory announces, "Such is your friend and companion, oh moneylenders! You have indeed ended your life with its vain pursuit of usury. Pains and hunger trouble you as you accumulate an inheritance of eternal punishment and leave your children penniless."[252]

Gregory's final statement to the usurer is a call to alter their pernicious ways, but he ends on a less hopeful note than did Basil, as Gregory acknowledges those in his audience who are "murmuring under their lips"[253] about his words, and that such persons are likely to "shut their doors to persons in need."[254] Faced with this threat, he advocates either the lending of money without interest or simple acts of charity, but his final words on the subject are that any who do otherwise act in a manner "hostile to God."[255] In a postscript, Gregory acknowledges that he will not address the plight of the debtor, and notes in a humble and demure statement that "our holy father Basil" has already quite sufficiently covered this problem.[256] This is not the first time Gregory adds a statement which draws the attention from himself to his brother, and Anthony Meredith points to the opening of *On Virginity*, which he considers to be a reference to Basil:

> Since it is customary for everyone to participate more eagerly in a pursuit in which he sees someone especially outstanding, we have, of necessity, recalled the glorious unmarried saints; and since descriptions aimed at establishing virtue are not as powerful as the living voice and the actual examples of what is good, we have, perforce, referred at the end of the discourse to our most reverend bishop and father as the only one capable of teaching these things. We did not mention him by name, but the treatise refers to him enigmatically, so that the advice bidding the young man to follow in the footsteps of one who has gone before them may not seem incomprehensible to those who have access to the treatise.[257]

---

were proud to have something of substance to leave to their children. This puts one in mind of Theophrastus, "penny-pincher"; see chapter 2.

252. Gregory of Nyssa, *Contra usurarios* (PG 46:452), in McCambley, "Against Those Who Practice Usury by Gregory of Nyssa," 301.

253. Ibid.

254. Ibid.

255. Ibid.

256. Ibid., 302.

257. Gregory of Nyssa, *De virginitate* (PG 46.317–416), *On Virginity*, in Callahan (trans.), *Saint Gregory of Nyssa: Ascetical Works*, 7.

Gregory's light is often cast in relation to that of Basil, the bright star of this famous Cappadocian family, who often commands the greatest attention—and the two examples above are clear evidence that Gregory would consider this to be appropriate. But, if one accepts that the phrase mentioned earlier, to "descend to the contest at hand,"[258] might imply a vague competition, as well as the statements of the scholars above that Gregory took on the task of completing and complementing his brother's works, then one might grant that Gregory set himself a task of moving the Christian ethical position on usury beyond his brother's previous homily on the same subject. While Gregory cannot have wanted to openly contend either with Basil or his memory, still, when the opportunity presented itself, he rose to the occasion, or—in his own words—"descended." If one accepts that Gregory sought to improve upon what Basil had done before, to write more thoroughly, to address other angles of the same problem which accompany usury and the sin which accompanies such a foul deed, then quite contrary to Cleary's allegation that Gregory considered Basil's text and then "borrow[ed] freely from it,"[259] Gregory's homily on usury stands independently from Basil's homily.

Conclusion

The goal of this chapter was to offer analysis of Basil of Caesarea's *Homilia in psalmum* 14 and Gregory of Nyssa's *Contra usurarios* to reveal noteworthy mutual qualities and differences, and to provide the answer to the question: To what extent does Gregory's homily depend on Basil's? This chapter began by offering a synopsis of their lives in Cappadocia; the opinions of Gregory and Basil regarding poverty, debt and usury as they have been refined in selections of their ascetic writings were considered, including one of Gregory's aforementioned two sermons against the poor, and Basil's *Homilia dicta tempore famis et siccitatis*. Finally, this chapter examined each of the brother's texts on usury in turn. As well, differing attitudes of the brothers towards the financial responsibilities of the poor or the debtor, and the degree to which they admonished the wealthy have been identified.

Without question, Basil and Gregory wrote two distinctly different homilies on usury, independent from one another, with different audiences

258. Gregory of Nyssa, *Contra usurarios* (PG 46:433), in McCambley, "Against Those Who Practice Usury by Gregory of Nyssa," 294.

259. Cleary, *The Church and Usury*, 49.

in mind, and with different foundational influences. Their distinctions are evident from the very first paragraphs: first, Basil's homily addresses usury because he is completing a two-part homily on Psalm 14, whereas Gregory has been asked to address specifically the subject of usury; this difference alone would indicate that they would take two distinct approaches. Second, Basil begins his homily by humbling himself, and introduces the subject to his audience as one of such importance that he dare not neglect it for the sake of his audience; on the other hand, Gregory begins reluctantly, indicating that he does not wish to have to speak on this subject, either because Basil has already covered the material or perhaps he knows that his audience will not be receptive. Previously noted factors also indicate that his "reluctance" might have been a rhetorical device contrived to humble oneself appropriately before adding additional teaching to what is a pressing issue in the community of Caesarea.

Textually there are differences: Basil does not chastise the debtor for relying on human ability rather than God, while Gregory provides stunning scriptural examples of humans who did to their benefit: Moses, Elizabeth, Hannah and Mary. Gregory, in fact, relies more on Scripture than does Basil, who references a few passages from Scripture and then moves on. In all, there are twenty-six scriptural references in Gregory's homily,[260] to Basil's seventeen references,[261] with five passages in common. The passages which they share in their homilies—Deuteronomy 23:19–20; Ezekiel 22:12; Psalm 14:5; Proverbs 19:17; Matthew 5:42—are even used in different ways: Gregory cites passages against usury found in Deuteronomy 23:20 and Psalm 14:5 in a section in which he notes the shameful way that usurers cite injunctions against usury as if to demonstrate that they are not impious folk who engage in such heinous activities, for such activities are banned in Scripture;[262] Basil, whose entire homily is based on the text found in Psalm 14:5, utilizes Deuteronomy 23:19 at the beginning

260. Exodus 16:15, 17:6, 22:24–25 (twice); Deuteronomy 23:20; 1 Samuel 1:20; Ezekiel 22:12; Isaiah 6:10; Amos 8:4–5; Psalm 14:5; Proverbs 19:17; Matthew 3:7, 5:42 (twice), 6:12 (twice), 18:28–34 (twice), 19:27; Luke 1:13, 2:7, 6:34–38 (four times), 8:13.

261. Deuteronomy 23:19; Ezekiel 22:12; Psalm 14:5 (twice), 54:12; Proverbs 5:15, 19:17, 23:27, 24:34, 29:13; Jeremiah 9:6; Isaiah 5:20; Judges 14:14, Matthew 5:42 (twice), 7:16–17 (twice).

262. "Have you heard them [the usurers] cry out in one voice about love and compassion saying 'To your brother you will not lend interest' (Deut 23:20), 'He has not given his money on usury' (Ps 14:5)" (Gregory of Nyssa, *Contra usurarios* [PG 46:449], in McCambley, "Against Those Who Practice Usury by Gregory of Nyssa," 300).

of his homily, citing it as evidence of the law against the practice.[263] Both brothers enlist Ezekiel's condemnation in 22:12 within the first paragraph of their homilies, with neither of them quoting the prophet directly, but merely paraphrasing his words.[264] Proverbs 19:17 is merely alluded to in Gregory's text,[265] while Basil quotes more specifically;[266] either way, they are both using the text as assurance to the lender that God will be bountiful in return to one who extends his fortune to include others. The final Scripture that the brothers have in common is Matthew 5:42, again alluded to in Gregory,[267] and cited in Basil.[268] Gregory, whose homily is saturated more heavily with Scripture quotes little, while Basil, who relies equally on Scripture and Plutarch, quotes Scripture explicitly but parrots the philosopher. Accompanying specific Scripture, Gregory provides allusions to

263. "You shall not lend at interest to your brother, and to your neighbour." Basil, *Homilia in psalmum* 14 (PG 29:265), in Schroeder, *On Social Justice*, 89.

264. "This sin has been censured in many places in Scripture. Indeed, Ezekiel places it among the greatest of evils to take interest or any profit, and the law expressly forbids it," Basil, *Homilia in psalmum* 14 (PG 29:265), in Schroeder, *On Social Justice*, 89. "Hence we are assembled here today to hear God's commands and to pay close attention to the prophet [Ezekiel]. He slew the evil of moneylending whose child is usury and has banished from his life money gained through trade." Gregory of Nyssa, *Contra usurarios* (PG 46:433), in McCambley, 294.

265. "Make a pledge to him who is immortal and believe in his reliable bond which can never be sundered. Do not demand gain but give bountifully and without corruption (Prov 19:17)" (Gregory of Nyssa, *Contra usurarios* [PG 46:440], in McCambley, "Against Those Who Practice Usury by Gregory of Nyssa," 297).

266. "When you are about to give to a poor person on the Lord's account, that same gift is also a loan: it is a gift, because you do not hope to receive it back again, but a loan because the Master in his great beneficence undertakes to make repayment for the poor person. He receives a little in the guise of the poor, but gives back much on their behalf. 'The one who has mercy on the poor lends to God.' Would you not like to have the Master of all as your guarantor for full repayment?" (Basil, *Homilia in psalmum* 14 [PG 29:277], in Schroeder, *On Social Justice*, 97–98).

267. "On the other hand we have the Apostle's admonition concerning person who give not through charity but out of greed (cf. Mt 5:42)" (Gregory of Nyssa, *Contra usurarios* [PG 46:436], in McCambley, "Against Those Who Practice Usury by Gregory of Nyssa," 296).

268. "Thus, the Lord explicitly commanded us, saying 'Do not refuse anyone who wants to borrow from you'" (Basil, *Homilia in psalmum* 14 [PG 27.265] in Schroeder, *On Social Justice*, 90).

Genesis[269] and Luke,[270] which allows his audience to recall the Scriptures, even if he does not specifically refer to them.

In addition to scriptural influence, their philosophical influences are different, too: Plato, Plutarch and Philo for Basil, and Plato and Aristotle for Gregory. Fialon's assessment in 1869 that Plutarch "parle dans la chaire chretiénne par la bouche de Basile"[271] should be accepted as accurate, with the addendum that in no way does Basil simply mimic the philosopher but—as Fialon also correctly noted—dimpled Plutarch's text with a distinctly Christian impression, and provides the added "new and unexpected" emphasis on the loss of personal freedom which accompanies debt. Overt evidence of Gregory's philosophical influence is primarily limited to his introduction, but though he begins with a definition of virtue his scripture-bound text indicates that he understands either the limits of his subject, his audience, or both. Less candid—but perhaps still present—is the influence of *Phaedo*, which shapes Gregory's concerns for the afterlife of the usurer, tainted by his actions in this present world.

One could easily make the claim that the brothers made use of similar themes in their sermons; this is a true statement, but they approached the same themes differently, as was demonstrated above. First, both authors claim that usurers are well aware of the sinfulness of their actions. However, their methods of revealing the known sin of the usurer are completely different: in Basil's homily, the usurer concocts an elaborate ruse, pretending to have no money and then producing the money by sheer coincidence, proof that they know that their actions are despicable; Gregory, however, observes that the usurers turned Scripture upon one another, chastising each other as if the reproofs were meant for another and not for themselves. The brothers both compare usurers to murderous physicians who treat their ill patients by afflicting them with further illnesses, wounding a man when they should be healing him, and killing under the mien of offering a balm. Basil and Gregory each describe the anxieties that abound when money is lent or borrowed, but while Basil portrays the mental woes of the one in debt, Gregory focuses on the distress of the usurer. Similar to other early Christian authors who touch on the subject of usury, Basil asserts the primacy of "heavenly usury" to that of any interest gained on

---

269. Genesis 4:7b, in Gregory of Nyssa, *Contra usurarios* (PG 46:437), in McCambley, "Against Those Who Practice Usury by Gregory of Nyssa,"295–96.

270. Luke 16:19–31, in Gregory of Nyssa, *Contra usurarios* (PG 46:436), in McCambley, "Against Those Who Practice Usury by Gregory of Nyssa," 295.

271. Fialon, *Étude historique et littéraire sur Saint Basile*, 196.

earth; Gregory does this as well, but pushes this concept further, referring explicitly to God as a "Debtor." Finally, both draw from the natural world to describe the characteristics of the usurer, but while Basil describes the usurer in feral terms, like a wild beast, Gregory casts the usurer in the role of the hunter of the beasts themselves, destroying nature and the free abundance of God.

While we know how Gregory's sermon was received—"For I know you are murmuring under your teeth,"[272]—less is known about the reception of Basil's homily. The fact that Gregory delivered what was a second homily on the same subject for the same city does indicate the possibility of the extreme hard-heartedness of the wealthy in Caesarea,[273] even though we know through Gregory of Nazianzus that Basil was able to work near miracles among the stingy in his see.[274]

Skirmishes with the stingy were just one of the many problems that both of these bishops faced, but the unfortunate and unforgiving social conditions of Cappadocia required that even the most esoteric of bishops turn from theological battles being waged about the Christian doctrine to attend to more finite concerns. These homilies show that both Basil and Gregory attended to the immediate and genuine ills in their communities, and they did so with considerably thoughtful theological reflection. Further, in no way did they simply mirror what had been said before them; instead, they used influences readily available, each one improving upon what was said previously, with the result being that the "fruit of these labors, even though it is contained in the roots, is always something new and unexpected."[275]

---

272. Gregory of Nyssa, *Contra usurarios* (PG 46.452), in McCambley, "Against Those Who Practice Usury by Gregory of Nyssa," 301.

273. González notes in *Faith and Wealth* that "it is impossible to know how this particular sermon of Basil was received. We do know that he and a number of his colleagues were able to induce significant liberality, at least from a number of their parishioners" (González, *Faith and Wealth*, 176).

274. Gregory of Nazianzus, *Oration* 43 (PG 36).

275. Balthasar, *Presence and Thought*, 17.

Conclusion

THE GOAL OF THIS project has been to contribute towards filling the lacuna of early Christian attitudes towards lending and debt, respectfully supplementing and updating previous work done by eminent scholars, and by offering an in-depth analysis of the texts of early Christian authors cited in studies of usury—but neglected with respect to theological content. This work has exclusively focused on a selection of early Greek Fathers foundational to the Byzantine and Eastern Christian theological and historical traditions, for the purpose of offering a more nuanced understanding of sermons that addressed the reality of debt and the responsibility of wealthy Christians. In addition, a second goal has been the elevation of Gregory of Nyssa's sermon *Contra usurarios* with respect to usury scholarship. This position has been defended by a detailed, systematic and loosely narrative comparison of the two texts, in which I considered scriptural and philosophical influences, the distinct ways in which they used common themes of theft, falsehood, anxiety, the natural world, and heavenly usury, and the possible motives for their sermons.

The above has been accomplished by having completed the following tasks: In chapter 1 I provided a brief historiography of scholarship that addresses the sermons of Basil and Gregory, for the purpose of considering to what degree Gregory's sermon has been offered scholarly consideration. In chapter 2, I provided a foundation for theological reflection on usury, by offering explanation of attitudes towards lending in Greece and Rome, centuries before and up until the fifth century CE, including general practices, laws and abuses; as well, this chapter examined philosophical reflection on the problems of usury in the works of Plato, Aristotle, Plutarch, Demosthenes, Cato, Marcus Tullias Cicero, and Seneca. In this chapter we learned that while citizens protested loans with interest, business communities recognized the economic value and benefits of such loans; that while interest on a loan continued to be legal, laws continued to be enacted to control the interest ceiling; that philosophers consistently denounced the practice of taking interest on a loan, and that the preferred loan was the ἔρανος, a loan gathered and controlled among groups of peers. The third chapter addressed Hebrew Bible and New Testament positions on usury. For the Israelites, though usury was part of the world of business they attempted to incorporate lending into the community in ways which were morally acceptable and which demonstrated righteous behavior before God. Although the New Testament offers little information on the practice, still, one can draw the conclusion from the Gospel authors that Jesus's statements on money suggest that usury is not consistent with his ethical responses to poverty and scarcity. Chapter 4 considered the ways in which references to "usury" were included in the various writings of a selection of early Greek Church authors, and determined that by the term "usurer" the authors intend to finger the individual who was often extracting a life-threatening degree of interest from someone else, most often someone known to them, likely someone from within the Christian community. The "usurer" was considered by these authors to be a parasite, a destroyer of society, someone who engaged in an activity that was an offence before God. It was concluded that the term "usurer" was not used lightly, or indiscriminately, but was connected directly with the crime. A further question was considered: Was Deuteronomy 23:19–20 used as defense for the practice of usury outside of the community, or was the practice of usury prohibited to all, regardless of relationship? Although exceptions were found, generally usury was prohibited to all, and there did not appear to be any distinction made between Christian and Jew, with respect to the practice of usury.[1] Therefore, I concluded that the scriptural or legal defense for the condemnation of usury among these Greek Fathers tended to draw from the spirit of the New Testament. Clement and Cyril rested their condemnation firmly in the Hebrew Bible, while Theodoret, Gregory of Nazianzus and John Chrysostom used the parables and statements of Jesus to bolster declarations against a morally offensive but legal practice that was simultaneously causing economic destruction in their communities, divisions among Christians, and thinning the ranks for heaven. Chapter 5 offered a detailed, critical examination of Basil of Caesarea's *Homilia in psalmum 14* and Gregory of Nyssa's *Contra usurarios*,

---

1. It is possible to conclude that some bishops suggest that usury rates set within legal limits were acceptable; we note the loophole that Clement of Alexandria leaves, in his adaptation of Philo's words against usury (*Stromata*, PG 8:1023). Similar to Clement, St. Ambrose allows for the same distinction, but in much less ambiguous language (Ambrose, *De Tobia*, 15.51 [PL 14:779]).

revealed noteworthy mutual qualities and differences, and provided the answer to the question: To what extent does Gregory's homily depend on Basil's? This chapter offered a synopsis of their lives in Cappadocia; the opinions of Gregory and Basil regarding poverty, debt and usury as they were refined in selections of their ascetic writings; and each of the brother's texts on usury was examined in great detail. It was determined that Basil and Gregory wrote two homilies on usury that were different from each other in manifold ways, including their foundational influences, use of Scripture, their independent motivations or occasions for the sermons, their use of point of view, their divergent sympathies for lender/debtor, and their distinct uses of similar themes.

While it was Maloney's desire to improve upon and update Seipel's work from early in the century, so too the goal for this project was to further Maloney's contribution. Writing in 1973, Maloney points out in "Teaching of the Fathers on Usury" that there had been no full treatment of "the origins of the early Christian teaching on usury."[2] According to Maloney, Seipel's work on this subject had grown outdated due to the greater accessibility of sources on the subject of usury. While Maloney covered "the origins," perhaps this thesis has furnished a more thorough understanding of the specific teachings on usury themselves. It would be foolish to suggest that I could improve upon the work done by Moser, as his text contributes enormously towards understanding the great synthesis of intellectual thought that provided the foundation for the Fathers. But this analysis has contributed by providing the following: a critical examination of writings from the Greek Fathers, critical consideration of Gregory of Nyssa's *Contra usurarios* alongside with and in comparison to Basil's *Homilia in psalmum 14*; a reunion of the important conclusions of Fialon with respect to Basil's sermon.

This text, however, does not accomplish everything with respect to this topic. It will not take this text for people to be reminded of the importance of ethics and economics. For economics—like religion—is not a structure of society, but something one "does"[3] everyday; each dollar extracted from a wallet is an opportunity to make a morally correct choice, and each supplicant encountered presents one with the opportunity to give freely to God's people, "the poor among you."

The "poor among you" surely includes a woman named "Heraclous," who, in the year 112 CE, being described by herself in her own receipt as "aged about 66 years, with a scar in the middle of her forehead," and being

2. Maloney, "The Teaching of the Fathers on Usury," 241.

3. Sahlins, *Stone Age Economics*, 76.

accompanied by her son Sabinus, who also had "a scar in the middle of his forehead," acknowledged in writing the recovery of a loan from a woman named Tasoucharion for the amount of one thousand, six hundred and twelve silver drachmae, as well as the interest on that loan.[4] This Tasoucharion, the daughter of Petermouthis, son of Posidonius, who also had a scar, was one of the fortunate ones: she had taken a loan and managed to repay both the loan and the interest to Heraclous, her creditor. Sadly, evidence remains that many loans did not end with the same level of satisfaction. If they had, it is likely that neither the Roman law nor the Christian bishops would have taken up legal and verbal arms against the usurer.

According to the Hebrew Scriptures, the problems of scarcity, toil[5] and envy[6] have long plagued society: the one who has and the one who has not will ever be at odds with one another, to moral and mortal detriment. Hebrew lawmakers sought to reduce the possibility for such situations and dealt with the problem of scarcity—and the problems created *by* scarcity— by creating a variety of solutions by which they hoped their community could live in economic peace. For Christianity, Frank Crüsemann notes that the arbitrary treatment of Torah by Christians resulted in an abandonment of "the biblical ethical tradition within the history of the Christian church and its theology."[7] He cites as his example the ready adaptation of the love of neighbor,[8] but the convenient denial of the command for love of strangers.[9] Pointing to the absurdity between forbidding theft and covetousness as applied to daily life but not with regard to business (interest on loans), Crüsemann accurately notes that the "arbitrary treatment of Torah is also amazing because it is controlled by self-interest."[10]

Self-interest too often motivates the moral centre, including the moral centre of the Christian who—conveniently separating the theological from the secular—would claim that "business is business" regardless of circumstances. A Christian powered by self-interest would assert that an individual has a right to take usury first of all because it is legal to do so, and second, because the Christian has been released from the law. This is the same logic Paul encountered in Corinth; his response to the rhetorical

---

4. P.Ryl. 174, in Hunt and Edgar, *Select Papyri*, 1:213.

5. Genesis 3:17b–19.

6. Genesis 4:3–9.

7. Crüsemann, *The Torah*, 5.

8. Leviticus, 19:18.

9. Leviticus, 19:34.

10. Crüsemann, *The Torah*, 5.

statement that "All things are lawful for me"[11] was a reminder that despite this freedom, "not all things are beneficial."[12] While it is dangerous to make sweeping statements, I will risk it with the following: none of the early Greek authors considered usury beneficial. Despite the rare occasion when interest gained on a loan might be turned to the advantage of the faithful,[13] the risks taken far outweighed the probability of success. From this, one can safely conclude that they did not consider usury to be either a moral, justifiable, or advantageous action, but in fact, almost unanimously argued against the practice. In addition to the denunciation of usury, common themes emerged among the early Greek authors: first, they all employed the term "usurer" to designate an individual who is extracting interest—perhaps a life-threatening degree of interest—from someone else, ensnaring an individual in a contractual agreement in which "the borrower's necessities deprive him of freedom in contracting and place him at the mercy of the lender."[14] Because of this contract, the designated "usurer" failed to follow Hebrew Bible prohibitions as well as the injunctions of Jesus to "lend, expecting nothing in return."[15] Second, contrary to my suspicion, they did not employ the term "usurer" as either an insult or as an indication of a sinful individual, but applied it specifically to the individual engaged in such practice. Third, they addressed the problem of usury specifically within their own communities, and denounced it as it infected their individual communities.

Knowing that early Greek authors continued in this tradition of denunciation, and knowing that they borrowed heavily from biblical, philosophical, philological and legal precedents, one might legitimately question what, if anything, did they contribute to the discussion? Two layers were affixed to the condemnation of usury by the early Greek authors: first, legal status does not justify or sanction behavior; rather than argue against the legal protection conceded to usury, they concentrated their attention on the behavior of those who had to live in a society that offered protection under the law for a variety of actions that should have been considered unlawful, just as we do today. The second element they added to the discussion is furthering the reverse concept of usury, in which a

11. 1 Corinthians 6:12a.

12. 1 Corinthians 6:12b.

13. Recall Bishop Desideratus, who, securing a loan through the charity of King Theudebert, carefully managed the loan to the benefit of his community: "the business people of Verdun became rich and they still remain so today" Gregory of Tours, *History of the Franks* (trans. Thorpe), 190–91.

14. Ryan, *Usury and Usury Laws*, 22.

15. Luke 6:34–35.

Christian lends without interest or gives freely to the poor, and, to their benefit, gains credit for themselves in heaven rather than on earth (seen as early as in New Testament texts, and reinforced in the subapostolic tradition). This is taken one step further by Basil and especially Gregory of Nyssa, who both write of God as the one in "debt" to the human creation; within this new definition of "debtor" one hears of a debtor not enfeebled by the position, but anxious to repay a hundred times over those who burden themselves with the responsibility of "my people, to the poor among you."[16] A final thing worth thinking about with respect to the Cappadocian contribution is to what extent *their* writing on usury will be influential for the overall Christian body. We know that Ambrose made generous use of Basil's sermon, and that Ambrose is foundational for the condemnation of usury in the works of medieval theologians. It might be time to return to scholarship that focuses on that era to reconsider the evidence for Cappadocian contribution to the history of Christian attitudes towards lending in the West.

As individuals continued to employ the sermon as a means to attack economic injustices, a further question is the effectiveness of such measures. At the risk of sounding cynical, it did Greek philosophers, Roman emperors and historians, or Greek bishops little good to write, draft laws, or preach against usury, as the practice continued to prevail despite measures taken to reduce unwavering problems of poverty. Greed will always be stronger than the desire to help the poor. But despite the continued presence of usury, enduring denunciations against the practice led to the inability of the usurer ever to gain a reputation as being anything other than completely foul.[17] The usurer might well escape legal retribution, but—if the bishops are correct—that will be sorry consolation when salvation is placed on the scales.

---

16. Exodus 22:25.

17. Perhaps the most well-known and most-imitated usurer is Charles Dickens's Ebenezer Scrooge from *A Christmas Carol*. It is not by accident that Dante places the usurers in the third round of the seventh level of hell; he classifies usury as a sin of violence rather than fraud, and includes usurers among the company of blasphemers and perverts (Dante, "Canto 11," *Dante's Inferno* [trans. Musa] 89–94). If the modern, post-Holocaust reader is able to look beyond the stereotypical negative traits so long and so unfortunately attributed to Jewish persons, then Shakespeare's *The Merchant of Venice* delivers a brilliantly vengeful and greedy creditor in his character Shylock. Another fine example of a usurer devoid of a soul is Edward Lewis Wallant's Sol Nazerman, from *The Pawnbroker*. And in 2000, award-winning mystery writer Lynn Hightower published a murder mystery in which an entire family is brutally murdered in repayment for a defaulted debt. See Hightower, *The Debt Collector*.

Bibliography

Primary Sources

Alciphron. In *The Greek Praise of Poverty: Origins of Ancient Cynicism*, by William D. Desmond. Notre Dame: University of Notre Dame Press, 2003.

Ambrose, Saint. *S. Ambrosii De Tobia*. (PL 14.759–94; CSEL 32.2.469–516). *St. Ambrosii, De Tobia: A Commentary with an Introduction and Translation*. Translated by Lois Miles Zucker. Patristic Studies 35. Washington, DC: Catholic University of America, 1933.

Ancient Roman Statutes: A Translation. Translated by Allan Chester Johnson et al. Austin: University of Texas Press, 1961.

Ancient Texts and Translations. Vol. 2, *The Babylonian Laws*. Edited and translated by G. R. Driver and John C. Miles. Ancient Codes and Laws of the Near East. Oxford: Clarendon, 1955.

Apollonius. In *The History of the Church from Christ to Constantine*, by Eusebius. Translated by G. A. Williamson. London: Penguin, 1965.

———. In Jerome. *De viris illustribus*. 40 (PL 23.655).

Apostolic Constitutions. In *ANF*, vol. 7. Edited by Alexander Roberts and James Donaldson. Peabody, MA: Hendrickson, 1999.

Appian. *Bella civilia, De bello Mithridatico*. Leipzig: Teubner, 1879.

Aristides of Athens. *Apologie: Mit Berücksichtigung der griech. und armenischen Bruchstücke aus dem Syrischen übersetzt von K. Julius*. In: *Fruhchristliche Apologeten und Martyrerakten*. Bibliothek der Kirchenväter 12. Munich: Kösel, 1913.

Aristophanes. *The Clouds*. In *Four Plays by Aristophanes*. Translated by William Arrowsmith et al. New York: Meridian, 1994.

Aristotle. *The Athenian Constitution*. In *Aristotle*. Vol. 20. Translated by H. Rackham. LCL. Cambridge: Harvard University Press, 1935.

———. *Constitution of Athens and Related Texts*. Translated by Kurt von Fritz and Ernst Kapp. Hafner Library of Classics 13. New York: Hafner, 1964.

———. *Politics*. Translated by Benjamin Jowett. Oxford: Clarendon, 1920.

———. *Politics*. In *The Basic Works of Aristotle*. Edited by R. McKeon. New York: Random House, 1941.

———. *The Works of Aristotle in English*. Vol. 9, *Ethica Nicomachea*. Translated by D. G. Ross. Oxford: Oxford University Press, 1963.

Athanasius. *Expositio in psalmum*, 14.2–5 (PG 27:100).

Augustine. *Enarratio in Ps.*126 (PL 37:1692).

———. *De baptismo contra Donatistas*, 4.9 (PL 43:162).

———. *Enarratio in psalmum* 36 (PL 36:386). Edited by J.-P. Migne.

———. *Epistula* 154 (153) (PL 33:665). Edited by J.-P. Migne.

———. *Sermon* 38 (PL 38:239–40). Edited by J.-P. Migne.

———. *Sermon* 86 (PL 38:525–26). Edited by J.-P. Migne.

———. *Sermon* 206 (PL 38:1041). Edited by J.-P. Migne.

———. *Sermon* 239 (PL 38:1128). Edited by J.-P. Migne.

Basil of Caesarea. *Against Those Who Lend at Interest* (PG 29:263–80). In *On Social Justice: St. Basil the Great.* Popular Patristics. Translated by C. Paul Schroeder. Crestwood, NY: St Vladimir's Seminary Press, 2009.

———. *Homilia de invidia* (PG 31:371–86). *Homily 11, Concerning Envy.* In *Saint Basil: Ascetical Works*, vol. 9. Translated by M. Monica Wagner. Washington, DC: Catholic University of America Press, 1950.

———. *Homilia dicta tempore famis et siccitatis* 325 (PG 31:303-28). *In Time of Famine and Drought.* In *The Hungry Are Dying: Beggars and Bishops in Roman Cappadocia.* Translated by Susan R. Holman. Oxford Studies in Historical Theology. Oxford: Oxford University Press, 2001.

———. *Homilia in divites* 4 (CPG 2581). In *Faith and Wealth: A History of Early Christian Ideas on the Origin, Significance, and Use of Money*, by Justo L. Gonzales. San Francisco: Harper & Row, 1990.

———. *Homilia in illud dictum evangelii secundum Lucam: "Destruam horrea mea, et maiora aedificabo"; itemque de avaritia* 322 (PG 31:261–78). In *Basil of Caesarea*, by Philip Rousseau. The Transformation of the Classical Heritage 23. Berkeley: University of California Press, 1994.

———. *Homilia in psalmum* 14 (PG 29:263–80). *Homily 12: A Psalm of David Against Usurers; On Psalm 14.* In *Saint Basil: Exegetical Homilies.* Translated by Agnes Clare Way, CDP. The Fathers of the Church. Washington, DC: Catholic University of America Press, 1963.

———. *Homilia quod Deus non est auctor malorum* 336 (PG 31:329-54). In Philip Rousseau. *Basil of Caesarea.* Berkeley: University of California Press, 1994.

———. *Homilia quod rebus mundanis adhaerendum non sit, et de incendi extra Ecclesiam facto* (PG 31:539–64). *Homily 21, On Detachment From Worldly Goods and Concerning the Conflagration Which Occurred in the Environs of the Church.* In *Saint Basil: Ascetical Works*, vol. 9. Translated by M. Monica Wagner. Washington, DC: Catholic University of America Press, 1950.

———. *Letter 58, To Gregory, His Brother.* In *Saint Basil, the Letters.* Translated by Roy J. Deferrari. LCL. Cambridge: Harvard University Press, 1930.

———. *Letter 100, To Eusebius, Bishop of Samosata.* In *Saint Basil, the Letters.* Translated by Roy J. Deferrari. LCL. Cambridge: Harvard University Press, 1930.

———. *Letter 188, To Amphilochius, on the Canons* (PG 32:220–1112). In *Saint Basil: The Letters.* Translated by Roy J. Deferrari. LCL. Cambridge: Harvard University Press, 1930.

———. *Letter 199, To Amphilochius, on the Canons.* In *Saint Basil, the Letters.* Translated by Roy J. Deferrari. LCL. Cambridge: Harvard University Press, 1930.

———. *Letter 204, To the Neocaesareans.* In *Saint Basil, the Letters.* Translated by Roy J. Deferrari. London: Heineman, 1930.

———. *Letter 217, To Amphilochius, on the Canons.* In *Saint Basil, the Letters.* Translated by Roy J. Deferrari. LCL. Cambridge: Harvard University Press, 1930.

———. *Letter* 223, *Against Eustathius of Sebaste*. In *Saint Basil, the Letters*. Translated by Roy J. Deferrari. LCL. Cambridge: Harvard University Press, 1930.

———. *Question* 42, in *The Long Rules* (PG 31:890–1052). In *Saint Basil: Ascetical Works*, vol. 9. Translated by M. Monica Wagner. Washington, DC: Catholic University of America Press, 1950.

———. *Sermo de ascetica disciplina, quomodo monachum ornari oporteat* (PG 31:647–52). *Discourse on Ascetical Discipline: How the Monk Should Be Equipped*. In *Saint Basil: Ascetical Works*, vol. 9. Translated by M. Monica Wagner. Washington, DC: Catholic University of America Press, 1950.

Cato. *On Agriculture*. Book I. Translated by William Davis Hooper and Harrison Boyd Ash. LCL. Cambridge: Harvard University Press, 1934.

Cicero. *Letters to Atticus*, volume 1. Edited and translated by D. R. Shackleton Bailey. LCL. Cambridge: Harvard University Press, 1999.

———. *Letters to Atticus*. Vol. 1. Translated by E. O. Winstedt. LCL. Cambridge: Harvard University Press, 1928.

———. *On the Republic. On The Laws*. Translated by Clinton Walker Keyes. LCL. Cambridge: Harvard University Press, 1928.

———. *Three Books of Offices, or Moral Duties*. Translated by Cyrus R. Edmonds. London: Bell, 1916.

Clement of Alexandria. *Pædagogus* (PG 8:363). In *The ANF* 2. Edited by Alexander Roberts and James Donaldson. 10 vols. Peabody, MA: Hendrickson, 1999.

———. *The Stromata* (PG 8:685–1382). In *ANF* 2. Edited by Alexander Roberts and James Donaldson. 10 vols. Peabody, MA: Hendrickson, 1999.

———. *Who Is the Rich Man That Shall be Saved?* (PG 9:602–52). Translation by G. W. Butterworth. LCL. Cambridge: Harvard University Press, 1919.

Codex Justinianus. In *The Civil Law*, by S. P. Scott. Cincinnati: Central Trust, 1932.

Commodianus. *The Instructions*, 65 (PL 59:163). In *ANF* 4. Edited by Alexander Roberts and James Donaldson. 10 vols. Peabody, MA: Hendrickson, 1999.

Cornelius Nepos. *Epaminondas*. In *Lives of Miltiades and Epaminondas*. Edited by G. H. Nall. London: Macmillan, 1900.

Cyprian. *De lapsis*, 6 (PL 4:470–71). In *Works*, vol. 3. Edited by G. Hartel, 1868. CSEL 3.

———. *Testimoniorum*, 3.48 (PL 4:675.). In *Works*, vol. 3. Edited by G. Hartel. 1868. CSEL 3.

Cyril of Jerusalem. *Catechesis* 4: *De Decem Dogmatibus* (PG 33.454–504). *Lecture* 4; *On the Ten Points of Doctrine. Colossians* 2.8. In *NPNF²* 7. Edited by Philip Schaff and Henry Wace. 14 vols. Peabody, MA: Hendrickson, 1999.

Dante. *Dante's Inferno, The Indiana Critical Edition*. Edited and translated by Mark Musa. Indiana Masterpiece Editions. Bloomington: Indiana University Press, 1995.

Demosthenes. *Against Neara*. In *Orations*, Vol. 6, *Orations* 50–58: *Private Cases. In Neaeram*. Translated by A. T. Murray. LCL. Cambridge: Harvard University Press, 1988.

———. *Against Pantaenetus*. In *Orations*, Vol. 4, *Orations* 27–40: *Private Cases*. Translated by A. T. Murray. Cambridge: Harvard University Press, 1965.

———. *De falsa legatione*. In *Orations*, Vol. 2, *Orations* 18–19: *De Corona, De Falsa Legatione*. Translated by C. A. Vince and J. H. Vince. LCL. Cambridge: Harvard University Press, 1926.

Dickens, Charles. *A Christmas Carol*. In *A Christmas Carol and Other Christmas Writings*. Penguin Classics. 2010.

Didache. In *The Apostolic Fathers*, Vol. 1, *I Clement. II Clement. Ignatius. Polycarp. Didache*. Translated by Kirsopp Lake. LCL. Cambridge: Harvard University Press, 1912.

Dio Chrysostom. *The Forty-Sixth Discourse: A Protest against Mistreatment by His Fellow Citizens*. In *Dio Chrysostom: Discourses 37–60*. Translated by H. Lamar Crosby. LCL. Cambridge: Harvard University Press, 1930.

Diodorus of Sicily. *Bibliotheca historica*. In *Diodorus Siculus: Library of History, V olume I, Books 1–2.34*. Translated by C. H. Oldfather. LCL. Cambridge: Harvard University Press, 1933.

"Elephantini Papyri," 10 and 11. In *Aramaic Papyri of the 5th Century B.C*. Edited by A. E. Cowley. 1923. Reprint, Ancient Texts and Translations. Eugene, OR: Wipf & Stock, 2005.

Epistle to Diognetus. In *The Apostolic Fathers*. Vol. 2, *The Shepherd of Hermas, The Martyrdom of Polycarp, The Epistle to Diognetus*. Translated by Kirsopp Lake. LCL. Cambridge: Harvard University Press, 1913.

Epistle of Barnabas. In *The Apostolic Fathers*. Vol. 1, *I Clement. II Clement. Ignatius. Polycarp. Didache*. Translated by Kirsopp Lake. LCL. Cambridge: Harvard University Press, 1912.

Euripides. *Helena*. Edited by G. G. A. Murray Oxford: Clarendon, 1902.

Eusebius. *The History of the Church from Christ to Constantine*. Translated by G. A. Williamson. London: Penguin, 1965.

Gaius. *The Institutes*. In *The Civil Law*, by S. P. Scott. Cincinnati: Central Trust, 1932.

Gratian. *Decretum Gratiani*, 14.4.12. In *The Scholastic Analysis of Usury*, by John T. Noonan. Cambridge: Harvard University Press, 1957.

Gregory Nazianzen, Saint. *Letter 197*. In *The Fathers Speak: St Basil the Great, St Gregory Nazianzus, St Gregory of Nyssa*. Translated by Georges A. Barrois. Crestwood, NY: St. Vladimir's Seminary Press, 1986.

———. *Oratio 16, In patrum tacentum propter plagam grandinis* (PG 35.934–64). *Introduction To Oration 16. On His Father's Silence, Because Of The Plague Of Hail*. In *NPNF²* 7. Edited by Philip Schaff and Henry Wace. 14 vols. Peabody, MA: Hendrickson, 1999.

———. *Oration 14: On the Love of the Poor and Those Afflicted with Leprosy*. In Vol. 4 of *The Sunday Sermons of the Great Fathers: A Manual of Preaching, Spiritual Reading and Meditation*. Edited and translated by M. F. Toal. Chicago: Regnery, 1963.

———. *Oratio 43, In laudem Basilii magni* (PG. 36:494–606). *Oration 43: The Panegyric on St. Basil*. In *NPNF²* 7. Edited by Philip Schaff and Henry Wace. 14 vols. Peabody, MA: Hendrickson, 1999.

Gregory of Nyssa, Saint. *Concerning Beneficence* (PG 46:543–64). In *The Hungry are Dying: Beggars and Bishops in Roman Cappadocia*. Translated by Susan R. Holman. Oxford: Oxford University Press, 2001.

———. *For the Abuse You Did Against Them You Did Against Me* (PG 46:472–89). In *The Hungry Are Dying: Beggars and Bishops in Roman Cappadocia*. Translated by Susan R. Holman. Oxford: Oxford University Press, 2001.

———. *On Pilgrimages*. In *NPNF²* 5. Edited by Philip Schaff and Henry Wace. 14 vols. Peabody, MA: Hendrickson, 1999.

———. *Vita S. Macrinæ Virginis* (PG 46:959–1000). *The Life of Macrina*. In *Handmaids of the Lord: Contemporary Descriptions of Feminine Asceticism in the First Six*

Christian Centuries. Edited and translated by Joan M. Peterson. Cistercian Studies Series 43. Kalamazoo, MI: Cistercian, 1996.

———. *Letter* 13.5 (MG 46:1049A). In *The Cappadocians*, by Anthony Meredith. Crestwood, NY: St. Vladimir's Seminary Press, 1995.

———. *De Anima et Resurrectione Dialogus* (PG 46:11–160). *On the Soul and Resurrection*. Translated by Catharine P. Roth. Crestwood, NY: St. Vladimir's Seminary Press, 1993.

———. *In Ecclesiasten, homilia* 4 (PG 44:615–754). In *Gregory of Nyssa, Homilies on Ecclesiastes: An English Version with Supporting Studies. Proceedings of the Seventh International Colloquium on Gregory of Nyssa (St. Andrews, 5–10 September 1990)*. Edited by Stuart George Hall. Translation by Stuart George Hall and Rachel Moriarty Berlin: de Gruyter: 1993.

———. *Contra usurarios* (PG 46:433–52). In "Against Those Who Practice Usury by Gregory of Nyssa." Translated by Casimir McCambley. *Greek Orthodox Theological Review* 36/3–4 (1991) 287–302.

———. *Epistola Canonica AS S. Letoium Melitines Episcopum* (PG 45:233B). In "Against Those Who Practice Usury by Gregory of Nyssa," by Casimir McCambley. *Greek Orthodox Theological Review* 36/3–4 (1991) 287–302.

———. *De Vita Moysis* (PG 44:298–430). *The Life of Moses*. Translated by Abraham J. Malherbe and Everett Ferguson. Classics of Western Spirituality. New York: Paulist, 1978.

———. *Saint Gregory of Nyssa: Ascetical Works*. Translated by Virginia Woods Callahan. Washington, DC: Catholic University of America Press, 1967.

———. *De virginitate* (PG 46:317–416). *On Virginity*, in *Saint Gregory of Nyssa: Ascetical Works*. Translated by Virginia Woods Callahan. Washington, DC: Catholic University of America Press, 1967.

———. *Contra Eunomium* (PG 45:243–1122). In *Gregorii Nysseni Opera Ascetica*. Edited by W. Jaeger. Gregorii Nysseni Opera 8.1. Leiden: Brill, 1967. *Against Eunomius*. In *NPNF²* 5. Edited by Philip Schaff and Henry Wace. Peabody, MA: Hendrickson, 1999.

———. *In Inscriptiones Psalmorum*. Edited by J. MacDonough and P. Alexander. Gregorii Nysseni Opera 5. Leiden: Brill, 1962.

——— *In Inscriptiones Psalmorum*. In *Gregory of Nyssa: Ascetical Works*. Translated by Virginia Woods Callahan. Washington, DC: Catholic University of America Press, 1967.

———. *In Canticum Canticorum*. Edited by J. Langerbeck. Gregorii Nysseni Opera 6. Leiden: Brill, 1962.

———. *Sermon* 5, *Forgive us our debts, as we forgive our debtors. And lead us not into temptation. But deliver us from evil*. In *The Lord's Prayer; The Beatitudes*. Translated by Hilda C. Graef. ACW 18. Westminster, MD: Newman, 1954.

———. Gregory of Nyssa *In laudem Basillii* 17. In *Encomium of Saint Gregory, Bishop of Nyssa, on His Brother Saint Basil, Archbishop of Caesarea*. Translated by Sister James Aloysius Stein Patristic Studies 17. Washington, DC: Catholic University of America Press, 1928.

———. *In Praise of Gregory Thaumaturgus* (PG 46:893–958). Edited by J.-P. Migne. 161 vols.

Gregory of Tours. *History of the Franks*. Translated by Lewis Thorpe London: Penguin, 1974.

Hesiod. *Works and Days*. Translated by David W. Tandy and Walter C. Neale. Berkeley: University of California Press, 1996.

Hieronymus. *In Ezechielem Commentarii* 6.18 (PL 25:176). Edited by J.-P. Migne. 217 vols.

Hilary of Poitiers, Saint. *Tractatus in psalmos* 14 (PL 9:231). Edited by A. Zingerk. CSEL 22. N.p.: 1891.

Hunt, A. S., and C. C. Edgar, translators. *Select Papyri: In Five Volumes.* Vol. 1, *Non-Literary Papyri: Private Affairs.* LCL. Cambridge: Harvard University Press, 1959.

———. *The Tebtunis Papyri*, Vol. 3, Part 1. London: Frowde, 1933.

Isocrates. *Isocrates II: On the Peace. Areopagiticus. Against the Sophists. Antidosis. Panathenaicus.* Translated by George Norlin. LCL. Cambridge: Harvard University Press, 1929.

Jerome, Saint. *De viris Illustribus* 40 (PL 23:655). Edited by J.-P. Migne. 217 vols.

———. *In Ezechielem Commentarii* 6:18 (PL 25.176). Edited by J.-P. Migne. 217 vols.

John Chrysostom, Saint. *Epistolam primam ad Corinthios*; *Homilia* 13, PG 61:107–14. In *The Nicene and Post- Nicene Fathers*, 1st series. Vol. 12. Edited by Philip Schaff. 14 vols. Peabody, MA: Hendrickson, 1999.

———. *Epistolam secundam ad Corinthios*; *Homilia* 3, PG 61:405–18. In *NPNF*[1] 12. Edited by Philip Schaff. 14 Vols. Peabody, MA: Hendrickson, 1999.

———. *Epistolam primam ad Corinthios*; *Homilia* 43 (PG 61.367–74). In *NPNF*[1] 12. Edited by Philip Schaff. 14 vols. Repr. Peabody, MA: Hendrickson, 1999.

———. *Epistolam ad Romanos*; *Homilia* 11, PG 60:331–564. In *NPNF*[1] 11. Edited by Philip Schaff. 14 vols. Peabody, MA: Hendrickson, 1999.

———. *Epistulam primam ad Thessalonicenses*; *Homilia* 10 (PG 62:460). Edited by J.-P. Migne. 161 vols.

———. *Epistulam primam ad Thessalonicenses*; *Homilia* 56 (PG 58:558). Edited by J.-P. Migne. 161 vols.

———. *Epistolam primam ad Timotheum*, *Homilia* 11, 2.20 (PG 62:501–662). Edited by J.-P. Migne. 161 vols.

———. *Homiliæ in Matthævm*, *Homilia* 5 (PG 57:55–62). *NPNF*[1] 10. Edited by Philip Schaff. 14 Vols. Repr. Peabody, Mass.: Hendrickson, 1999.

———. *Homiliæ in Matthævm*, *Homilia* 18 (PG. 57:265–74). In *NPNF*[1] 10. Edited by Philip Schaff. 14 vols. Peabody, MA: Hendrickson, 1999.

———. *Homiliæ in Matthævm*, *Homilia* 28 (PG 57:349–58). In *NPNF* [1] 10. Edited by Philip Schaff. 14 vols. Peabody, MA: Hendrickson, 1999.

———. *Homiliæ in Matthævm*, *Homilia* 37 (PG 57:419–28). In *NP1NF*[1] 10. Edited by Philip Schaff. 14 vols. Peabody, MA: Hendrickson, 1999.

———. *Homiliæ in Matthævm*, *Homilia* 45 (PG 58.471–76). *NPNF*[1]10. Edited by Philip Schaff. 14 vols. Peabody, MA: Hendrickson, 1999.

———. *Homiliæ in Matthævm*, *Homilia* 56 (PG 58:549–58). In *NPNF*[1] 10. Edited by Philip Schaff. 14 vols. Peabody, MA: Hendrickson, 1999.

———. *Homiliæ in Matthævm*, *Homilia* 64 (PG 58.609–18). In *NPNF*[1] 10. Edited by Philip Schaff. 14 vols. Peabody, MA: Hendrickson, 1999.

———. *Homiliæ in Matthævm*, *Homilia* 78 (PG 58:711–18). In *NPNF*[1] 10. Edited by Philip Schaff. 14 vols. Peabody, MA: Hendrickson, 1999.

———. *Homiliæ in Genesin* 41 (PG 53:375–86). In *Saint John Chrysostom, Homilies on Genesis*: 18–45, 400–417. Translated by Robert C. Hill. Washington, DC: Catholic University of America Press, 1990.

Juvenal. *Saturae.* Edited by C. F. Hermanni. Leipzig: Teubner, 1911. In Maloney, Robert P. "Usury in Greek, Roman, and Rabbinic Thought." *Traditio* 27 (1971) 92.

Lactantius. *Epitome* 64 (PL 6:1076). Edited by J.-P. Migne. 217 vols.

———. *Institutiones divinae*, 6.18 (PL 6.698–99). Edited by S. Brandt and G. Laubmann CSEL 19. Vindobonae: Tempsky, 1890.

Leo the Great. *Nec hoc quoque* (PL 54:613). Edited by J.-P. Migne. 217 vols.

———. *Sermo* 17, *Lending to the Lord Is a Better Bargain than Lending to Man* (PL 54.180–82). Edited by J.-P. Migne. 217 vols.

Lessius, Leonard. *De Jure et Justitia.* 20:88. Venice, 1617.

Libanius. *Orations* 11:230. In Hendy, Michael F. "Economy and State in Late Rome and Early Byzantium." In *The Economy, Fiscal Administration, and Coinage of Byzantium.* Northampton: Variorum, 1989.

———. *Orations*, 1:205, 226, 29, *passim.* In Jones, A. H. M. *The Roman Economy: Studies in Ancient Economic and Administrative History.* Oxford: Blackwell, 1974.

Livy. *History of Rome.* Translated by B. O. Foster. LCL. Cambridge: Harvard University Press, 1919.

Lucian. *Epigram* 43. In *Philostratus and Eunapius: The Lives of the Sophists.* Translated by Wilmer Cave Wright. LCL. Cambridge: Harvard University Press, 1922.

Lysias. *Subversion of the Democracy*, 25.13. In *Merit and Responsibility: A Study in Greek Values*, by A. W. H. Adkins, 202. Oxford, Clarendon, 1960.

Martyrius of Antioch. *Ex laudatione in Sanctum Patrem Nostrum Johannem Chrysostomum Archiepiscopum Constantinopoleos.* In *Nova patrum biblithecae.* Vol. 2. 1782–1854.

Mekiltha on Exodus. Edited by Jacob Z. Lauterback. Philadelphia: Jewish Publication Society of America, 1933.

Mishnah. Translated by Herbert Danby. Oxford: Oxford University Press, 1933.

Mishpatim, Exodus Rabbah. In Susan R. Holman, *The Hungry Are Dying: Beggars and Bishops in Roman Cappadocia.* Oxford: Oxford University Press, 2001.

Origen. *In psalmum 36, homiliae.* 3.11 (PG 12:1347). Edited by J.-P. Migne. 161 vols.

Philo. *The Special Laws.* In vol. 7 of *On the Decalogue. On the Special Laws, Books* 1-3 and in vol. 8 of *On the Special Laws, Book* 4. *On the Virtues. On Rewards and Punishments.* Edited by G. P. Goold. Translated by F. H. Cohen. LCL. Cambridge: Harvard University Press, 1999.

———. *On The Virtues.* In vol. 8 of *On the Special Laws, Book* 4. *On the Virtues. On Rewards and Punishments.* Edited by G. P. Goold. Translated by F. H. Cohen. Loeb Classical Library. Cambridge: Harvard University Press, 1999.

Pindar. *Pythia.* Edited by B. Snell. Leipzig: Teubner, 1959.

Plato. *The Republic.* Vol. 1, Books 1-5. Translated by Paul Shorey Cambridge: Harvard University Press, 1978.

———. *The Laws of Plato.* Translated by Thomas L. Prangle New York: Basic Books, 1980.

Pliny. *Epistle* 3. In *Trade, Transport and Society in the Ancient World: A Sourcebook.* Edited and translated by Fik Meijer and Onno van Nijf. London: Routledge, 1992.

———. *Letters and Panegyrics*, vols. 1 and 2. Translated by Betty Radice. LCL. Cambridge: Harvard University Press, 1969.

Pliny the Elder. In vol. 4 of *Natural History Books* 12–16. Translated by H. Rackham. LCL. Cambridge: Harvard University Press, 1960.

Plutarch. *Sulla.* In vol. 4 of *Lives: Alcibiades and Coriolanus. Lysander and Sulla.* Translated by Bernadette Perrin. LCL. Cambridge: Harvard University Press, 1914–26.

————. *Solon*. In *The Rise and Fall of Athens: Nine Greek Lives by Plutarch*. Translated by Ian Scott-Kilvert. London: Penguin, 1979.

————. "That We Ought Not to Borrow (*De vitando aere alieno*)." In *Love Stories: That a Philosopher Ought to Converse Especially With Men in Power. To an Uneducated Ruler. Whether an Old Man Should Engage in Public Affairs. Precepts of Statecraft. On Monarchy, Democracy, and Oligarchy. That We Ought Not to Borrow. Lives of the Ten Orators. Summary of a Comparison Between Aristophanes and Menander*. Vol. 10 Translated by Harold North Fowler. LCL. Cambridge: Harvard University Press, 1936.Scott, S. P. *The Civil Law*. Cincinnati: Central Trust, 1932.

Seneca. *De Tranquillitate Animi*. In vol. 2, *Moral Essays, De Consolatione ad Marciam. De Vita Beata. De Otio. De Tranquillitate Animi. De Brevitate Vitae. De Consolatione ad Polybium. De Consolatione ad Helviam*. Translated by John W. Basore. Loeb Classical Library. Cambridge: Harvard University Press, 1969.

————. *Epistle* 14. In vol 3 of the *Epistles*, 93–124. LCL. Cambridge: Harvard University Press, 1967.

————. *Of a Happy Life*. In *The Morals of Seneca: A Selection of His Prose*. Edited by Walter Clode. London: Walter Scott, 1888.

————. *On Benefits*. In vol. 3 of *Moral Essays, De Beneficiis*. Translated by John W. Basore. LCL. Cambridge: Harvard University Press, 1935.

Seven Ecumenical Councils of the Undivided Church; Their Canons and Dogmatic Decrees, Together with the Canons of All the Local Synods which have received Ecumenical Acceptance. In NPNF² 14. Edited by Philip Schaff. 14 vols. Peabody, MA: Hendrickson, 1999.

Shakespeare, William. *The Merchant of Venice*. N.p.: Simon & Brown, 2011.

Shepherd of Hermas. In *The Apostolic Fathers*, Vol. 1, *I Clement. II Clement. Ignatius. Polycarp. Didache*. Translated by Kirsopp Lake. LCL. Cambridge: Harvard University Press, 1912.

Siphra on Leviticus. In J. Bonsirven. *Textes Rabbiniques*. Rome: Pontifical Biblical Institute, 1955. In Maloney, Robert P. "Usury in Greek, Roman, and Rabbinic Thought." *Traditio* 27 (1971) 105.

Siphra on Deuteronomy. In Bonsirven, J. *Textes Rabbiniques*. Rome: Pontifical Biblical Institute, 1955. In Maloney, Robert P. "Usury in Greek, Roman, and Rabbinic Thought." *Traditio*, 27 (1971) 97.

Sozomen. *The Ecclesiastical History of Sozomen*. In NPNF² 2. Edited by Philip Schaff and Henry Wace. 14 vols. Peabody, MA.: Hendrickson, 1999.

Tacitus. *The Annals*. Translated by John Jackson. LCL. Cambridge: Harvard University Press, 1937.

Talmud Bavli. B'rakhot 35a. In *With All Your Possessions: Jewish Ethics and Economic Life*, by Tamari Meir. New York: Free Press, 1987.

Tertullian. *Aduersus Marcionem*, (PL 2:428). Edited by J.-P. Migne. 217 vols.

Theodoret. 77 (PG 83:1252–56). *To Eusebius, bishop of Persian Armenia*. In NPNF² 3. Edited by Philip Schaff and Henry Wace. 14 vols. Peabody, MA: Hendrickson, 1999.

The Theodosian Code and Novels, and the Sirmondian Constitutions. Translated by Clyde Pharr, with Theresa Sherrer Davidson and Mary Brown Pharr. The Corpus of Roman Law 1. Princeton. Princeton University Press, 1952.

Theophanes. *The Chronicle of Theophanes*. Translated by Harry Turtledove. The Middle Ages. Philadelphia: University of Pennsylvania Press, 1982.

Theophrastus. *Characters*. Edited and translated by Jeffrey Rusten and I. C. Cunningham. LCL 225. Cambridge: Harvard University Press, 2002.

Thucydides. "Pericles' Funeral Oration." In *The Peloponnesian War*, 2:37. Quoted in Sir Alfred Eckhard Zimmern. *The Greek Commonwealth: Politics and Economics in Fifth-Century Athens*. 5th ed. rev. London: Oxford University Press, 1961.

Secondary Sources

Abrams, Mary E. *Moving the Rock: Poverty and Faith in a Black Storefront Church*. Lanham, MD: AltaMira, 2009.

Allen, Pauline. "Challenges in Approaching Patristic Texts." In *Reading Patristic Texts on Social Ethics: Issues and Challenges for Twenty-First-Century Christian Social Thought*, edited by Johan Leemans et al., 30–42. CUA Studies in Early Christianity. Washington, DC: Catholic University of America Press, 2011.

Andreades, A. M. *A History of Greek Public Finance*. Translated by C. N. Brown. Cambridge: Harvard University Press, 1933.

Andreau, Jean. *Banking and Business in the Roman World*. Translated by Janet Lloyd. Key Themes in Ancient History. Cambridge: Cambridge University Press, 1999.

Avila, Charles. *Ownership: Early Christian Teaching*. 1983. Reprinted, Eugene, OR: Wipf & Stock, 2004.

Ballard, Bruce. "On the Sin of Usury: A Biblical Economic Ethic." *Christian-Scholar's Review* 24 (1994) 210–28.

Balthasar, Hans Urs von. *Presence and Thought: An Essay on the Religious Philosophy of Gregory of Nyssa*. Communio Books. San Francisco: Ignatius, 1995.

Barker, Sir Ernest. *Greek Political Theory: Plato and His Predecessors*. London: Methuen, 1918.

Baron, S. W. *A Social and Religious History of the Jews*. Vol. 1. New York: Columbia University Press, 1952.

Barlow, Charles Thomas. "Bankers, Moneylenders and Interest Rates in the Roman Republic." PhD diss., University of North Carolina, 1978.

Barthet, Bernard. *S'enrichir en dormant: L'argent et les religions*. Paris: Brouwer, 1998.

Beauchet, Ludovic. *Histoire du droit privé de la républic athénienne*. Paris: Chevalier-Marescq et Cie, 1897.

Belloc, Hilaire. *Usury*. King's Land: Sheed & Ward, 1931.

Benvenisti, J. L. *The Iniquitous Contract: An Analysis of Usury and Maldistribution*. London: Burns, Oats & Washbourne, 1937.

Berger, Adolf. 'Leges Semproniae,' 'Leges Semproniae.' In *The Encyclopedic Dictionary of Roman Law*. American Philosophical Society, 1980.

Bernardi, Jean. *La predication des peres cappadociens: le predicateur et son auditoire*, Publications de la Faculté des lettres et sciences humaines de l'Université de Monpellier, 30. Paris: Presses Universitaires de France, 1968.

Billeter, Gustav. *Geschichte des Zinsfusses*. Leipzig: Teubner, 1898.

Bradshaw, Matt, and Christopher G Ellison. "Financial Hardship and Psychological Distress: Exploring the Buffering Effects of Religion." *Social Science & Medicine* 71 (2010) 196–204.

Brown, Peter. *The World of Late Antiquity: AD 150–750*. Library of World Civilization. New York: Norton, 1989.

Buckley, Susan L. *Teachings on Usury in Judaism, Christianity and Islam.* Texts and Studies in Religion 85. Lewiston, NY: Mellen, 2000.

———. *Usury Friendly? The Ethics of Moneylending: A Biblical Interpretation.* Grove Ethics Studies 110. Cambridge, UK: Grove, 1998.

Bury, J. B. *History of the Later Roman Empire: From the Death of Theodosius I to the Death of Justinian.* Vol. 2. London: Macmillan, 1923.

Cameron, Rondo E., and Larry Neal. *A Concise Economic History of the World: From Paleolithic Times to the Present.* 4th ed. New York: Oxford University Press, 2003.

Charanis, Peter. *Social, Economic and Political Life in the Byzantine Empire.* London: Variorum, 1973.

Cleary, Patrick. *The Church and Usury: An Essay on Some Historical and Theological Aspects of Money Lending.* Dublin: Gill, 1914.

Constantelos, Demetrios J. *Byzantine Philanthropy and Social Welfare.* Rutgers Byzantine Series. New Brunswick, NJ: Rutgers University Press, 1968.

Cox, Donald M. "The History of Interest and Usury to the Nineteenth Century." Colorado College, 1950.

Coxe, A. Cleveland. "Introductory Note to Clement of Alexandria." In *ANF* 2. Edited by Alexander Roberts and James Donaldson. Peabody, MA: Hendrickson, 1999.

Cross, F. L., and E. A. Livingston, editors. *The Oxford Dictionary of the Christian Church.* Oxford: Oxford University Press, 1997.

Crüsemann, Frank. *The Torah: Theology and Social History of Old Testament Law.* Translated by Allan W. Mahnke. Minneapolis: Fortress, 1996.

Daley, Brian E. "Building a New City: The Cappadocian Fathers and the Rhetoric of Phil-anthropy." *Journal of Early Christian Studies* 7 (1999) 431–61.

———. *The Hope of the Early Church: A Handbook of Patristic Eschatology.* Peabody, MA: Hendrickson, 2003.

Daniélou, Jean. "Chronologie des sermons de Saint Grégoire de Nysse." *Revue des Sciences Religieuses* 29 (1955) 346–72.

———, editor. *From Glory to Glory: Texts from Gregory of Nyssa's Mystical Writings.* Translated by Herbert Musurillo. London: Murray, 1962.

Dawson, David. *Allegorical Readers and Cultural Revision in Ancient Alexandria.* Berkeley: University of California Press, 1992.

Deconto, Jesse James. "The People's Interest: A New Battle against Usury." *Christian Century* January 12, 2010, 20–24.

Dempsey, Bernard. *Interest and Usury.* Washington, DC: American Council on Public Affairs, 1942.

Derrett, J. D. M. "Fresh Light on St. Luke 16. The Parable of the Unjust Steward." *New Testament Studies* 7 (1960–61) 198–219.

Desmond, William D. *The Greek Praise of Poverty: Origins Of Ancient Cynicism.* Notre Dame: University of Notre Dame Press, 2006.

Drinkwater, Francis H. *Money and Social Justice.* London: Burns, Oates & Washbourne,1934.

———. *Why Not End Poverty?* London: Burns, Oates & Washbourne, 1935.

Duke, Anna et al. "Natural Disasters as Moral Lessons: Nazianzus and New Orleans." Presentation at the American Academy of Religion regional meeting, University of Victoria, Victoria, B.C. May, 2010.

Durham, John. *Exodus.* Word Biblical Commentary 3. Waco, TX: Word, 1987.

Eissfeldt, Otto. *The Old Testament: An Introduction.* Translated by Peter R. Ackroyd. Oxford: Blackwell, 1965.

Ellis, I. P. "The Archbishop and the Usurers." *Journal of Ecclesiastical History* 21 (1970) 33–42.

Fedwick, Paul J., editor. *Basil of Caesarea: Christian, Humanist, Ascetic.* A Sixteen-Hundredth Anniversary Symposium, Vol.1. Toronto: Pontifical Institute of Medieval Studies, 1981.

Fialon, Eugene. *Étude historique et littéraire sur Saint Basile suivie de l'hexameron.* Paris: Durand, 1865.

Figulla, H. H., and W. J. Martin. *Letter and Documents of the Old-Babylonian Period.* Ur Excavation Texts 5. British Museum and the University Museum, University of Pennsylvania, 1953.

Finley, M. I. *Economy and Society in Ancient Greece.* Edited with an introduction by Brent D. Shaw and Richard P. Saller. Harmondsworth: Penguin, 1983.

Fish, T. "The Sumarian City Nippur in the Period of the Third Dynasty of Ur." *Iraq* 5 (1938) 157–79.

Fitzmyer, Joseph. "The Story of the Dishonest Manager (Lk. 16:1–13)." *Theological Studies* 25 (1964) 23–42.

Frank, Tenney. *An Economic Survey of Ancient Rome.* 6 vols. Paterson, NJ: Pageant, 1959.

French, Alfred. *Growth of the Athenian Economy.* London: Routledge & Paul, 1964.

Fuks, Alexander. *Social Conflict in Ancient Greece.* Jerusalem: Magnes, 1984.

Geisst, Charles R. *Collateral Damaged: The Marketing of Consumer Debt to America.* New York: Bloomberg, 2009.

Giet, Stanislas. "De Saint Basile à Saint Ambroise: La condamnation du prêt à intérêt au IVᵉ siècle." *Science Religieuse: Travaux et Recherches* 33 (1944) 95–128.

———. *Les idées et l'action sociales de saint Basile.* Paris: Lecoffre, 1941.

Gilbreath, W. J. S. "Martin Luther and John Calvin on the Ethics of Property." *Crux* 22 (1986) 10–18.

Glare, P. G. W., editor. *The Oxford Latin Dictionary.* New York: Oxford University Press, 1983.

Glotz, Gustave. *The Aegean Civilization.* New York: Knopf, 1925.

———. *Ancient Greece at Work: An Economic History of Greece from the Homeric Period to the Roman Conquest.* Translated by M. R. Dobie. New York: Norton, 1967.

———. *The Greek City and Its Institutions.* New York: Barnes & Noble,1965.

Goetze, Albrecht. *The Laws of Eshnunna.* Annual of the American Schools of Oriental Research 31. New Haven: The Department of Antiquities of the Government of Iraq and the American Schools of Oriental Research, 1956.

Gofas, Demetrios. "The Byzantine Law of Interest." In *The Economic History of Byzantium: From the Seventh through the Fifteenth Century,* edited by Angeliki E. Laiou et al. Washington, DC: Dumbarton Oaks Research Library and Collection, 2000.

González, Justo L. *Faith and Wealth: A History of Early Christian Ideas on the Origin, Significance, and Use of Money.* San Francisco: Harper & Row, 1990.

———. *The Story of Christianity.* Vol. 1, *The Early Church to the Dawn of the Reformation.* San Francisco: Harper & Row, 1984.

Gordon, Barry. *The Economic Problem in Biblical and Patristic Thought.* Supplements to Vigiliae Christianae 9. Leiden: Brill, 1989.

Grayzel, Solomon. *The Church and the Jews in the XIIIth Century.* Edited by Kenneth R. Stow. New York: Hermon, 1989.

Grieg, Lucy. "Throwing Parties for the Poor: Poverty and Splendor in the Late Antique Church." In *Poverty in the Roman World*, edited by Margaret A. Atkins and Robin Osborne. Cambridge: Cambridge University Press, 2006.

Hamilton, Jeffries M. "*Ha'ares* In the Shemitta Law." *Vetus Testamentum* 42 (1992) 214–22.

Hands, A. R. *Charities and Social Aid in Greece and Rome.* Aspects of Greek and Roman Life. London: Thames & Hudson, 1968.

Harris, Rivkah. "Old Babylonian Temple Loans." *Journal of Cuneiform Studies* 14 (1960) 126–37.

Heichelheim, Fritz M. *Ancient Economic History: From the Palaeolithic Age to the Migrations of the Germanic, Slavic, and Arabic Nations.* Vol. 1. Translated by Joyce Stevens. Leiden: Sijthoff, 1965.

Heil, Johannes, and Bernd Wacker, editors. *Shylock? Zinsverbot und Geldverleih in jüdischer und christlicher Tradition.* Munich: Fink, 1997.

Hendy, Michael F. "Economy and State in Late Rome and Early Byzantium." In *The Economy, Fiscal Administration, and Coinage of Byzantium.* Northampton: Variorum Reprints, 1989.

Hengel, Martin. *Property and Riches in the Early Church: Aspects of a Social History of Early Christianity.* Translated by John Bowden. London: SCM, 1973.

Hightower, Lynn. *The Debt Collector.* New York: Dell, 2000.

Holman, Susan R. "The Entitled Poor: Human Rights Language in the Cappadocians." *Pro Ecclesia* 9 (2000) 476–89.

———. *God Knows There's Need: Christian Responses to Poverty.* Oxford: Oxford University Press, 2009.

———. *The Hungry Are Dying: Beggars and Bishops in Roman Cappadocia.* Oxford Studies in Historical Theology. Oxford: Oxford: University Press, 2001.

———, editor. *Wealth and Poverty in Early Church and Society.* Holy Cross Studies in Patristic Theology and History. Grand Rapids: Baker Academic, 2008.

———. "'You Speculate on the Misery of the Poor': Usury as Civic Injustice in Basil of Caesarea's Second Homily on Psalm 14." In *Organised Crime in Antiquity*, edited by Keith Hopwood, 207–28. London: Duckworth, 1998.

Homer, Sidney, and Richard Sylla. *A History of Interest Rates.* 3rd. New Brunswick, NJ: Rutgers University Press, 1996.

Horsley, Richard A. *Covenant Economics: A Biblical Vision of Justice for All.* Louisvlle: Westminster John Knox, 2009.

Houkes, John M. *An Annotated Bibliography on the History of Usury and Interest from the Earliest Times through the Eighteenth Century.* Lewiston, NY: Mellen, 2004.

Ihssen, Brenda Llewellyn. "Basil and Gregory's Sermons on Usury: Credit Where Credit is Due." *Journal of Early Christian Studies* 16 (2008) 403–30.

———. "'That Which Has Been Wrung from Tears': Usury, the Greek Fathers, and Catholic Social Teaching." In *Patristic Texts on Social Ethics: Issues and Challenges for Twenty-First-Century Christian Social Thought*, edited by Johan Leemans et al., 124–60. Washington, DC: Catholic University of America Press of America. 2011.

Jacobs, Louis, editor. *The Jewish Religion: A Companion.* Oxford: Oxford University Press, 1995.

Jaeger, Werner. *Two Rediscovered Works of Ancient Christian Literature: Gregory of Nyssa and Macarius*. Leiden: Brill, 1954.

Jeremias, Joachim. *Jerusalem in the Time of Jesus: An Investigation into Economic and Social Conditions during the New Testament Period*. Translated by F. H. Cave and C. H. Cave. London: SCM, 1969.

Johnson, Paul. *A History of the Jews*. London, Orion, 1993.

Johnston, Leonard. *A History of Israel*. New York: Sheed & Ward, 1964.

Jones, A. H. M. *The Later Roman Empire 284–602: A Social Economic and Administrative Survey*. 3 vols. Oxford: Blackwell, 1964.

———. *The Roman Economy: Studies in Ancient Economic and Administrative History*. Edited by P. A. Brunt. Oxford: Blackwell, 1974.

Jones, Arthur. *Capitalism and Christians: Tough Gospel Challenges in a Troubled World Economy*. New York: Paulist, 1992.

Jones, David W. *Reforming the Morality of Usury: A Study of the Differences that Separated the Protestant Reformers*. Dallas: University Press of America, 2004.

Jones, Norman. *God and the Moneylenders: Usury and Law in Early Modern England*. Oxford: Blackwell, 1989.

Jones, T. B., and J. W Snyder. *Sumerian Economic Texts from the Third Ur Dynasty*. Minneapolis: University of Minnesota Press, 1961.

Karayannopoulos, Ioannes. "St. Basil's Social Activity: Principles and Praxis." In *Basil of Caesarea: Christian, Humanist, Ascetic*. A Sixteen-Hundredth Anniversary Symposium. Vol. 1. Edited by Paul Jonathan Fedwick. Toronto: Pontifical Institute of Medieval Studies, 1981.

Keiser, C. E. *Selected Temple Documents of the Ur Dynasty*. Yale Oriental Series: Babylonian Texts 4. New Haven: Yale University Press, 1919.

Kelly, J. N. D. *Golden Mouth: The Story of John Chrysostom, Ascetic, Preacher, Bishop*. Grand Rapids: Baker, 1998.

Kelly, Joseph F. *The World of the Early Christians*. Message of the Fathers of the Church 1. Collegeville: Liturgical, 1997.

Kidner, Derek. *Ezra and Nehemiah*. Tyndale Old Testament Commentary 11. Downers Grove, IL: InterVarsity, 1981.

Kolb, Robert. "No Christian Would Dare Practice Usury." *Concordia Historical Institute Quarterly* 48/4 (1975) 127–41.

Krinsky, R. "Halakah." In *The New Catholic Encyclopedia*, 6:624. 15 vols. Detroit: Thomson/Gale, 2003.

Laiou, Angeliki. "Church, Economic Thought and Economic Practice." In *The Christian East: Its Institutions & Its Thought*, edited by Robert F. Taft. Orientalia Christiana analecta 251. Rome: Pontificio Istituto Orientale, 1996.

———. "Economic Ideology." In *The Economic History of Byzantium: From the Seventh through the Fifteenth Century*, edited by Angeliki E. Laiou. Washington, DC: Dumbarton Oaks Research Library and Collection, 2002.

Landry, David, and Ben May. "Honor Restored: New Light on the Parable of the Prudent Steward (Luke 16:1–8a)." *Journal of Biblical Literature* 119 (2000) 287–309.

Landsberger, B. *Die Serie ana ittisu*. Rome: Pontifical Biblical Institute, 1937.

Langholm, Odd Inge. *The Aristotelian Analysis of Usury*. Bergen: Universiteitsforlaget, 1984.

———. *Price and Value in the Aristotelian Tradition: A Study in Scholastic Economic Sources*. Bergen: Universiteitsforlaget, 1979.

———. *Wealth and Money in the Aristotelian Tradition: A Study in Scholastic Economic Sources*. Bergen: Universiteitsforlaget, 1985.

Lecky, William Edward Hartpole. *The History of the Rise and Influence of the Spirit of Rationalism in Europe*. New York: Braziller, 1955.

Legrain, Leo, editor. *Business Documents of the Third Dynasty of Ur*. Ur Excavation Texts 3. British Museum and University Museum of the University of Pennsylvania, 1947.

Levy, Ernst. *Weströmisches Vulgarrecht: Das Obligationenrecht*. Weimar: Bohlhaus Nachfolger, 1956.

Lewis, Naphtali, editor. *The Documents from the Bar Kochba Period in the Cave of Letters: Greek Papyri*. Judean Desert Studies 2. Jerusalem: Israel Exploration Society/The Hebrew University of Jerusalem/The Shrine of the Book, 1989.

Liddell, H. G. *A Lexicon: Abridged from Liddell and Scott's "A Greek-English Lexicon."* Oxford: Clarendon, 1958.

Liddell, H. G., and R. Scott, editors. *A Greek-English Lexicon*. Oxford: Clarendon, 1996.

Liebeschuetz, J. H. W. G. *Barbarians and Bishops: Army, Church and State in the Age of Arcadius and Chrysostom*. Oxford: Clarendon, 1991.

Long, Stephen D. "Bernard Dempsey's Theological Economics: Usury, Profit, and Human Fulfilment." *Theological Studies* 54 (1996) 690.

Louis, Paul. *Ancient Rome at Work: An Economic History of Rome from the Origins to the Empire*. New York: Knopf, 1927.

Luttrell, G. S. "Usury." In *The Encyclopedia of Biblical and Christian Ethics*. Edited by R. K. Harriston. Nashville: Nelson, 1987.

Malina, Bruce J., and Richard L. Rohrbaugh. *Social-Science Commentary on the Synoptic Gospels*. Minneapolis: Fortress, 1992.

Maloney, Robert P. "The Background for the Early Christian Teaching on Usury." Ann Arbor: University Microfilms, 1969.

———. "Early Conciliar Legislation on Usury: A Contribution to the Study of Christian Moral Thought." *Recherches de théologie ancienne et médiévale* 39 (1972) 145–57.

———. "Teaching of the Fathers on Usury: An Historical Study on the development of Christian thinking." *Vigiliae Christianae* 27 (1973) 241–65.

———. "Usury and Restrictions on Interest-Taking in the Ancient Near East." *Catholic Biblical Quarterly* 36 (1974) 1–20.

———. "Usury in Greek, Roman, and Rabbinic Thought." *Traditio* 27 (1971) 79–109.

Mango, Cyril, *Byzantium: The Empire of New Rome*. New York: Scribner, 1980.

Mark, Jeffrey. *Analysis of Usury*. London: Gordon, 1935.

Marshall, I. H. *The Gospel of Luke*. Exeter: Paternoster, 1978.

Mayer, Wendy, and Pauline Allen. *John Chrysostom*. The Early Church Fathers. London: Routledge, 2000.

McCambley, Casimir. "Against Those Who Practice Usury, by Gregory of Nyssa." *Greek Orthodox Theological Review* 36 (1991) 287–302.

McGuckin, John. *St. Gregory of Nazianzus: An Intellectual Biography*. Crestwood, NY: St. Vladimir's Seminary Press, 2001

McLaughlin, T. P. "The Teaching of the Canonists on Usury (12th, 13th, and 14th Centuries)." *Medieval Studies* 1 (1939) 81–147.

———. "The Teaching of the Canonists on Usury (12th, 13th, and 14th Centuries)." 2 (1940) 1–22.

Meikle, Scott. "Modernism, Economics and the Ancient Economy." In *The Ancient Economy*, edited by Walter Scheidel and Sitta Von Reden. New York, Routedge, 2002.

Meislin, B. J., and M. L. Cohen. "Backgrounds of the Biblical Law against Usury." *Comparative Studies in Society and History* 6 (1963–64) 250–67.

Meredith, Anthony. *The Cappadocians*. Crestwood, NY: St. Vladimir's Seminary Press, 1995.

———. *Gregory of Nyssa*. The Early Church Fathers. Routledge, 1999.

Michell, H. *The Economics of Ancient Greece*. 2nd ed. Cambridge: Heffer, 1957.

Millett, Paul. *Lending and Borrowing in Ancient Athens*. Cambridge: Cambridge University Press, 1991.

Mills, Paul. "The Ban on Interest: Dead Letter or Radical Solution?" *Cambridge Papers* 2/1 (March 1993).

———. *Interest in Interest: The Old Testament Ban in Interest and Its Implications for Today*. Cambridge: Jubilee Centre Publications, 1993.

Mitteis, Ludwig. *Reichsrecht und Volksrecht in dem östlichen Provinzen des römischen Kaiserreichs. Mit Beiträgen zur Kenntniss des griechischen Rechts und der spätrömischen Rechtsentwicklung*. Hildesheim: Olms, 1963.

Morley, Neville. "The Early Roman Empire: Distribution." In *The Cambridge Economic History of the Greco-Roman World*, edited by Walter Scheidel et al. Cambridge: Cambridge University Press, 2008.

Moser, Thomas. *Die patristische Zinslehre und ihre Ursprünge: Vom Zinsgebot zum Wucherverbot (The Patristic Interest Precepts and Its Origin: From the Birth of Interest to the Prohibition of Usury)*. Winterthur: Schellenberg. 1997.

Mott, Stephen Charles. "Interest on Loans as a Sin." *Christian Social Action* 12 (Fall 1999) 31.

Moxnes, Halvor. *The Economy of the Kingdom: Social Conflict and Economic Relations in Luke's Gospel*. Overtures to Biblical Theology 23. 1988. Reprinted, Eugene, OR: Wipf & Stock, 2004.

Murdoch, Iris. *The Nice and the Good*. London: Chatto & Windus, 1968.

Murphy, F. X. "Moral and Ascetical Doctrine in St. Basil." In *Papers Presented to the Sixth International Conference on Patristic Studies Held in Oxford* 1971, edited by Elizabeth A. Livingstone 3:320–26. 3 vols. Studia Patristica 14. Berlin: Akademie, 1976.

Nelson, Benjamin. *The Idea of Usury: From Tribal Brotherhood to Universal Otherhood*. Princeton: Princeton University Press, 1949.

Neufeld, Edward. "Socio-Economic Background of Yobel and Semitta." *Revista degli studi orientali* 33 (1958) 53–124.

———. "Prohibitions against Loans at Interest in Ancient Hebrew Laws." *Hebrew Union College Annual* 26 (1955) 355–412.

Nicholson, E. W. *Deuteronomy and Tradition: Literary and Historical Problems in the Book of Deuteronomy*. Philadelphia: Fortress, 1967.

Noonan, John T. *The Scholastic Analysis of Usury*. Cambridge: Harvard University Press, 1957.

Oakman, Douglas. *Jesus and the Economic Questions of His Day*. Studies in the Bible and Early Christianity 8. Lewiston, NY: Mellon, 1986.

———. *Jesus and the Peasants*. Matrix: The Bible in Mediterranean Context 4. Eugene, OR: Cascade Books, 2008.

Olivier, H. "The Effectiveness of the Old Babylonian Mesarum Decree." *Journal of Northwest Semitic Languages* 12 (1984) 107–13.

Ostrogorsky, George. *History of the Byzantine State.* Rev. ed. Rutgers Byzantine Series. New Brunswick, NJ: Rutgers University Press, 1969.

Patlagean, Evelyne. *Pauvreté économique et pauvre é sociale à Byzance, 4e–7e siecles.* Civilisations et societes 48. Paris: Mouton, 1977.

Phan, Peter C. *Social Thought.* Message of the Fathers of the Church 20. Wilmington, DE: Glazier, 1984.

Preston, Ronald H. *Religion and the Ambiguities of Capitalism.* London: SCM, 1991.

Rakover, Nahum. *Unjust Enrichment in Jewish Law.* Jerusalem: Library of Jewish Law, 2000.

Reuther, Rosemary Radford. *Gregory Nazianzus, Rhetor and Philosopher.* Oxford: Clarendon, 1969.

Roll, Eric. *A History of Economic Thought.* New York: Prentice-Hall, 1952.

Rose, H. Shields. *The Churches and Usury, Or the Morality of Five per Cent.* London: Sealey Clark, 1931.

Rostovtzeff, Michael Ivanovich. *The Social & Economic History of the Hellenistic World.* Vol. 1. Oxford: Clarendon, 1959.

———. *Rome.* Oxford: Oxford University Press, 1927.

Rousseau, Philip. *Basil of Caesarea.* The Transformation of the Classical Heritage 20. Berkeley: University of California Press, 1994.

Ryan, Franklin W. *Usury and Usury Laws: A Juristic-Economic Study of the Effects of State Statutory Maximums for Loan Chargers upon Lending Operations in the United States.* Boston: Houghton Mifflin, 1924.

Sahlins, Marshall. *Stone Age Economics.* Chicago: Aldine-Atherton, 1972.

Sayers, Sean. *Plato's Republic: An Introduction.* Edinburgh: Edinburgh University Press, 1999.

Schumpeter, Joseph A. *History of Economic Analysis.* New York: Oxford University Press, 1954.

Seipel, Ignaz. *Die wirtschaftsethischen Lehren der Kirchenväter.* Graz: Akademische Druck-u. Verlagsanstalt, 1907.

Siepierski, Paulo. "Poverty and Spirituality: Saint Basil and Liberation Theology." *Greek Orthodox Theological Review* 33 (1988) 313–26.

Soddy, Frederick V. *Wealth, Virtual Wealth and Debt.* New York: Allen & Unwin, 1926.

Soss, N. M. "Old Testament Law and Economic Society." *Journal of the History of Ideas* 34 (1973) 323–44.

Starr, Chester G. *The Economic and Social Growth of Early Greece: 800–500 B.C.* New York: Oxford University Press, 1977.

Stein, Siegfried. "Laws on Interest in the Old Testament." *Journal of Theological Studies* 4 (1953) 161–70.

Stone, Mary Alice. "The Portrayal of Contemporary Usury in the Elizabethan Drama." PhD diss., University of Chicago, 1923.

Sutherland, John R. "The Debate concerning Usury in the Christian Church." *Crux* 22 (1986) 3–9.

———. "Economic Development and Usury Laws." PhD diss., Trinity Evangelical Divinity School, 1982.

———. "Usury: God's Forgotten Doctrine [Ex 22:25–27; Lev 25.35–37; Deut 23.19–20]." *Crux* 18 (1982) 9–14.

Tamari, Meir. *"With All Your Possessions": Jewish Ethics and Economic Life.* New York: Free Press, 1987.

Telfer, W. *Cyril of Jerusalem and Nemesius of Emesa,* LCC 4. London: SCM, 1955.

Tenny, Frank. *An Economic Survey of Ancient Rome.* Vol. 1, *Rome and Italy of the Republic.* 6 vols. Paterson, NJ: Pageant, 1959.

Tscherikower, V., and F. M. Heichelheim. "Jewish Religious Influence in the Adler Papyri." *Harvard Theological Review* 35 (1942) 25–44.

U.S. Congress. *Credit Card Accountability Responsibility and Disclosure Act of* 2009, HR 627, 111th Cong. Online: http: http://www.gpo.gov/fdsys/pkg/PLAW-111publ24/pdf/PLAW-111publ24.pdf/.

Wallant, Edward Lewis. *The Pawnbroker.* New York: Harcourt, Brace and World, 1961.

Watt, Lewis. *Usury in Catholic Theology.* Oxford: Catholic Social Guild, 1945.

Wee, Paul A. "Biblical Ethics and Lending to the Poor." *Ecumenical Review* 38 (1986) 416–30.

Whybray, R. N. *Introduction to the Pentateuch.* Grand Rapids: Eerdmans, 1995.

Williams, Jay. *Understanding the Old Testament.* New York: Barron's Educational Series, 1972.

Williamson, H. G. M. *Ezra, Nehemiah.* Word Biblical Commentary 16. Waco: Word, 1985.

Williston, Samuel. *A Treatise on the Law of Contracts.* 4th ed. Rochester, NY: Lawyers Cooperative Publishing, 1990.

Wilson, Robert McNair. *Defeat of Debt.* London: Routledge, 1935.

———. *Promise to Pay.* London: Routledge, 1934.

Winslow, Donald F. "Gregory of Nazianzus and Love for the Poor." *Anglican Theological Review* 47 (1965) 348–59.

Wiseman, D. J. *The Alalakh Tablets.* London: British Institute of Archaeology at Ankara, 1953.

Wright, C. T. "Some Conventions Regarding the Usurer in Elizabethan Literature." *Studies in Philology* 31 (1934) 179–97.

———. "The Usurer's Sin in Elizabethan Literature." *Studies in Philology* 35 (1938) 178–94.

Woodhouse, W. J. *Solon the Liberator: A Study of the Agrarian Problem in Attika in the Seventh Century.* New York: Octagon, 1965.

Yarnold, Edward. *Cyril of Jerusalem.* The Early Church Fathers. London: Routledge, 2000.

Young, Frances M. *Biblical Exegesis and the Formation of Christian Culture.* Cambridge: Cambridge University Press, 1997.

Zipperstein, Edward. *Business Ethics in Jewish Law.* New York: Ktav, 1983.